South view of House, from Drive.

A History of London's
Most Celebrated Salon

HOLLAND
HOUSE

Linda Kelly

I.B. TAURIS

LONDON · NEW YORK

Published and reprinted in 2013 by I.B.Tauris & Co Ltd
6 Salem Road, London W2 4BU
175 Fifth Avenue, New York NY 10010
www.ibtauris.com

Distributed in the United States and Canada
Exclusively by Palgrave Macmillan
175 Fifth Avenue, New York NY 10010

ISBN: 978 1 78076 449 8

A full CIP record for this book is available
from the British Library
A full CIP record for this book is available
from the Library of Congress

Library of Congress catalog card: available

Typeset by Tetragon, London
Printed and bound by CPI Group (UK) Ltd, Croydon, CR0 4YY

Contents

List of Illustrations

To our grandchildren:
Edward, Sasha, George, Nadya, Tara,
Katherine, Dyala, Charlotte and Arthur

Preface

ONE of the last great balls in London in the summer of 1939 took place at Holland House. George VI and Queen Elizabeth were among the guests, and the queue of cars to the gates on Kensington High Street stretched back to Hyde Park Corner. It was a magnificent finale. War was looming and a few weeks later the then owner, the sixth Earl of Ilchester, removed the most valuable paintings, books and furniture, as well as the priceless collection of family manuscripts, to his country home at Melbury in Dorset. We can only be thankful for his foresight. On 27 September 1940 Holland House was largely destroyed by enemy bombs.

Lord Ilchester wrote two books based on family papers about the history of Holland House, *The Home of the Hollands, 1605–1820* and *Chronicles of Holland House, 1820–1900*. He also edited the journals and Spanish journals of Elizabeth, Lady Holland, her letters to her son, Henry Edward Fox, and Henry Fox's own journals as a young man, each in their way reflecting the excitement of the years when Holland House was the centre of Whig politics. A devoted guardian of the family archive, Ilchester was determined that the vast collection of Holland House papers, with their far-reaching coverage of political and family history, should not leave Britain, and after his death in 1959 they were acquired, as he had wished, by the British Library. The Holland House paintings, books and furniture – together with busts of Fox and others which were rescued from the fire – are still at Melbury and I am enormously grateful to Charlotte Townshend, granddaughter of the seventh Earl of Ilchester, for her kindness in showing them to me. They brought the third Lord Holland's circle to life in a way that nothing else could have done.

I am very grateful, too, to the staff of the British Library, the Kensington Central Library, the London Library, the National Portrait Gallery and the Public Record Office of Northern Ireland; to Francis Russell for making my visit to Melbury possible and for sharing his knowledge of its treasures; to Theodore Wilson Harris for allowing me to quote from his novel *Da Silva da Silva's Cultivated Wilderness*, and to Tim Cribb for introducing me to it; to Peter Cochran for allowing me to quote from his transcription of Hobhouse's comments in Doris Langley Moore's copy of Moore's *Life of Byron*, now in the collection of Jack Wasserman; to my agent and former publisher, Christopher Sinclair-Stevenson; to my editors Lester Crook, Joanna Godfrey and Nadine El-Hadi at I.B.Tauris, and Alex Billington and Alex Middleton at Tetragon; to friends and relations for their help and encouragement: Henry Anglesey, Marina Camrose, Raymond Carr, Rosanna and Anthony Gardner, Mark Girouard, Rachel Grigg, Erskine Guinness, Nicholas Kelly, Anthony Malcolmson, Chip Martin, Douglas Matthews, Mollie and John Julius Norwich, Valerie Pakenham, Antonia Pinter, Mehreen Saigol, the late Christine Sutherland, Hugh Thomas, John Train, Katharine Wakefield and Frances Wilson; and last but certainly not least to my husband Laurence Kelly for his constant interest and support.

1

Nephew of Fox

T HE leafy expanses of Holland Park, 52 acres of gardens and woodland in the heart of Kensington, are all that remain of the once great estate that surrounded Holland House. The house itself, a palatial red-brick Jacobean mansion, was destroyed beyond repair in the last war, but the seated statue of its best-known owner, the third Lord Holland, still marks the meeting point of four main avenues, looking out across lawns towards the remains of his former home. He is an affable, indeed welcoming figure, somewhat stout, with rumpled gaiters and the same shaggy eyebrows as his uncle Charles James Fox. The plinth of the statue is in water, a stone-edged pond where ducks swim languidly, and the tangled undergrowth around is home to every sort of wildlife, not least the fox from which the Holland family took its name.

For the third Lord Holland the name of Fox had an almost religious significance. Brought up in the principles of his beloved uncle, Holland saw himself as heir to Fox's political ideals and guardian of the family flame. Together with his wife, Lady Holland, beautiful, capricious and demanding, he presided over the most celebrated salon of the age. During the first 30 years of the nineteenth century, when the party was almost constantly out of office, Holland House was the unofficial centre of the Whig opposition. Devoted to the memory of Fox and enriched by the progressive views of a new generation of writers, critics and politicians, its influence permeated the political climate. At a time of revolutions across Europe, the Whig tradition of aristocratic liberalism, avoiding the extremes of radicalism and reaction, would be one of the chief factors in the peaceful achievement of parliamentary reform.

Fox had not begun life as a liberal. He had entered Parliament at the age of 19 in 1769 and had rapidly sprung to the fore as a debater, speaking off the cuff, with a careless brilliance that amazed his hearers. But his political conduct had been wayward. Appointed to the government in 1770, he had incurred the wrath of the mob by attacking the freedom of the press (on the grounds that Parliament should be pre-eminent), then infuriated the king by resigning in opposition to the Royal Marriages Bill, forbidding members of the royal family to marry without the king's consent. The subject of forbidden marriages had always been a sensitive one in the Fox family. Fox's father, Henry Fox, a shrewd but parvenu politician, had made a runaway marriage with the Duke of Richmond's daughter, a great-great-granddaughter of Charles II. This act of near *lèse-majesté* had created a major scandal at the time though Henry Fox, having acquired an enormous fortune as Paymaster General during the Seven Years War and become the first Lord Holland, proved not such a bad match after all.

Fox was back in office as a junior Lord of the Treasury when his nephew Henry Fox was born in October 1773. The baby was jokingly hailed as a second Messiah, 'born for the destruction of the Jews',[1] for his father Stephen Fox was in failing health, and Fox, who would otherwise have been his brother's heir, had gambling debts of over £100,000 (approximately £12 million today). The birth of his nephew, removing his security with the moneylenders, threatened Fox with bankruptcy. He was rescued in the nick of time by his father, who painfully raised the money to pay off his debts before dying in February 1774; Lady Holland followed her husband a few weeks later. Stephen, the second Lord Holland, survived his parents for only five more months. Henry inherited his father's title and estates, the latter heavily encumbered, when he was less than a year old.

The string of family tragedies did not stop here, for Henry's mother Mary, 'the most amiable woman that ever lived',[2] died four years later, leaving two children, Henry and his elder sister Caroline. Caroline found a home with her maternal aunt, Lady Lansdowne; Henry was brought up by his mother's brother, the Earl of Upper Ossory, with Fox, who adored the 'young one', as he called him, as a benevolent figure on the sidelines.

Henry was still a baby when the American War of Independence broke out. Over the next eight years, abandoning his role in government, Fox made his name as a champion of the American rebels and a staunch opponent of the war. He took to wearing the buff and blue of the American forces – a blue jacket and buff waistcoat – and inveighed against the prime minister, Lord North, in a series of devastating speeches. Behind the prime minister he sensed the far more dangerous influence of George III. For Fox, the king's desire to dominate his ministers was a return to royal despotism and a threat to the parliamentary freedoms won in the Glorious Revolution of 1688. It was the start of a continuing battle against the power of the Crown and the encroachments of the executive. If not always carried out consistently by Fox himself it would become an article of faith for his nephew.

Fox's dislike of George III was heartily reciprocated by the king. Although Fox's father, the first Lord Holland, had been a useful hatchet man in the first years of his reign, George III had always disapproved of his son. Fox's rakish habits were a byword. Unperturbed by his earlier losses, he continued to gamble recklessly, spending whole nights at the faro table, or returning muddied and hotfoot from the racecourse to take his place in the House of Commons. Worse still, in George III's opinion, he had infected the Prince of Wales with his bad principles. At the age of 18, with a household of his own, the prince had reacted spectacularly against his strait-laced upbringing, running up huge debts, pursuing actresses, drinking 'like a leviathan', and imbibing opposition politics from Fox.

On 23 November 1781 came the news of the British surrender at Yorktown. It was now clear to everyone except the king that the war in America had been lost. In March 1782 the harassed Lord North resigned. A new administration, entrusted with the peace negotiations, was formed under Lord Rockingham, with Fox and Lord Shelburne as joint Secretaries of State. But the antipathy between Fox and Shelburne, an old political opponent of his father's, made it impossible for the two men to work together. The death of Rockingham in July 1782 brought matters to a head. Fox refused to serve under Shelburne who, without him, was unable to command a majority in the House of Commons. Shortly after, to the amazement of those who had listened to his nightly diatribes against him, Fox formed an alliance with Lord North. 'It is not my nature to bear malice or live in ill will,' he explained blandly. 'My friendships are eternal, my enmities not.'[3]

The alliance of Fox and North made the defeat of the government inevitable. In February 1783 Shelburne resigned. After five weeks of vainly seeking an alternative, the king was forced to form a new government under the nominal leadership of the Duke of Portland, with Fox as Foreign Secretary and North in charge of Home Affairs. But, as one observer remarked, it was clear the administration would not last long, for the king, on Fox's kissing hands, 'turned back his eyes and ears just like the horse at Astley's when the tailor he had determined to throw was getting on him.'[4]

It took less than a year for the king to unseat Fox. The occasion was a bill to regulate the East India Company, placing the control in the hands of seven commissioners nominated by the government. The bill, in practice giving the patronage of the East India Company to Fox's friends, was passed by a majority in the House of Commons. The king, however, was determined to defeat it. Having secretly ensured that the young William Pitt would be prepared to form a ministry if the coalition fell, he let it be known that any person who voted for the bill in the House of Lords would be considered by him an enemy. Although his intervention was clearly unconstitutional the king had sufficient power and patronage to ensure that the bill was overthrown. Fox and his fellow ministers were forced to resign, and Pitt became the First Lord of the Treasury, in practice the prime minister.

Fox would never forgive this act of treachery, as he saw it, though he could not foresee how long he would spend in the political wilderness as a result. Within three months of taking office, using a skilful mixture of patronage and coercion, Pitt had reduced the coalition's majority to only one vote and forced them to call an election. The result was a disaster for Fox. One hundred and sixty of the coalition's candidates, Fox's martyrs as they were called, lost their seats. Fox himself, after a rowdy and hard-fought election in which for the first time he presented himself as a popular or 'people's' candidate, was returned as one of the two members for Westminster.

At this point Pitt still called himself a Whig. But he relied on the support of Tory and royalist members and gradually, as the party system became more defined, he came to be seen as the leader of the Tories, as Fox was of the Whigs. Hatred of Pitt and mistrust of the king were part of the mythology with which the young Henry Holland grew up, and the great betrayal of 1784, when the king intervened to overthrow the government, would remain a reference point for ever after.

Henry spent a happy childhood in the care of his uncle, Lord Upper Ossory, a gentle, studious man in whose library he laid the foundations of his lifelong love of reading. He was educated at Eton where, as a junior boy, he had his first experience of oppression when his fag master insisted he toast bread for him with his bare hands; Henry's fingers had a withered appearance for the rest of his life. Despite this unpromising beginning he went on to become a member of the sixth form and made friends with some of the cleverest students of the day, among them the future prime minister George Canning and Robert 'Bobus' Smith, an outstanding classical scholar whose younger brother, the clerical wit and polemicist Sydney Smith, would be one of the brightest ornaments of Holland House.

But his most important intellectual influence was Fox, whose warmth, intelligence and charismatic personality were irresistible to the fatherless child. From Fox he acquired a passion for poetry and the classics, as well as a precocious interest in the great political and constitutional issues of the day. 'So thoroughly was he imbued with the views and sentiments of his uncle on these subjects,' wrote the editor of his correspondence, Lord John Russell,

> that he had only to dive into his own bosom, to find the motives on which Mr Fox would have acted... During his own political career, when any doubt or difficulty perplexed him, the first thought that occurred to him was, how would Mr Fox have felt... on the occasion?[5]

Since the defeat of 1784, Fox had been the leader of the Whig opposition, a far more coherent body than had hitherto existed in English politics. In 1788 George III's first attack of madness (or porphyria) had briefly offered a chance of returning to power, with the Prince of Wales as regent, but the king's unexpected recovery had dashed their hopes, returning them to the wilderness again. Then, in 1789, came the defining moment in Fox's political career, the fall of the Bastille.

'How much the greatest event it is that ever happened in the world! and how much the best!'[6] was his famous response to the French Revolution, a position from which he never wavered through the years of bloodshed and upheaval which followed.

Henry was still at Eton when the Revolution broke out. But he was able to see something of it for himself when he visited Paris, with his tutor, the Reverend William Morris, on holiday from Oxford in September 1791. Three months earlier Louis XVI and the royal family had been captured at Varennes and brought back ignominiously to Paris; they were now virtual prisoners in the Tuileries. Henry heard the king's speech in the legislative assembly pledging loyalty to the Constitution, 'in a clear but tremulous voice', and, not yet 'steeled, by experience of their hollowness, to royal speeches,'[7] was deeply moved. The king, at that very moment, he learnt later, was secretly seeking help abroad to overthrow the Constitution.

Welcomed in progressive circles as the nephew of Fox, Henry made friends with those, like Talleyrand and Lafayette, who hoped to combine reform with a constitutional monarchy; as aristocratic moderates they were the nearest equivalent to the Whigs in France. But he was never in sympathy with the extremer elements – the Girondins and Jacobins – who were beginning to dominate events. Only a year later Talleyrand was forced to flee from Paris; Lafayette was languishing in an Austrian dungeon; and the king, imprisoned in the Temple, was awaiting trial.

These were dramatic happenings and it was not surprising that Henry found his time at Oxford, where he was at Christ Church, something of an anticlimax. 'In no town in which I ever resided did I see less of men distinguished for learning and literature than in Oxford during the two years I spent in that University,' he wrote later. For Fox, who regarded Oxford as the 'very capital and centre of Toryism', there was nothing surprising in this view.[8]

His real education would be travel, his uncles rightly feeling that he should see something of the world before taking his place in the House of Lords. From the autumn of 1792 till the spring of 1796, he toured Europe, visiting Sweden, Denmark, Prussia, Portugal, Spain (the start of an abiding interest in Spanish politics and literature) and Italy. As well as fluent French, Italian and Spanish and a working knowledge of Portuguese and German he acquired a cosmopolitan breadth of outlook which would stand him in good stead in the years when Holland House was a centre of European as well as British liberal thought. The French Revolution and the war which followed had thrown much of Europe into turmoil, but the old freemasonry which linked the European aristocracy from country to country still worked in the places which the war had not affected. Henry had enough connections and introductions to give him an entry to the best society, whether in the courts of Berlin and Madrid, or the salons of Naples, Rome and Florence; there were encounters too with other aristocratic English tourists, bent on improving their taste and widening their horizons despite the restrictions of the war.

He remained in affectionate communication with his uncle throughout his travels. 'You talk very foolishly in making excuses for egotism,' wrote Fox, 'for in letters from you it is precisely what I want; I wish to know everything about you.'[9] Sadly Henry's letters to Fox have been lost, but we catch their echoes in his uncle's to him, careless, easy and intimate, with no hint of talking down. Their great shared interests were literature and politics, with literature taking first place, Lope de Vega and Cervantes when Henry was in Spain, Ariosto when he reached Italy, Homer at every stage of Henry's journeys. 'It is a long time since I wrote to you,' wrote Fox in one letter; 'when I wrote last, I was in the ninth book of the Odyssey, which I have since finished and read eighteen books of the Iliad, so that it must be a good while since.'[10]

But the French Revolution was pursuing its course, and politics was impossible to avoid. The death of Robespierre, in July 1794, put an end to the worst of the Terror, but the war with France, involving half of Europe, continued. In the House of Commons, Fox continually put the case for peace and attacked the government's repressive policies at home, but he found himself increasingly isolated. In 1794, after agonized discussion, the bulk of the Whig party defected to Pitt, leaving Fox with less than 50 followers in the House of Commons. It had been a painful break on both sides; Portland, the official leader of the Whigs, was in tears at the parting. For Fox it was a shattering blow. 'I cannot forget,' he wrote to Henry, 'how long I have lived in friendship with them, nor can I avoid feeling the most severe mortification, when I recollect the certainty I used to entertain that they never would disgrace themselves as I think they have done.'[11] He longed for his nephew to support him in the House of Lords. 'I hope you will come home soon,' he told him,

> and if you make the figure I cannot help thinking that you will, it will make amends to me for everything, and make me feel alive again about politics; which I am now quite sick of, and attend to only because I feel I have a duty to do so.[12]

Fox would continue to fight, convinced as he was that only the party system and an articulate opposition could save Britain from falling into 'the euthanasia of an absolute monarchy'.[13] But his nephew Henry, now installed in Florence, was in no hurry to plunge into the hurly-burly of opposition. He had fallen in love, and was living through his own private dramas; for the time being, even his beloved uncle must take second place.

2

Lovers' Meeting

D ESPITE the difficulties caused by the war with France, Henry's European travels had not been so different from those of any young nobleman on the Grand Tour in previous years. No doubt, as with other young Englishmen on the loose, they included a number of amorous episodes. The Grand Tour, among other things, was meant to be a journey of initiation. But we hear no echoes of that side of his life in his letters from his uncle, nor of the absorbing love affair that began when he arrived in Florence in January 1794. He was travelling with a friend, Lord Granville Leveson-Gower, the two of them having come from Spain. Lord Granville was brilliantly good-looking, a social star who had taken Paris by storm in the days before the Revolution. Henry, black-browed and heavy-featured, was 'not in the least handsome'[1] and moreover known to share his uncle's unfashionably pro-French views. But he radiated such gaiety and good humour, his manners were so open and unassuming, that he was soon as much a favourite as his friend in the little circle of English aristocrats who were living there.

They were a fluctuating group, whose leading figures, apart from the English minister Lord Hervey, were Sir Godfrey and Lady Webster, the latter a tall, voluptuous beauty of 23, with dark eyes and a restlessly enquiring mind. The two were unhappily married. Elizabeth Webster, paired off at 15 with a husband of 49, had rapidly grown discontented with her lot, drowning her unhappiness in travelling and the adoration of numerous admirers. She was now pregnant with her third child, whose father may have been Sir Godfrey's political patron, Thomas Pelham, or Sir Godfrey himself, both men fondly believing themselves responsible. When she and Sir Godfrey left Florence for Naples in February, Henry and Lord Granville followed them. They found themselves in a society which included the Duchess of Devonshire's sister Lady Bessborough and her husband, her mother Lady Spencer and a cheerful band of young Englishmen, whose chief occupations, according to Elizabeth, were gambling and gallantry. The consul was Sir William Hamilton, with the famous Emma as his hostess: 'Of all the most vulgar, vain and disagreeable women I ever saw,' wrote Henry, 'the fair Ambassadress is the most so.'[2]

Because of her pregnancy Elizabeth Webster did not go out much in Naples, preferring to see friends at home in her apartments, where Henry and Lord Granville were soon constant visitors. It was Lord Granville who first took Elizabeth's fancy, but it soon became clear that he had fallen for the riper charms of Lady Bessborough (she was 12 years his senior), with whom he would embark on a long-lived affair. Henry, however, was a delightful substitute, his high spirits so infectious that she and Lady Bessborough christened him 'Sal Volatile'. Above all he shared Elizabeth's intellectual interests. In her years of travel she had done much to make up for a neglected education, reading widely, assiduously visiting galleries and monuments, learning French and Italian, and taking courses in chemistry, biology and mineralogy. The two spent happy hours sightseeing or discussing poetry, Henry introducing her to the works of William Cowper, Elizabeth sharing her enthusiasm for Ariosto and the Italian poets of the sixteenth century. Sir Godfrey, bored by literary discussions, was usually out on his wife's evenings at home. The quarrels of the

Websters were becoming common knowledge. 'They do not agree together,' wrote Lord Granville when he first met them, 'and their jarrings might as well not be made a matter of public observation.'[3]

After six or seven weeks in Naples, the Webster party moved to Rome, where they took a villa on the Pincian Hill. They were followed by most of their Naples set, including Henry and the Bessboroughs, though Lord Granville and two others had returned to England – 'where nothing short of compulsion shall ever drag me,'[4] wrote Elizabeth firmly. They lingered there visiting chapels and churches, and saw the Pope (Pius VI) give his blessing to the multitude. 'He is an excellent actor,' noted Elizabeth. 'Garrick himself could not have represented the part with more theatrical effect.'[5]

It was now nearly time for Elizabeth's baby to be born; at the end of May she returned to Florence, bidding a fond farewell to Lady Bessborough, who was returning to England – perhaps to follow Lord Granville. On 12 June 1794, Elizabeth gave birth to a little girl, Harriet, her first daughter. Henry turned up for the christening, and remained in Florence on and off for the rest of the year, celebrating his 21st birthday there with a great ball in November. Elizabeth was 24 the following March, and Henry composed a graceful ode for the occasion. It was a custom he would continue for the rest of his life.

By now it was obvious that Henry was deeply in love with Elizabeth. He was not the first to be so, but hitherto she had always kept a cool head in the midst of her affairs. This time, reading between the lines in her diary, with its frequent references to Henry, it is clear that she was beginning to return his feelings. Sir Godfrey, jealous and bad-tempered, resentful at his wife's neglect, was no match for Henry's ardent wooing.

Elizabeth was a considerable heiress, an only child, with family money coming from the West Indies; Sir Godfrey had married her as much for her prospects as her beauty. In February 1795 her father,

Richard Vassall, died leaving her in possession of a fortune. 'Detestable gold,' she wrote on receiving the news. 'What a lure for a vil[l]ain and too dearly have I become the victim to him.'[6] Sir Godfrey was now eager that she should leave with him for England, where he was planning to stand as a parliamentary candidate for his home constituency of Battle. It would have been natural for his wife to accompany him, if only to see her widowed mother and look after her affairs. Elizabeth, however, pleaded ill health; she was in the first stages of pregnancy and unfit, she said, to travel. 'To say the truth,' she confided to her journal, 'I made as much as I could of that pretext... as I enjoyed myself too much here to risk the change of scene.'[7] Despairing of persuading her to follow him, Sir Godfrey left for England in May 1795.

Elizabeth spent the next year in Italy, with Henry almost always in her entourage. She had taken a house in Florence, a 'delicious residence' in the midst of the Mattonaia gardens, where she entertained three times a week, attracting the leading artists and intellectuals of the town to her salon: the template for the Holland House gatherings was already there. On their evenings alone, Henry read aloud to her; in the daytime they would go on sightseeing expeditions in the surrounding countryside, or travel further afield to visit the galleries and churches of other cities. In Turin, for instance, they visited the chapel of the monastery of St Agnes, with its painting of the saint's martyrdom by Domenichino. 'Lord Holland read a passage to me out of a letter from Charles Fox, from which it appears that he reckons the picture almost the best in Italy,'[8] wrote Elizabeth in her journal.

The autumn of 1795 was darkened by the death of her newborn baby in October – 'a lovely boy... never again shall I become mother to such a child,' she mourned. But Henry's company helped distract her from her sadness, and by the spring of 1796 she was pregnant once again. The child she had lost might well have been Sir Godfrey's; this time she was carrying Henry's. It was clear that the situation had to be resolved. On 11 April, Elizabeth bade farewell to Florence, 'that lovely spot where I enjoyed a degree of happiness that for a whole year was too exquisite to be permanent',[9] and set out towards England with her lover and three children. She had not seen her husband for a year.

Eighteenth-century aristocratic morality, especially Whig morality, was easy-going where liaisons outside marriage were concerned. The Duke of Devonshire had lived for years in a *ménage à trois* with his wife and Lady Elizabeth Foster; Granville Leveson-Gower would be Lady Bessborough's lover for over 15 years. Children were sometimes born, 'children of the mist' as someone called them, and brought up either as distant relations or conveniently, during the confusion of the French Revolution, as the orphaned children of French aristocrats. But the marriage bond was usually preserved. Elizabeth and Henry wanted more than a discreet liaison; they wanted to live together openly, if possible to marry.

For Elizabeth this would mean great sacrifices. Not only would she face social ruin if she separated from her husband, but under the laws of the day she would also lose her three children. Godfrey, or 'Webby', the eldest, was seven, Henry, the second, three, and Harriet, the youngest, still a baby. It was bad enough to lose the boys, but to part with her daughter at such a tender age was more than she could bear. She had always had a reckless streak, and with or without her lover's knowledge she now devised a desperate scheme. On the first stage of their journey home, she and Henry separated outside Florence, arranging that they would meet in Padua. She had already sent most of her servants ahead there, taking a slower route via Modena, accompanied by her three children, a nursery maid and her Italian maid who had a small child of her own. A few miles outside Bologna, she pretended that Harriet had been taken dangerously ill with measles and must stay behind with her, while the nursery maid and the two boys went on to Modena. The next step was to fake Harriet's death. Having filled a guitar case, which could pass for a small coffin, with stones and a pillow dressed with clothes, she told her footman to take it to the British consul in Leghorn with instructions to arrange for its burial in the British cemetery. Meanwhile she had disguised her daughter as a boy, and arranged for the Italian maid to take her and her own child to a rendezvous in Hamburg, using a false passport which she had previously obtained in Florence. As Harriet was said to have died from measles, no one would wonder that Elizabeth had left her maid behind to nurse her own child, supposedly also suffering from the illness.

On reaching Modena Elizabeth broke the news of Harriet's death to her entourage, before continuing to Padua where her lover joined her from Florence. They then travelled on through Austria and Germany, and eventually reached Hamburg, where Elizabeth met up with her Italian maid (and Harriet) before crossing to Yarmouth from Cuxhaven. They arrived there in mid June. Harriet, still disguised as boy, was presumably left in lodgings with the maid, while Elizabeth and her lover proceeded to London.

Rumour of course had gone before them. Henry's sister Caroline, six years older than her brother, had heard the news of his attachment the year before and had written to warn him gently of the scandal it was causing. Henry would have none of it: 'Do not imagine, my dearest little sister,' he told her,

> that I am or ever can be the least angry with you, but I confess I am very unhappy at hearing you abuse a person I love so much... I may be like Antony – & beg the privilege of saying,

> > But on your life
> > No word of Cleopatra, she deserves
> > More worlds than I could lose.[10]

Caroline, who adored her brother, had quickly changed her tune, and now on the lovers' return to London she was the first to offer her support. But Henry had no illusions about the social difficulties that lay ahead. His chief concern was to mitigate their consequences for Elizabeth, who would inevitably bear the greatest share of blame. 'As to what I have done,' he told his sister,

> it was in some respects contrary to the advice of my friends, but as her situation rendered an éclat sooner or later almost certain & any management for her character quite desperate... my only object was to live with her in the way most comfortable & to *her* feelings most creditable... I would not have taken such a step as this without feeling that I never could be happy were I not to live with her upon the only terms that would make her some compensation for it. [11]

It might have helped to quieten scandal if, as some of their friends suggested, Elizabeth had concealed her pregnancy, and discreetly farmed out the baby afterwards. But Elizabeth, who was already losing her sons, and could only see Harriet in secret, was determined not to part with her child. Henry agreed. Its situation would be difficult, he told Caroline, 'yet surely even that is better than if any concealment had taken place & it had been condemned for years never to have known its mother.' [12] Both he and his sister, motherless children themselves, knew what a deprivation that could be.

On arriving in London the lovers set up house in Brompton Row. Holland House, which had been let during Henry's minority, had recently become available, but Elizabeth felt it might be thought 'a kind of *effrontery*' [13] if she moved there before their marriage. Even this was still uncertain; if her divorce did not go through, it would be socially impossible to stay in England and they would be forced to live abroad. Everything now rested with Sir Godfrey. Within days

of Elizabeth's return to England he had announced that he was insti-
tuting divorce proceedings against her. In fact he vacillated for many
months, at one point tearfully promising to help her by speeding up
proceedings, at another flatly refusing to divorce her on the grounds
that it would injure his sons' prospects. It was only after much hard
bargaining – 'every paltry chicane that could extort money from us
was had recourse to,'[14] wrote Elizabeth – that he finally agreed to go
ahead.

In the meantime the lovers had to come to terms with their relations. Elizabeth's mother, widowed 17 months earlier, had found a
new husband; in July 1796 she married a Suffolk baronet, Sir Gilbert
Affleck. Unwilling to jeopardize her new position, she flatly refused
to see Elizabeth till she was married. On Henry's side, things were
slightly better. He could count on the support of Caroline, and though
Lord Upper Ossory made no immediate signal, his mother's other
brother, General Fitzpatrick, was kindly and encouraging, and invited
them to stay. So too did the Duke of Bedford, another friendly kinsman on his mother's side. Fox, however, remained strangely silent.
He disapproved of his nephew's choice, though it can hardly have
been on moral grounds. He had been living with a former courtesan,
Mrs Armistead, for the last ten years.

For Elizabeth, hitherto always fêted and admired, these were ter-
rible humiliations. She was miserably conscious of coming between
Henry and his family, and her own mother's disapproval must have
been a further blow. But Henry's devotion never wavered, and the
birth of their baby in October was a chance to build a bridge with Fox.
The child was christened Charles after his great uncle, with Caroline
as his godmother.

Under the laws of the day a marriage could only be dissolved by an
act of Parliament, preceded by a case in the civil court. The proceedings began in February 1797, Sir Godfrey making it a condition of the

divorce that his wife should give up the bulk of her yearly income of £7,000 to him, retaining only £800 for herself; he also claimed damages of £10,000 (later reduced to £6,000) from Henry. These terms were denounced as 'iniquitous' by the Lord Chancellor, Lord Loughborough, when the bill to dissolve the marriage came up before the House of Lords in June. But Sir Godfrey threatened to drop the case if his conditions were not met, and rather than risk his withdrawal, Henry, together with the Duke of Bedford, his friend Charles Ellis and his future father-in-law Sir Gilbert Affleck, signed a bond guaranteeing that they would be responsible if Lady Webster did not hand over her estate within two days of her divorce. Meanwhile Fox, belatedly coming to the rescue, persuaded Loughborough not to upset things by insisting on Lady Webster's rights.

On 4 July, at long last, Elizabeth's 'wretched marriage' was annulled by Parliament. The next day she signed over her whole fortune, with the exception of £800 a year, to Sir Godfrey. On 6 July, she married Henry in Rickmansworth Church. Fox did not attend, but her new stepfather, Sir Gilbert Affleck, gave her away, and Henry's old tutor, the Reverend William Morris, officiated. 'I have been supping with *Lady Holland*', wrote Lady Bessborough to Lord Granville that evening.

> They were married at eight this morning, and I never saw creatures so happy. He flew down to meet me, *kiss'd* me several times, ne vous déplaise, and can do nothing but repeat her name. Such perfect happiness as theirs scarcely ever was instanc'd before[.]
>
> Un tel hymen c'est le Ciel sur la terre.[15]

3

In Opposition

⁓

THREE and a half years after their first meeting, Lord and Lady Holland, as we shall now refer to them, had finally reached the safe haven of marriage. For Lady Holland, reflecting on the wedding in her journal, there was only one cause for regret. She was 26, her husband only 23. 'The difference in age is, alas! two years and eight months – a horrid disparity.'[1] But all else, scandal, the loss of her fortune, even separation from her children, was as nothing when contrasted with her present state. 'My own individual happiness,' she wrote, 'is so perfect, that I can scarcely figure to myself a blessing that I do not possess.'[2]

Looking back on her neglected early life, she recalled her lack of any kind of formal or religious education. She had been saved by her intellectual curiosity and her passion for books, but had been too eager to learn to follow any regular system and was more ignorant in some areas than a ten-year-old schoolboy. And then, at 15, 'with youth, beauty and a good disposition all to be so squandered', she had been thrown into marriage with a 'pompous coxcomb.'[3]

The connexion was perdition to me in every way; my heart was good, but accustomed to hear and see everything that was mean and selfish,

I tried to shut it to the calls of humanity and used my reason to teach me to hate mankind... At Florence, in 1794, I began to think there were exceptions to my system, and every hour from that period to this, which now sees me the happiest of women, have I continued to wonder and admire the most wonderful union of benevolence, sense and integrity in the character of that excellent being whose faith is pledged to mine. Either he has imparted some of his goodness to me or his excellence has drawn out the latent good I had as certainly I am a better person now and a more useful person than I was in my years of misery.[4]

It was a touchingly humble confession from someone normally so high-handed. In fact she was even luckier than she knew. Three years later a law making it impossible for anyone who was divorced to marry the person who had caused the divorce was put before the House of Commons; fortunately it was dropped after the second reading. Had it come into existence she and Holland would have been condemned to spend their life abroad, tossed here and there by the changing fortunes of the Napoleonic wars.

Meanwhile, secure in her new happiness, she could begin to rebuild her social position. Lady Bessborough, who called on them a few days after their wedding, found her 'in famous beauty and he wild with joy the whole time'.[5] They were surrounded by family, Sir Gilbert and Lady Affleck, the latter all smiles now her daughter was safely married, Holland's aunt by marriage Lady Upper Ossory, and Elizabeth's son Henry, whom Sir Godfrey, as a rare concession, had allowed to visit her for a week.

The Hollands' relations were rallying round. One of their first invitations was from Holland's uncle by marriage, the Marquess of Lansdowne,[6] to stay at Bowood, his splendid country house in Wiltshire. Formerly Lord Shelburne, Lansdowne had been Fox's hated rival in 1780, but time and their shared political sympathies – opposition to Pitt and the war with France – had done much to reconcile them. Lansdowne's marriage to Holland's aunt, Lady Louisa Fitzpatrick, as his second wife was a further link. It had been she who brought up Caroline Fox, who after her aunt's death in 1789 became the adopted daughter of the house. Also living there were Lord Lansdowne's unmarried sisters-in-law from his first marriage, Elizabeth and Caroline Vernon, step-aunts to Henry and his sister.

Two step-aunts, an uncle and a sister-in-law: for Lady Holland, who would meet them for the first time, it was a daunting prospect. Even her husband was a little nervous: 'I must entreat you to look upon the first hour of her acquaintance as a blank because like many other shy people she is extremely awkward,' he wrote to Caroline; 'her shyness takes the form almost of impudence and she says all sorts of foolish things… as you may easily believe, my dearest little sister… I shld. feel miserable were the first impressions of her acquaintance upon your mind to be unfavourable.'[7]

In the event the visit went off very well. Lady Holland, wrote her husband, was delighted by the kindness of her new relations, and they in turn, his sister assured him, 'were all pleased beyond our expectation by finding her manners accord so well with ours & entirely free from that pedantry & affectation which idle report had taught us to expect.'[8] Lord Lansdowne was instantly won over. 'My dearest Ld. Holland,' he wrote when they had left. 'Why shld. you not make an inn of this house or any other use you think proper. I shall be sorry if you and Lady Holland do not find it the same as Holland House.'[9]

Fox's attitude was more reserved and Lady Holland would always be a little frightened of him. Five years earlier, his enormous debts had been paid off by his friends; he had now forsworn gambling, and was living a domesticated life with Mrs Armistead (whom he had secretly married three years before) at his Surrey villa, St Anne's Hill. Even in her journal, Lady Holland did not dare to breathe a word against her husband's hero, but she was dismissive of his companion who, having begun her career in a 'certain notorious establishment'[10] in Marlborough Street, had run through a series of celebrated lovers, including the Prince of Wales, before settling down with Fox. 'Mrs Armstead...' she wrote loftily,

> possesses still those merits which, when united to the attractions of youth... placed her above her competitors for the glory of ruining and seducing the giddy youth of the day. She has mildness and little rapacity, but these negative merits, when bereft of the other advantages, constitute but an insipid resort... But I have often noticed that very superior men are easier satisfied with respect to the talents of those they live with than men of inferior talents.[11]

Holland had returned home at a dismal point in the Whig fortunes. Two years earlier, encouraged by the French Convention's replacement by the Directory, Pitt's government had put out feelers for peace, only to find that France's external ambitions had not changed. Regardless of the threat to Britain's security, she insisted on keeping her conquests up to the Rhine, and negotiations eventually broke down. One by one Britain's allies signed separate peace treaties with France. In October, her last important ally, Austria, having been driven out of Italy by Bonaparte's invading army, bought peace at the Treaty of Campo Formio. Britain now confronted France alone.

Pitt's willingness to negotiate for peace – the main plank of the opposition's policy – had taken the wind out of the Foxites' sails. France's refusal to give up her conquests made it impossible for them to go on arguing that the government was deliberately prolonging the war. At the same time, a motion for parliamentary reform, put forward by Fox's disciple, Charles Grey, was so convincingly defeated that it would not be raised again for many years. Despairing of continuing the fight, Fox announced that his party would cease to attend the House of Commons in protest.

The decision to secede was taken at Holland House. 'The 14th October [1797],' wrote Lady Holland in her journal, 'Mr Fox, D. of Bedford, etc. dined here, and it was then finally concluded among them that none of the shattered remains of their party should attend the meeting of Parliament.'[12]

It was the first time since the death of Holland's grandfather that Holland House had been the setting for political discussion. Fox's Surrey villa was too far out for party meetings; Holland House, two miles from Hyde Park Corner yet surrounded by woods and fields, combined the advantages of a town house and a stately home. Born into the heart of the Whig aristocracy – 'they are all cousins,' someone remarked – and imbued with his uncle's political ideals, Holland fell naturally into the role of host for Fox's friends. It was one that had previously belonged to the Duchess of Devonshire, famed for canvassing for Fox in the Westminster elections of 1784, when she was said to have exchanged kisses for votes. But domestic and financial troubles and a series of agonizing eye operations had done much to curtail her activities. Lady Holland, who had first known her in Italy five years earlier, was shocked by the change in her. 'Scarcely has she a vestige of those charms that once attracted all hearts. Her figure is corpulent, her complexion coarse, one eye gone, and her neck immense. How frail is the tenure of beauty!'[13]

There was still a friendly overlap of guests with Devonshire House, but Holland House was very different in character. For one thing there was no gambling; unlike the Duchess of Devonshire, who had lost many millions in today's currency at the gaming table, the Hollands had no interest in high play. Nor was there the same atmosphere of feminine intrigue. The Duchess and Lady Bessborough, like other ladies of the great Whig families, were familiar visitors, but even though Lady Holland was now married, the stiffer ladies of the aristocracy stayed away and the majority of the guests were men. Lady Holland felt it but not too bitterly. She had her own position as mistress of a splendid house, her husband, lively and ebullient, was an enchanting host, and she herself, in the full glow of her youth and beauty, could once more exercise her social skills. Together they made Holland House a magnet for those politicians still attached to Fox's tattered standard, few in number, but making up in talent what they lacked in votes.

Among them was the future prime minister, Charles Grey, whose brilliant début as a speaker at the age of 22 had propelled him to the forefront of the party. Now in his early thirties, he had been the lover of the Duchess of Devonshire, eight years before; it had been she, according to Lady Holland, who had first attached him to the Foxite Whigs. In 1792 he had been a founder of the Society of the Friends of the People, an aristocratic left-wing group devoted to electoral reform. Discredited by the excesses of the Revolution, it lasted only a few years; in the long run, however, it pointed the way to the Reform Bill of 1832, when Grey, who lived to carry it through Parliament, would refer to his membership with pride.

Richard Brinsley Sheridan, another habitué of Holland House, had also been a founding member of the group, though he was increasingly at odds with Grey, who regarded him as devious and unreliable. From his dazzling beginnings as a playwright, and still linked to the theatre as manager of Drury Lane, he had gone on to an equally dazzling career in politics, at his best outshining even Fox as an orator. Frequently the worse for drink – 'Sheridan lost his dinner,' Lady Holland noted on one occasion – he made himself forgiven by 'a sort of cheerful frankness and pleasant wittiness'[14] she found impossible to resist.

Sheridan's loyalty to Fox's self-denying ordinance deprived him of the chance to show his powers in public, a sacrifice made worse by the fact that George Tierney, another Foxite MP, had ignored the call to defect and was now stealing much of his thunder in the House of Commons. Sheridan loathed Tierney as a result. Tierney, meanwhile, had taken an embarrassing fancy to his hostess. Lady Holland had not lost her instinct for flirtation, but she had no intention of endangering her marriage for his sake. 'I told Lord H. of Tierney's persecution,' she wrote; 'we jointly laughed at his vain presumption, and imputed it to his opinion of the depravity and corruption he believes exists among women of fashion.'[15]

With the withdrawal of Fox's supporters from the House of Commons, Holland became one of their chief spokesmen in the House of Lords. Unlike his uncle he was not a natural parliamentary speaker. His manner was hesitant and sometimes confused, from a rush of too many ideas at once; he was better in the brief exchanges of debate. Fox, who had retired, not at all unwillingly, to his books at St Anne's Hill, did not attend his nephew's maiden speech, a protest against increases in assessed taxes and the 'calamitous' war policies that made them necessary. 'No person that got through his speech at all was ever, I believe so frightened,'[16] confessed Holland to his sister. But Fox was full of praises for its content. 'I think your speech, whether well or ill given reads very well indeed,' he told him, 'but it was not the goodness of the speech only that I alluded to [in a previous letter] it was the stoutness of fighting so well, all alone against them all, and I really was delighted full as much as I said and more.'[17]

It was true that Holland was fighting a lonely battle in the House of Lords; there was only a handful of other members who remained loyal to Fox. This did not prevent him from speaking out against the government whenever he could: its incompetence in running the war, its suppression of habeas corpus and civil liberties, above all its disastrous policies in Ireland, where a national uprising was already preparing in secret.

The failure of a French expeditionary force to land in Ireland in 1796 – only averted when the fleet was scattered by a hurricane – had dramatically pointed up the country's vulnerability to invasion. The threat had spurred the government to drastic action. Their policy of disarming potentially disaffected areas had led to widespread abuses, the victims, mainly Catholic, responding with violence and assassination. By the beginning of 1798 the country was on the brink of anarchy. It was not until May that the storm broke, but it is hard to acquit Fox, contentedly studying the classics at St Anne's Hill, of abdicating his responsibilities, leaving it to Sheridan to break his party's silence and attack the government's policies in the Commons.

For the Fox family the Irish rebellion would have a tragic personal dimension. On 19 May, Fox's first cousin Lord Edward Fitzgerald, the leader of the rebel forces, was arrested in Dublin where he had been in hiding. His apprehension hurried on the revolt, first in scattered outbreaks round Dublin, then more seriously in Wexford, where a force of largely Catholic insurgents captured the town. From then on the revolution snowballed; for a few days the fate of Ireland hung in the balance as the rebels marched towards Dublin.

Meanwhile, Lord Edward, who had been wounded in the struggle to arrest him, was awaiting trial in prison. Fox and Holland both offered to go to Ireland to speak on his behalf, and were still trying desperately to save him when they heard that he had died of septicaemia from his wounds. 'Death has placed the gallant Ld. Edward beyond the reach of his enemies,'[18] wrote Lady Holland sadly.

By the end of August 1798, the Irish insurrection had been crushed by superior government forces, leaving a toll of 30,000 dead and a legacy of bitterness which has lasted to this day. Its immediate result was to open the way for reunion with Britain. For 17 years Ireland had had its own parliament, which, though confined to the Protestant ascendancy, at least had a modicum of independence. But its failure to deal with the grievances of the Catholics, culminating in the horrors of the rebellion, had convinced Pitt that it must be abolished. By bringing its members into the wider context of a British parliament, the proportion of Catholics to Protestants would shift, and with the Irish Protestants no longer a minority, the question of Catholic Emancipation could be addressed. It had been Pitt's original intention to make emancipation a keystone of the Act of Union, but seeing difficulties ahead he decided to deal with the two issues separately.

At first sight the government's solution had all the virtues of expediency; in practice it would prove a disaster for both countries, sowing the seeds of discord for the next two centuries. While Sheridan, in the Commons, fought a hopeless battle against the loss of Irish independence, Holland was one of the few who protested against it in the House of Lords. There was no evidence, he insisted, that the proposed union was the right solution to Ireland's discontents; to impose such a hasty and ill-considered measure on a population still 'inflamed by civil animosity' would merely exacerbate its grievances. Its main effect would be an enormous increase in the influence of the Crown, with no corresponding benefits for Ireland.

Like Sheridan's, his was a Cassandra voice. The Act of Union, forced through by massive bribery of the Irish members, was passed in 1801. The hope of Catholic Emancipation proved illusory, blocked by the flat refusal of the king to countenance what he saw as a violation of his coronation oath. Pitt, to his credit, resigned over the matter; for Holland, it was a reaffirmation of the Foxite view of George III's nefarious role in politics.

Although such political issues, taking place against the turbulent background of a European war, were constantly discussed at Holland House, it was far more than just a forum for the opposition. Both the Hollands, through their travels abroad, were familiar with the European concept of a salon as a cosmopolitan meeting place where fashion, learning and the arts could mingle, new talents be encouraged, and ideas expanded in the give and take of conversation. It was Lady Holland who took the initiative in creating such a centre. She knew she faced ostracism in most London drawing rooms. Her husband was too content at Holland House to go out on his own. Society must come to them. 'Mixing with a wide variety of people,' she wrote,

> is an advantage to Lord H., because as he, thank God, lives constantly at home, unless I were active in collecting fresh materials he might be too apt to fall into a click [clique], a calamity no abilities can fight against. Ideas get contracted, prejudices strong and the whole mind narrowed... Mankind was made to live together; the more they mix with each other the better able a man is to judge them and conduct himself; otherwise it becomes what a priest once said of the universal truth, 'Orthodoxy is my doxy.'[19]

It was this open-mindedness, this readiness to embrace new people and ideas, which would make Holland House such a powerhouse in the years to come.

4

Foreign Adventures

APART from occasional references to the garden, 'delicious in summer', Lady Holland says little of her new surroundings in her journal for the first years of marriage. It was as if she took the splendours of Holland House for granted, preferring to concentrate on the politics and personalities around her. But she devotes several pages to the history of the house itself. 'This house,' she writes in March 1800, 'has contained many remarkable and interesting persons,' and she goes on to tell some of their stories.[1] Built by Sir Walter Cope in 1607 and originally known as Cope Castle, the house had passed by marriage to the first Earl of Holland, 'a most accomplished and gallant cavalier', who was executed during the Civil War for his support of Charles I. The first earl's grandson Edward, on the death of a cousin, took on the second title of the Earl of Warwick. Edward's widow, the Countess of Warwick, married her son's tutor, the poet, essayist and statesman Joseph Addison. The marriage was not a success. The countess, observes Lady Holland, 'always remembered her own rank and thought herself entitled to treat the tutor of her son with very little ceremony.' Lord Warwick, 'a disorderly young man', despite the moral exhortations of his tutor, died unmarried in 1721; his successor, also unmarried, died in 1759, leaving the earldom of Holland extinct. (That of Warwick passed to another line.)

The Holland title was revived, though only as a barony, by Henry Fox, who rented the house soon after his marriage in 1749, and bought it 18 years later. During his lifetime, the house was 'frequently the resort of the great politicians... Sir Robert Walpole, Lds Bute and Chatham, etc.' It was also the home of the first Lady Holland's sister, Lady Sarah Lennox, when the young Prince of Wales, later George III, fell in love with her, and but for 'her levity and total disregard for appearances' (the words are Lady Holland's) might have made her his queen. His subsequent marriage to a German princess disappointed the ambitious Henry Fox, but left Lady Sarah emotionally unscathed. She went on to a tumultuous career, marriage, elopement and divorce, before settling down with a brave but impoverished army officer, George Napier, and becoming the mother of heroes – three of her sons were famous generals.

On the death of the second Lord Holland in 1775 the contents of the house, with the exception of the library and a few treasured possessions, had been sold at auction, and the house had been let till his son's majority. As soon as they returned to England the Hollands set about putting it in order. The house itself was enormous – so large that William III had considered making it his palace when he first came to England – and had deteriorated badly. But their aim was to renovate rather than rebuild, letting its Jacobean character – its turrets, gables and tall chimneys, its mullioned windows and ornate plaster ceilings – speak for itself. Unfashionable at the time the first Lord Holland bought it, its picturesque qualities were now beginning to be appreciated, and the Hollands' architect and supervisor, George Saunders, a fellow of the Royal Society of Antiquaries, would have shared their feeling for its history.

First glimpsed through the trees from what is now Kensington High Street, the house was approached by a long elm avenue, culminating in an elaborate carved-stone gateway designed by Inigo Jones. As with many other great houses of the period, it was laid out roughly in the shape of an E, with a projecting entrance porch, and wings on each side. From an imposing front hall, peopled with marble busts, an inner hall led to the grand main staircase and the principal reception rooms on the first floor. The whole of the west, or left, wing of the house was taken up by the gallery or library, 90 feet long, with little cabinets for study set in along the walls, and portraits of writers and statesmen hung above the bookcases. Here Addison had paced as he mused over the next issue of the *Spectator*, here Fox had first acquired his passion for poetry and the classics, and here in the days of the third Lord Holland, 'all the antique gravity of a college library', as Macaulay put it, was blended with 'all that female grace and wit could devise to embellish a drawing room'.[2] For Macaulay, as for most visitors, the library was the heart of Holland House.

From the library on the south side, an arched recess led into the dining room, its red-silk walls hung with family portraits, its sideboard 'glittering with venerable plate' and its china cabinet gay with oriental porcelain. There were more family portraits, mostly by Reynolds, in the Crimson Drawing Room beyond: the first Lady Holland and her sisters, the Duchess of Leinster and Lady Louisa Connolly; the 14-year-old Charles James Fox in a conversation piece with his young aunt, Lady Sarah, and his cousin Lady Susan Fox-Strangways, another wayward lady, who scandalized her family by marrying an actor; the first Lord Holland; Caroline Fox as a little girl, with a puppy on her lap; Lady Holland as a 'Virgin of the Sun'; Holland on his Italian tour.

Two other formal reception rooms led off the Crimson Drawing Room and Dining Room respectively: the Gilt Room, once the 'Great Chamber' of the house, its magnificent carved panelling and gilded decorations supposedly commissioned for a wedding ball for Charles I, and used by the Hollands as a dining room on grand occasions; and the smaller Yellow Drawing Room, hung with Flemish and Italian old masters collected on the Hollands' travels. The east wing of the house was devoted to the family's own apartments. Elsewhere on the ground and upper floors, there was ample space for family and guests to stay, sometimes for weeks on end, sometimes, especially in winter, to dine and spend the night.

Caroline Fox, who longed to have more of her brother to herself, objected to the constant stream of visitors, many of them foreigners exiled by war or revolution, who came through the house. Their overnight stays – requiring conversation at the breakfast table – were a further trial. Her brother remonstrated with her gently (incidentally giving an insight into the discomforts of hired transport at the time):

> With regard to people staying to supper & to sleep and consequently returning to the charge at breakfast – now I ask you if you were a poor Emigrant, accustomed not only to the comforts but the luxuries of life and a climate much milder than ours, if you would like to go home of a night in the dark over a dirty and deep road in a Hackney coach (the horses of which have grown very bad from the dearness of corn and the short commons upon which they are consequently kept), the fares of which are double after sunset & the insides of which are stinking & disagreable & ill defended from the inclemency of the weather... and the springs of which are gone?[3]

Caroline could only withdraw gracefully. Despite her grumbles she continued to be a frequent visitor to Holland House – too frequent perhaps for Lady Holland since, as she noted in her journal, 'one half of my male and female intimates are placed at the top of Miss Fox's black list.'[4] But the house, as it had been in the first Lord Holland's time, was very much a family centre where relations could come and go as they pleased, and Fox spent the night on his rare visits to London. Here came Lord Edward Fitzgerald's brother, the Duke of Leinster, and his mother soon after Lord Edward's death, the Hollands entering wholeheartedly into their sorrows. The Duke of Bedford, devoted to Fox and one of Holland's few allies in the House of Lords, was another frequent visitor. So too was Lord Lansdowne, a special mark of favour since he had become something of a recluse and seldom ventured out. With him came his two sisters-in-law, one of whom, Caroline Vernon, had recently dismayed her family by marrying Holland's school friend Bobus Smith, 12 years her junior and with barely a penny to his name. The marriage, thought Lansdowne, was a 'profligate abandonment',[5] though he later relented enough to find Bobus a place with the East India Company. Lansdowne's eldest son Lord Wycombe, an old friend from the Hollands' days in Italy, was also a caller, till one day he saw his father's carriage at the gates of Holland House and left in dudgeon never to return. Father and son were at daggers drawn and the Hollands, who were fond of both, were unwillingly caught in the crossfire.

Lady Holland had her own share of family dramas at the time. In January 1799, she gave birth to a son, Stephen, 'a nice little boy, who is going on perfectly well';[6] there were now two children at Holland House. But she missed her other children terribly. She managed to see the two boys, Webby, now at Harrow, and Henry, on a few rare occasions, and to visit her daughter Harriet in secret. But in the summer of 1799 she decided she must give Harriet up; rumours of her existence were going round, and she was afraid of involving Holland in a further scandal. She used her mother as her go-between in telling Sir Godfrey that the daughter he had mourned was still alive. To do him justice, he behaved extremely well, immediately acknowledging her and welcoming her back. Lady Holland felt bereft. She knew that everyone was talking about her, but she paid no attention to their stories. 'I only feel I have renounced a darling child, and my heart aches for it.'[7] To make matters worse Harriet had been sent to boarding school, where her mother heard she was unhappy.

Then, on 4 June 1800, very early in the morning, the Hollands were awakened by a loud rapping on the bedroom door. It was Lady Affleck, who had come to tell them that Sir Godfrey had died, supposedly from a fit, the night before. 'I could not hear the news without emotion,' wrote Lady Holland,

> and was for some time considerably agitated. But, my God! how was I overcome when Drew [the family doctor] showed me a note written to him by Hodges to apprise me of the manner of his death. He shot himself, he added, in consequence of heavy losses at play… Unhappy man! What must have been the agony of his mind, to rouse him to commit a deed of such horror. Peace to his soul, and may he find that mercy I would bestow.

It transpired that Sir Godfrey had been suffering from some kind of mental disorder for the last six months, and that he had twice already tried to kill himself by taking laudanum. On the morning of his death, he had gone out to buy a pair of pistols, and having found various pretexts to get the servants out of the way had shot himself in his front drawing room. Lady Holland could only be grateful that his death had not taken place two years earlier, at the time of her divorce: 'The world and my own readiness to upbraid myself would have assigned my quitting him as the cause.'[8]

With the death of Sir Godfrey most of Lady Holland's fortune was returned to her. But any hopes she might have had of being reunited with her children were soon dashed. Even though Sir Godfrey had left no will, her former brother- and sister-in-law, Mr and Mrs Chaplin, obtained the guardianship of the children. They had originally been quite friendly to the Hollands, even congratulating them on their marriage, but their attitude had hardened after Sir Godfrey's shocking end, and they refused to allow the children any contact with their mother.

The following month, perhaps to distance themselves from these tragedies, the Hollands left on a tour of northern Germany, taking their eldest son Charles, now four, the Bessboroughs' 18-year-old son Lord Duncannon, Dr Drew, the Reverend Matthew Marsh (an old friend from their Italian days) and a numerous retinue of servants with them. They travelled extensively, visiting the courts of Brunswick, Hanover and Prussia and meeting notabilities and intellectuals, before returning – such were the privileges of wartime travel for English aristocrats – through the Netherlands and France on papers provided by the French authorities.

The last stages of their journey had been overshadowed by alarming news of their baby Stephen's health. They reached home in October to find that he was critically ill. He died a month later on his father's birthday, 10 November 1800. It was not until the end of January that Lady Holland could bear to take up her journal again. 'After passing many watchful nights, and latterly for 8 together, by the side of my dear boy, he was snatched from me, alas, for ever!' she wrote. She could not help feeling that if only she had not gone abroad he could have been saved, though the medical details of his illness – 'two tubercles on his lung, and a pint of water on his chest' – made this unlikely.[9] Three months later she was still mourning, though once again beginning to entertain and to take an interest in the changing political scene.

Even though he had withdrawn from Parliament, Fox was still a source of controversy. In January 1798 he had attended a dinner in his honour at the Whig Club at which the Duke of Norfolk, an ardent Foxite, proposed a toast to 'the Majesty of the People'. The toast, in Pitt's opinion, was little short of treason, and the duke was immediately dismissed from his post as Lord Lieutenant of the West Riding in Yorkshire. Unwilling to let him bear the odium alone, Fox repeated the toast at a Whig Club dinner shortly after. Wisely judging, however, that it was no use making him a martyr by bringing him to trial, Pitt had contented himself with advising the king that Fox's name should be struck off the list of privy councillors.

The episode confirmed the general view of Fox as an unpatriotic, even treasonable figure. Blue-jowled and black-browed, his image appeared in countless caricatures in which his pro-French sympathies and revolutionary leanings were constant themes. Protected by his aristocratic status and connections, and contentedly installed in the country, he could afford to ignore his unpopularity. He had embarked on a history of his thrice great-uncle, James II, and the Glorious Revolution by which the rights of Parliament had been established: historical precedents for his opposition to the Crown.

In February 1801 the Act of Union with Ireland was passed, without its accompanying measure of Catholic relief, and Pitt was morally obliged to resign. The new prime minister, Henry Addington, supported George III in opposing Catholic Emancipation, but the illness of the king – brought about by the worry of the Catholic question – put Addington's future in doubt. Once again the question of a regency was raised, and for a brief moment there seemed a possibility of the Whigs' return to power. Rumours and counter rumours abounded. 'The king is recovering as fast as he can, say the courtiers,' noted Lady Holland; 'Pitt's people cautiously say he may amend, but it must be slowly; Opposition declare he is as mad as the winds.'[10]

In March, the king's unexpected recovery put speculations at an end. But faced with the exhausted state of the economy, Addington proved as eager as the Whigs themselves to steer the country towards peace. The signing of the Treaty of Amiens in March 1802 was greeted with general jubilation, though the terms were highly advantageous to the French, and it was soon obvious that it would not last. It was, said Sheridan, in an epigram which Holland described him as having heard at Holland House two hours before and borrowed without leave, 'a peace which every man ought to be glad of but no man could be proud of'.[11]

Meanwhile the Hollands had had another son, Henry Edward. Born with a slight malformation of the hip, his health was fragile from the first, while Charles, his elder brother, had barely survived a series of bronchial infections the previous winter. They determined to travel to a warmer climate for the next one, leaving Caroline Fox to keep an eye on Holland House.

As well as their usual retinue of servants, they were accompanied by Frederick Howard, the 16-year-old son of Lord Carlisle, his tutor Matthew Marsh and, since Dr Drew was too unwell to travel, a Scottish physician, John Allen. Recommended by Bobus Smith, whose brother Sydney had known him in Edinburgh, Allen had been part of the brilliant intellectual circle who were soon to found the *Edinburgh Review*, sharing their literary interests and ardent belief in political reform. He was 'a stout strong man', wrote the Hollands' son Charles, recalling his first impressions of him, 'with a very large head... enormous round silver spectacles before a pair of peculiarly bright and intelligent eyes... his accent Scotch, his manner eager but extremely good natured'.[12] His travels with the Hollands were the start of a lifelong friendship with the family, with Allen becoming not only resident physician, but librarian, confidant and social secretary of Holland House.

The Hollands intended to spend the winter of 1802–3 in Spain, but the signing of the Peace of Amiens made a visit to Paris a natural beginning to their journey. Two and a half years earlier, in the coup of 18 Brumaire (9 November) Bonaparte had become First Consul, an appointment which had just been confirmed for life. A host of English aristocrats, long starved of travel on the Continent, flocked to Paris to see the new dictator and the pomps of his military regime for themselves. Fox and Mrs Armistead (now revealed to the world as Fox's wife) were among them; as well as surveying the political scene, Fox was planning to research in the Paris archives for his projected history of the reign of James II.

Holland, who considered that even the horrors of the Terror were no justification for a return to Bourbon rule, was cautiously approving of the new regime. It was true, he wrote to his sister, that the First Consul was a king in all but name, but he was 'at least less likely to produce reaction, confusion and bloodshed than any Bourbon king would do'.[13] Many of the advantages resulting from the Revolution, such as the equalization of taxes, the abolition of obstacles to internal trade and the opening of careers to all talents, were perfectly compatible with a strong, not to say an arbitrary, government – but all would be lost if the arbitrary government were in Bourbon hands.

When Fox was first presented to the First Consul at a reception in September, Bonaparte greeted him with a speech which he had obviously learnt by heart. Its purport, reported Lady Holland, was that Fox was 'the greatest man of one of the greatest countries, and that his voice had always been exerted on the side of humanity and justice, and that to its influence the world owed the blessings of peace'.[14] Despite these flowery compliments there was no real meeting of minds between them. In a small but telling moment when the two men talked in private, Bonaparte complained of the scurrilous attacks against him in the English papers. Fox, well used to press abuse, replied that in England such things were a necessary evil and that no one minded them. '*C'est tout autre chose ici*,'[15] said Bonaparte, who would not have dreamt of allowing their equivalent in France.

Both the Hollands were presented to the First Consul and his wife at an official reception in September, a balm to Lady Holland's feelings since in England she was not received at court. (She was not best pleased however that Mrs Fox was presented on the same occasion.) Later the Hollands would be notorious for their hero worship of Napoleon, but Lady Holland's first reaction was more measured. 'His head is out of proportion, being too large for his figure...' she told her sister-in-law. 'The gracious smile he puts on is not in unison with the upper part of his face: that is penetrating, severe and unbending.' As for Joséphine, her figure and clothes were perfect, but her face was ghastly, 'deep furrows on each side of her mouth, fallen-in cheeks... a worn-out hag prematurely gone, as she is not above 40 years old.'[16]

The Hollands spent three months in Paris, fêted in the new society which had sprung up round the First Consul, in which old members of the aristocracy, encouraged back from exile, mixed with generals, former revolutionaries and beauties of dubious reputation who, thanks to their looks and their protectors, had managed to survive the storm. Holland revived his friendship with Talleyrand, last seen as a penniless exile in London, and now entertaining lavishly as foreign minister; Lafayette, by contrast, was living in dignified retirement in the country. It was a vivid, fast-moving scene, to which Bonaparte's restless genius gave an edge of drama. It was clear that his expansionist plans had not abated. Already, when they left, there were rumours that the peace could not last, though the Hollands chose to disbelieve them. They set out for Spain at the end of September 1802, travelling in three large carriages; it was 12 years before they would see Paris again.

5

'The Best and Greatest Man...'

ONE of Holland's aims in going to Spain was to seek material for a life of the great Spanish dramatist and poet, Lope de Vega. A contemporary of Shakespeare, de Vega was an almost equally universal figure; from the vast range of his work (he was said to have written 2,000 plays) Holland eventually translated 15. But both he and his wife were passionately interested in the contemporary scene as well. Indefatigable travellers, they moved from town to town, braving uncomfortable lodgings, entertaining or being entertained by local dignitaries and intellectuals, visiting convents, libraries and palaces, attending a bullfight (whose cruelty disgusted Lady Holland) and avidly following the politics of the day.

The Hollands left two accounts of their journeys in Spain. Lady Holland's journal recorded day-to-day happenings, including the illnesses that punctuated their travels. Their children were both delicate, Holland was laid low by a prolonged attack of gout and Lady Holland herself almost died from a miscarriage. Her husband's reminiscences, written many years later, were less personal in nature, and paint a fascinating picture of the characters and intrigues of the Spanish court. The Bourbon king, Charles IV, weak and slow-witted, was dominated by his wife, Queen Maria Luisa, who despite being plain and toothless – she had a set of teeth from Paris, Holland noted – was famous for her amours. The chief minister was her former lover, Manuel Godoy, created 'Prince of the Peace' for his part in negotiating peace with France in 1795. An alluring figure, with graceful manners and brilliant dark eyes, he won the approval of the Hollands for his brave attempts to challenge the vested interests of the Church and army. In foreign affairs, however, he pursued a pro-French policy which would lead to Spain declaring war on England in December 1804. By that time the Peace of Amiens had already come to an end – Britain declared war on France in May 1803 – and all English travellers in France had been interned. This time there would be no question of the Hollands' going home through France, though they were in no hurry to return. They lingered on in Spain till the eve of the war, renewing and widening the circle of acquaintances Holland had made on his first visit there, Lady Holland now as fluent in Spanish as her husband.

At the end of November 1804, two weeks before Spain declared war on Britain, they crossed the frontier into Portugal, where after a brief stay in Lisbon they planned to take a house in the watering place of Las Caldas, in the hope that the baths would help Lord Holland's gout and the weakness in his small son Henry's leg. But the news that the French fleet had escaped from Brest, and that a packet boat was leaving immediately to take the information to England, offered too good a chance of getting home to miss. In 13 hours – 'a wonderful exertion', noted Lady Holland[1] – they were ready to sail. They embarked at midnight and after a stormy voyage, in constant fear of enemy attack, they landed safe in Falmouth on 2 April.

Fox was delighted at his nephew's return. 'I cannot tell you how happy your letter from Falmouth has made me,'[2] he told him. There were hopes for the opposition once again, and he was eager for Holland to play his part. Addington had resigned in April 1804, and three separate groups in the House of Commons, the Foxites, Pitt's followers and those of the former Foreign Secretary, Lord Grenville, were united on the issue of Catholic Emancipation. Their attitudes to the war had entered a new phase too, even the Foxites agreeing that Napoleon's aggressive policies – he had become emperor in 1804 – made its renewal inevitable. Pitt had tried to form a broad-based ministry, but it had foundered on the king's refusal to accept Fox under any circumstances, and Grenville's honourable decision not to accept office if Fox was excluded. Pitt had been forced to form his ministry without them, including not only Addington but a number of Addingtonians in his Cabinet, but the situation was fluid enough to bring the Foxites back into the fray.

Holland arrived home just in time to speak in support of a parliamentary motion by Lord Grenville to consider the removal of Catholic disabilities. Five years earlier, during the debates over the Act of Union, he had put forward a similar motion. Dismissed at the time, it was the first such initiative in the Lords. 'I may perhaps indulge a little pardonable complacency,' he wrote in his memoirs, 'in reminding my reader that the great measure, commonly called Catholic Emancipation, which so many of its inveterate opponents were driven to adopt in 1829, was first moved in the House of Lords by the writer of these pages.'[3]

Grenville's motion, though backed by heavier guns, and supported by a mass petition from the Irish Catholics, was rejected by a large majority. The mood of the country was against emancipation; and the Prince of Wales, though professing sympathy for the measure, was too nervous of reviving criticism of his relationship with the Catholic Mrs Fitzherbert to support it. His defection, wrote Holland later, was 'shabby and dishonourable'; however, the Foxites still had great hopes of the prince and he continued, as he had been before their absence, to be a regular guest at Holland House.

Lady Holland, always happiest in foreign climes, was sorry when their travels came to an end. She had been given an enthusiastic welcome by her family and friends, her mother, Fox and Lady Bessborough among them. 'I liked to see them mightily,' she wrote, 'but a *return* to this country always damps my spirits.'[4] Despite her initial gloom, however, she was soon back in the swing of entertaining and, what was more exciting, of political intrigue. The resignation of Addington from Pitt's Cabinet in July 1805 had once more opened the possibility of a coalition with the Foxites. Lady Holland was against it; she would have preferred an alliance with Addington against Pitt. 'We dined at Holland Ho. yesterday,' wrote Lady Bessborough to Lord Granville. 'I am afraid she [Lady Holland] will do mischief; she has taken violently to Politics lately, is a profess'd Addingtonian, influenced by Mr Tierney, and opposes with all her might (and certainly with might on Lord Holland's mind) all designs of Union with Mr Pitt.'[5]

In August 1805, after prolonged negotiations, Britain formed a coalition against France with Austria, Russia and Sweden. Its first result was to divert the French army, which for the last two years had been massed on the coast near Boulogne; only the British navy had stood between Britain and invasion. In a lightning march Napoleon moved his army to the Black Forest, and while British troops were still preparing to embark for Germany, and the Russians were moving up through Poland, forced the capitulation of 30,000 Austrian troops at Ulm. The news reached Pitt, already struggling from illness and exhaustion, only five days before that of Nelson's victory and death at Trafalgar. From now on Britain was invincible at sea, and the threat of invasion was at an end. But the coalition proved short-lived; on 2 December came the devastating blow of Napoleon's victory at Austerlitz. The Austrians surrendered four days later; the Russians and Swedes withdrew to their own borders. Napoleon's dominance in Europe seemed unassailable.

The news of Austerlitz, by general agreement, sounded Pitt's death knell. Fighting against increasing weakness, he lingered on till 23 January 1806. He was only 46. For Fox, the death of Pitt was the end of an era. For 22 years Pitt had been the great enemy, but neither had underestimated the other's qualities. 'Ah,' said Pitt, to someone who had never heard Fox speak, 'you have not been under the wand of the magician.'[6] And when Pitt died, Fox turned pale at the news. 'It is as if there was something missing in the world,' he told the Duke of Devonshire, 'a chasm, a blank that cannot be supplied.'[7]

Pitt's death at last brought Fox into office, and the king, overcoming his loathing of his character and politics, was forced to accept him as the Foreign Secretary. Grenville was First Lord of the Treasury and nominal prime minister, Addington, now Lord Sidmouth, was Lord Privy Seal. The new administration, in which Fox was the dominating figure, was christened 'the Ministry of All the Talents'; it was certainly one of all opinions.

Now at last seemed the moment to deal with the question of Catholic Emancipation. But Fox knew that he would not be able to carry it through Parliament, let alone convince the king, and that it would be better to postpone the matter till he could achieve his primary aim of making peace with France. On this, though not on the Catholic question, he would have the support of Sidmouth and the Addingtonians.

Fox was in charge of the peace negotiations, and talks in Paris began between Talleyrand and the British plenipotentiary, Lord Yarmouth. It was soon clear, however, that Napoleon was bent on further conquests and had no intention of offering concessions. Even Fox, who had so consistently argued for peace, could see no alternative to continuing the war. Meanwhile his health was beginning to fail. 'I had been struck, on my return to England, with the change in Mr Fox's countenance,' wrote Holland.

The cheerfulness of his spirits and the charms of his conversation, soon wore out this impression. He was, however, more liable to slight indispositions than he had been; and, at the funeral of Lord Nelson, which I attended with him, I observed that the length of the ceremony, and the coldness of the cathedral, overpowered him in a way that no fatigue which I had ever known him undergo had done heretofore.[8]

By May Fox was showing the symptoms of dropsy, probably caused by cancer of the liver. His friends urged him to retire but Fox, as he told his nephew, had 'two glorious things' to achieve, peace and the abolition of the slave trade. Peace was to prove beyond him, but he had the satisfaction, in his last speech in the House of Commons, of proposing a motion in favour of the abolition of the slave trade. The resolution was passed in both houses, and though the bill was not passed till after his death, he knew that it was safely set in train.

At the end of July Lord Lauderdale was sent to replace Lord Yarmouth as the government's chief negotiator in Paris. Fox had earlier spoken of appointing Holland to the post, but by this time he was too ill to attend Cabinet meetings, and the decision had been made without him. 'In his then state of health, I should certainly have declined it,' wrote Holland,

but I own that I was weak enough to feel two minutes' mortification on Lord Howick's [Grey's courtesy title on his father becoming Earl Grey] not giving me the option. I felt this more sensibly when, on approaching my uncle's bedside after he had heard of, and sanctioned, Lord Lauderdale's appointment, he said, with a melancholy smile of affection that I can never forget – 'So you would not leave me, young one, to go to Paris but liked staying with me better – there's a kind boy.' He thus gave me credit for refusing what had never been offered to me, and I did not like to explain the circumstances for fear he might misinterpret my explanation into an expression of disappointment at not going. I answered: 'Why, I hope I may be useful to you here; and I am sure if you like my being here, it would be very odd if I did not prefer staying.'[9]

The following month, however, brought a consolation prize when Holland and Lord Auckland were appointed as joint commissioners to an American delegation sent to London to sort out some of the problems caused by the British navy's high-handed treatment of American ships at sea. Holland was made a privy councillor at the same time. But his uncle's health was growing worse, and he was now spending several hours each day talking or reading to him at his rented house in Stable Yard, St James's. Lady Holland, 'whom he *will not* see', according to Fox's old friend Mrs Bouverie, hovered nearby and did her best to keep out other female visitors. 'She plants herself in one of the rooms below, under pretext of waiting for Lord Holland, and so prevents his admitting any other woman.'[10]

On 7 August, after trying various remedies, the doctors decided on cupping to draw off the fluid from Fox's distended legs and stomach: 'sixteen pints of amber-coloured water was drawn off,'[11] noted Lady Holland. For a few days he revived enough to think of returning to St Anne's Hill. But although it was only three hours from London, the doctors thought the journey was too much for him. Instead the Duke of Devonshire offered him the use of Chiswick House, the exquisite Palladian villa designed by Lord Burlington, as a halfway house. Four months earlier the Duchess of Devonshire, who had flung herself so gallantly into Fox's battles, had died in London, and Chiswick House was full of memories of their friendship. For Fox, it would be the final staging post. A second operation became necessary, which at first seemed to bring some relief. But the next day as he was led about

THE BEST AND GREATEST MAN

the rooms at Chiswick to look at the pictures, a gush of water burst
from his wound, and he fell into a state of alarming breathlessness
and weakness.

Mrs Fox sent for Holland, who from that time never left him. Lady
Holland of course came too, but though Fox behaved more affection-
ately to her than usual, even kissing her hand when she approached his
bedside, she remained in an outer room while Mrs Fox and Holland
kept vigil over him. He seemed to take comfort in seeing them, taking
his wife's hand continually, and opening his eyes with pleasure to see
Holland: 'Ah! young one, are *you* there? I have had had a hard tussle
for it, but all's well now.'[12] When he was given a little claret, he talked
cheerfully of having drunk five bottles in the past.

He had never been one for religious observances, but to please
Mrs Fox a clergyman was sent for who read a prayer while he listened
with clasped hands. Friends came to say goodbye, or waited in the
outer rooms for news. The end came on the evening of 13 September.
Fox's last intelligible words were for his wife: 'I die happy; bless you,
I pity you.' He died a few minutes later, apparently peacefully and
without pain. 'Poor Ld. H. had appear'd quite calm the whole Day,
but then he sank down on the bed and was oblig'd to be carried out,'
wrote Lady Bessborough to Lord Granville. Lady Holland meanwhile
had broken the news to those who were breathlessly waiting outside
by appearing among them with her apron thrown over her head.
Perhaps it was because of this, or some other unspecified eccentricity,
that her behaviour during Fox's last illness was greatly criticized. 'The
cry against her is dreadful,' wrote Lady Bessborough. 'A good deal of
this is *manner*, and neither want of feeling or intention but she really
does act foolishly.'[13]

Few public figures have ever been mourned more than Fox. Adored
by his followers, he was a symbol of free speech and the defence of
civil liberties to thousands who had never known him; his bust by

Nollekens was an icon in Whig households and debating clubs, not least his former gambling haunts at Brooks's. For his nephew he was quite simply the

> best and greatest man of our time, with whom the accident of birth closely connected me, from whose conversation and kindness I derived the chief delight of my youth and veneration for whose memory furnished me with the strongest motive for continuing in publick life, as well as the best regulation for the conduct therein.[14]

It was a path he would strive to follow in the years to come.

6

Edinburgh Reviewers

S HORTLY before his last illness, Fox paid a farewell visit to Holland House and walked all over the grounds, 'looking tenderly at each familiar spot, as if he wished to carry through the gates of death the impressions engraved on his soul during childhood.'[1] Here he had been brought up, and here, while his nephew was alive, his memory and his principles would be kept green.

The word 'Whig' had had many meanings during the previous century. At the outset the Whigs had been the party represented by that group of powerful families who had brought William and Mary to the throne in the Glorious Revolution of 1688, and asserted the rights of Parliament against the absolute monarchy of James II. It had been George III's desire to shift this balance by taking control into his own hands that Fox had consistently opposed, though the king's recurring illnesses, the French Revolution and the continuing war with France had greatly changed the picture since the so-called betrayal of 1784.

Till now the Whig objectives had been driven by the great landed families, interconnected by marriage and friendship, who saw themselves as the guardians of the country's liberties. It was a guardianship based on property; though there had always been brilliant outsiders, like Burke and Sheridan, the real power rested in the hands of the aristocrats, who regarded themselves as the natural leaders of the party. Paradoxically, the Tories had always been more open to talent; Holland's old friend Canning, the son of an actress, for instance, knew that he could never hope to obtain high office under the Whigs.

Until the beginning of the nineteenth century the chief forum for the Whigs had been the Houses of Parliament, and the press, though often scathing in its abuse of individual figures, from Fox and Sheridan to the increasingly corpulent Prince of Wales, had been more inclined to report on current issues than to widen the debate. But in October 1802, three brilliant young men from Edinburgh, Francis Jeffrey, Henry Brougham and the Reverend Sydney Smith, had opened up a whole new era in journalism with the foundation of their quarterly, the *Edinburgh Review*. Broadly Whig in politics, as reflected in the buff and blue (Fox's colours) of the cover, it rapidly acquired an enormous influence as a force for social change: Catholic Emancipation, electoral reform, the abolition of slavery, the end of flogging in the army and the repeal of the barbarous game laws were among the many causes it espoused. Fox had been the great precursor, but the *Edinburgh Review* would take his ideas further, and provide the intellectual framework for a new generation of Whig writers and politicians.

By the time the Hollands returned from Spain, both Smith and Brougham had moved to London, leaving Jeffrey, based in Edinburgh, as the official editor of the magazine. Brougham, studying law at Lincoln's Inn, was a tireless and versatile contributor, Smith almost equally so. Brougham's articles were savage and hard-hitting; Smith made ridicule his chief weapon. As well as contributing to the *Edinburgh Review*, he had recently embarked on a series of lectures on moral philosophy at the Royal Institution in Albemarle Street. The lectures were wildly successful, attracting such crowds that the street was blocked by carriages, and creating, said Smith, 'such an uproar as I never remember to have been excited by any other literary imposture.'[2]

It was natural that Brougham and Smith should gravitate to Holland House; both were friends of Allen, himself a contributor to the *Edinburgh Review*, and Smith's brother Bobus was married to Lord Holland's aunt. A little overawed at first, Smith was soon singing the praises of his hosts. 'With Lady Holland I believe you are acquainted,' he wrote to the Scottish jurist Sir James Mackintosh in the autumn of 1805. 'I am lately become so. She is very handsome, very clever and I think very agreeable.' As for Lord Holland:

> I hardly know a talent or virtue he has not, little or big. The devil himself could not put him out of temper, nor is he in any way inferior to him in acuteness. In addition to this, think of his possessing Holland House, and that he reposes every evening on that beautiful structure of flesh and blood, Lady H.[3]

It was the start of a lasting relationship with Holland House, Smith's witty tongue, stout figure and Fox-like black eyebrows becoming almost as much part of its legend as his hosts themselves. Brougham was less easily domesticated. He objected to Lady Holland's imperious ways. Smith would cheerfully give as good as he got, but Brougham was inclined to take umbrage. 'George Lamb says he [Brougham] always leaves Holland House the moment she begins ordering and giving herself airs,' reported a fellow guest.[4] But at least in his early days he enjoyed the patronage of Holland House, much valued for his clever pen and his consistent harrying of the Tories.

In the government reshuffle that followed Fox's death, Holland was made Lord Privy Seal. At one point Fox had hoped that his nephew would follow him as Foreign Secretary and had promised to oversee his progress. 'It will be nice too,' he had added with a smile, 'for it will secure my seeing you at St Anne's when I am there.'[5] But Fox's death had put paid to such plans and Lord Howick (Grey), Fox's successor as leader of the Foxite Whigs, succeeded him as Foreign Secretary as well.

Even though it was a lesser post, Holland's new appointment gave him a seat in the Cabinet. Lady Holland made the most of her husband's new position. 'She is much too *official* and boasts of knowing things, which either she does not know, or she proves by that very boast, that she ought not to have been told...'[6] wrote Lady Bessborough. 'On being ask'd what some papers were, she put on a mysterious air, saying, "Oh, these are Cabinet Secrets – some papers Ld. Grenville has sent Ld. Holland to look at before they are carried to the King."'

Lady Holland was now 34, still very beautiful in a full-blown way. But she had had eight children – a daughter, Mary, had been born in the spring of 1806 – and had reached an age when making new conquests was less interesting than political intrigue. Sydney Smith was one of the first beneficiaries of her wire-pulling; in 1806, she persuaded the Lord Chancellor Lord Erskine to give him the living of Foxton-le-Clay in Yorkshire. When Smith went to thank him, the Chancellor refused to take any credit: 'Oh don't thank *me*, Mr Smith. I gave you the living because Lady Holland insisted I should do so; and if she had desired me to give to the devil, *he* must have had it.'[7] Since Smith was able to put in a neighbouring curate till 1809, when the rules requiring clergymen to reside in their own parishes were tightened, he continued to be a regular guest at Holland House. We see him there, on an evening before Christmas, in a letter from Lady Bessborough to Lord Granville:

At the Hollands there were a motley company of Lawyers, statesmen, Critics and divines – Sydney Smith the only one of the latter class, in high glee attacking Mr Ward and Mr Allen telling them that the best way to keep a merry Xmas was to roast a Scotch Atheist as the most intolerant and arrogant of all two legged animals. Allen [a diehard atheist] did not look pleas'd, but kept clasping his hands together till his fingers crack'd (a great trick of his). S.S. call'd out, 'See! there's one beginning to crackle already.'[8]

As a clergyman Smith was something of an exception at Holland House. Most of the Whigs, and certainly the Hollands, were sceptics or at best conventionally religious. Tolerant themselves, they were committed to the idea of religious toleration, in particular Catholic Emancipation, not only as a matter of natural justice, but as the only hope of calming Irish discontents.

It was the question of Catholic Emancipation, or rather a small step towards it, which would bring about the downfall of the Ministry of All the Talents in March 1807. The immediate cause was a measure to conciliate the Irish by allowing Catholics to become senior officers in the British army. For the king it was a step too far, a potential violation of his coronation oath. He demanded a pledge from Grenville that the Cabinet would never reopen the Catholic question again. Grenville firmly but courteously refused, and after nine days of uncertainty while the king tried to form a new administration, the ageing Duke of Portland was prevailed upon to head a broadly Tory ministry. 'The time will come,' wrote Macaulay, admittedly a Whig historian,

> when posterity will do justice to the Whigs of England, and will faith-
> fully relate how they suffered for Ireland; how for the sake of Ireland
> they remained out of office for more than 20 years, braving the frowns
> of the court, braving the hisses of the multitude, renouncing power
> and patronage and salaries, and peerages, and garters, and yet not
> receiving in return even a little fleeting popularity.[9]

It was true that the Whigs got no credit for their principles, and the party was roundly defeated in the next election. The cry of 'no popery' was still potent; most people ignored or dismissed the problems of Ireland, and the age and infirmity of the king had only increased his popularity with the general public. But though out of office, they continued to fight for Catholic Emancipation from the sidelines, finding their most powerful spokesman, unexpectedly, in the person of the Church of England clergyman, Sydney Smith.

In the summer of 1807 the first of a series of satirical pamphlets, *The Letters of Peter Plymley*, was published. Supposedly sent by Plymley to his brother Abraham, a country clergyman, and written in a rumbustious style that closely resembled Smith's own conversation, they launched a devastating attack on the bigotry and folly of the government's attitude to Catholic Emancipation. The situation had never been more dangerous. There were nearly five million Catholics in Ireland; Napoleon was winning hearts and minds in other countries by his tolerance of all religions:

> To deny the Irish this justice now, in the present state of Europe, and in the summer months, just as the season for conquering kingdoms is coming on, is (beloved Abraham), whatever you may think of it, little short of insanity.[10]

But reason, as the pamphlets showed, had little to do with the public's – or Plymley's fellow clergy's – perception of the question:

> The moment the very name of Ireland is mentioned the English seem to bid adieu to common feeling, common prudence and common sense and to act with the barbarity of tyrants and the fatuity of idiots.[11]

The effect of the letters (ten in all) was compared to a spark on a heap of gunpowder; there had been nothing like them since the days of Swift, thought Holland. From the drawing rooms of London they quickly spread across the country, each new letter increasing the eagerness and curiosity of the public. The collected edition was reprinted 16 times in the first year, and cheaper editions were specially printed for sale in Ireland. 'Far more than to any other cause,' writes Smith's biographer Hesketh Pearson, 'the Catholics in Great Britain and Ireland could attribute the general feeling in favour of their emancipation, when at last it was manifested, to the common sense, wit and ridicule of Sydney Smith.'[12]

The letters were published anonymously, and despite all the efforts of the authorities, their authorship was not discovered till 30 years later when Smith included them in his collected works. Till then, remembering that Swift had lost a bishopric through being too witty, Smith wisely denied all responsibility for them, though it was an open secret among his friends at Holland House. But he kept up the pretence just the same. 'Mr Allen has mentioned to me the letters of a Mr Plymley, which I have... read with some entertainment,' he wrote to Lady Holland.

> My conjecture lies between three persons – Sir Samuel Romilly, Sir Arthur Pigott or Mr Horner – for the name of Plymley is evidently fictitious! I shall be very happy to hear your conjectures on this subject on Saturday, when I hope you will let me dine with you at Holland House.[13]

Despite their political setbacks the Hollands were continuing to receive on a grand scale. The French chef was paid a princely 110 guineas a year; the pastry cook got 60. The dinner book, kept by Allen, some-times recorded as many as 50 guests. In July the Prince of Wales came to dinner, and wittily routed Sydney Smith who, in the course of a conversation on 'wicked men', asserted that Philippe d'Orléans, regent in France between 1715 and 1723, was the wickedest man that ever lived – 'and he,' he said pointedly, 'was a *prince*.' 'No,' said the prince, 'the wickedest man that ever lived was Cardinal Dubois, the regent's prime minister, and he was a *priest*, Mr Sydney.'[14]

There was still fun and good conversation to be had at Holland House, but some of the urgency had gone out of things. 'The loss of all interest in public affairs was the natural effect of the change of Administration to me,'[15] noted Lady Holland. For her husband, as it had been for Fox, there was always consolation to be had in books. In 1806 he had published his biography of Lope de Vega, collecting many praises for its easy, lucid style, and at the same time adding to his library a unique collection of Lope de Vega manuscripts and printed books. He then set about editing and publishing his uncle's unfinished *Early Life of James II*, adding a preface of his own. But Fox, so magical as a speaker, was not a natural writer and the book was generally considered rather dull. Holland wrote far better than his uncle.

Meanwhile events in Europe had taken a new turn. Although the Spanish had declared war on Britain in 1804, the defeat of the French and Spanish fleets at Trafalgar in 1805 had dampened their enthusiasm – never very great – for continuing. Napoleon, triumphant in northern Europe, was now casting his eye on the Iberian peninsula. In November 1807 the French army invaded Portugal, though not before the Portuguese fleet and royal family had fled to Brazil. French troops, ostensibly intended for the invasion of Portugal, were also massed in Spain. In the spring of 1808 Godoy was overthrown, and following the disputed abdication of Charles IV in favour of his son Ferdinand, Napoleon seized the crown for his brother Joseph instead. Ferdinand was sent off to comfortable house imprisonment in France, but the Spanish people refused to accept their subjugation so tamely. The first of a series of risings took place in Madrid in May, banishing the French and sparking off a national resistance; the Portuguese too rose up against the invaders. The British, seeing their opportunity, sent troops to the peninsula under Sir Arthur Wellesley. In August 1808, after their defeat at the Battle of Vimeiro, the French were forced to evacuate their troops from Portugal, and to sign an armistice at the Treaty of Cintra.

Napoleon was now free to concentrate his energies on Spain, mustering an army of a quarter of a million men to carry out the invasion. For the Hollands, always passionately interested in Spanish affairs, it was a chance to take part in a national war of liberty against the French and perhaps to influence events. Ignoring the protests of friends and relations, from Brougham, who accused them of deserting the Whig cause, to Caroline, who thought they were abandoning their children, they determined to set out for Spain. 'Think of the Hollands going to Spain,' exclaimed Lady Bessborough to Lord Granville.

> Why for? as Ly. Harrington would say... I shd. not think Ly. H., with all her attendants and wants, a good follower of the camp. Neither she nor Ld. H. would make famous warriors; as to *counsel* in a civil capacity, much as I love Ld. Holland, I should be sorry to have him interfere, and still more *her*.[16]

The Tory government had no desire for Holland's services as an unofficial envoy, as Canning, then Foreign Secretary, made clear to the Spanish authorities and to Holland himself. His presence in a war zone could only be an embarrassment to the army. But the Hollands had the bit between their teeth. On 8 October 1808, accompanied by Dr Allen and the 16-year-old son of the Duke of Bedford, Lord John Russell, as well as two maids and six manservants, they left Holland House for Falmouth on the first stage of their journey. 'Well my dear little sister,' Lord Holland told Caroline,

though not launched we are off – they all say it is a wild scheme though
I cannot see why or how, and can only beg you in Dryden's words

> ...O defend
> Against your judgement your departed friend. [17]

On 4 November, after long delays caused by bad weather, they set sail
for Corunna on a British frigate.

7

Spanish Journeys

S INCE the outbreak of the Spanish rising Holland House had been a centre of hospitality for the representatives of the various Spanish juntas seeking help from Britain. Although as a member of the opposition Holland had no direct influence on government policy, he had advice and sympathy to offer, as well as a first-hand knowledge of their country. In some ways his support for their cause meant breaking ranks with his own party, for Grey, now the leader of the Whigs, was insistent on the necessity of making peace, and denounced the folly of a new campaign. But Holland had the precedent of his uncle's support for the war after the peace negotiations of 1806 had failed, and he saw the rising in Spain as a chance of breaking Napoleon's stranglehold on Europe.

Corunna was in a state of excitement when the Hollands arrived there on 3 November 1808. 'We have been received by honours, acclamations, serenades, fireworks that quite overcame us,'[1] wrote Holland to his sister. There were four British regiments stationed there, with fresh troops constantly arriving, and for the Hollands a social round that included visits to the theatre – 'not much less than the Haymarket', noted Lord John – and an expedition to see the monastery at Santiago de Compostela.

After a fortnight in Corunna the Hollands had intended to travel to Madrid, where the Central Junta (or provisional government) had its headquarters. But they were turned back on the second day of their journey by the news that the French were advancing on Madrid; the Spanish army had been defeated at Burgos, and the British troops under Sir John Moore were retreating towards the coast. Instead of participating in a triumph of the liberating armies the Hollands were witnessing the beginning of a rout.

Corunna, now in a state of alarm and confusion, was obviously no place for non-combatants to linger. Failing to find a British ship to take them to Cadiz by sea, they decided to go overland to Lisbon, and thence, provided the French did not get there first, to Seville. On 4 December, Madrid fell to the French after only one day's resistance, though Holland, who did not hear the news till the 20th, had been convinced it would be furiously and successfully defended. His sympathy for the cause of Spanish liberty made him overestimate the effectiveness of the Spanish resistance, at the same belittling the achievements and the difficulties of his own countrymen. Not unnaturally, his attitude aroused considerable resentment. 'I believe he would give the lives of ten Englishmen to save one Spaniard,'[2] wrote an English general bitterly.

As time went by even Holland was forced to modify his optimism about the war. The retreat of Sir John Moore to Corunna and the withdrawal of his army in January 1809 left Britain with only 16,000 troops on the peninsula, and these were committed to the defence of Lisbon. When the Hollands arrived in Seville, where the provisional Spanish government was now installed, Holland was pleased to meet its leading members, many of whom he had known before and one of whom, the statesman and philosopher Jovellanos, was drawing up plans for a constitution along British lines. But the general situation was discouraging. 'I must confess,' he wrote to his sister on 2 February 1809, that neither the political or the military state of the country affords much hope of any improvement in the state of affairs & the wretched condition as well as alarm of most of those to whom I am attached... is rather heightened than softened by the reflection that there are still materials to form a defence of the country but that owing to innumerable faults both Spanish & English they are not likely to be employed.[3]

The arrival in April of Sir Arthur Wellesley, with an expeditionary force of 26,000 men, put a new complexion on affairs. Within a month he had chased the French from Portugal and had carried the war into Spain; but it would take six years of bitter struggle, in which the Spanish resistance played a vital role, before the French were driven out. In the end Holland's belief in the determination of the Spanish people to throw off their conquerors would be justified; even in the short term he felt their contribution had been undervalued. As he wrote to Grey that May:

If the reports given by our Generals & officers of the apathy of the people, the ignorance of the Government, the treachery of individuals etc. etc. were true, how could the whole coast of Spain from Barcelona to Corunna & from Gerrol to St Ander be in the possession of the Spaniards four or five months after so hopeless a state of things [i.e. the withdrawal of Moore's army from Corunna]?[4]

The Hollands spent just over three months in Seville, retreating to Cadiz when news of enemy approaches made them seek the safety of the coast, then picking up courage to return. For Lady Holland, braving the discomforts and alarms of their situation, there was one piece of news that must have filled her heart with pride. Her son Webby, now Sir Godfrey Webster, had been the hero of a cavalry skirmish in which he and a fellow officer, at the head of 30 men, had attacked 100 of the enemy, killed 20 and taken five prisoner. "Twas a most gallant affair,'[5] wrote his commanding officer Lord Henry Paget, reporting the incident to Lord Holland.

By May 1809 the Hollands were ready to leave Spain; they had never thought of their journey, as Holland told his sister, 'as a serious *going abroad* but merely as an excursion.'[6] Lady Holland was pregnant (a daughter, Georgiana, would be born in November); Lord John was beginning to think about the next stage of his education; their friends and family were urging them to come home. But it was some time before they could find a ship to take them. After travelling to Cadiz, where they had hoped to sail on the *Ocean*, taking despatches to England, they found that the ship was held up on convoy duty, and were forced to retrace their steps to Seville. From here they made their way to Badajoz, where their party was greeted by cheering crowds, and thence to Lisbon, where they eventually set sail for England. 'On the 10th of August,' wrote Lady Holland, concluding her Spanish journal, 'got into St Helens and landed in a most boisterous gale and high seas at Portsmouth. Remained the whole day, set off on the following... On the 12th reached Holland House where we found the children and my mother perfectly well.'[7]

It had been an adventurous journey, and for Holland a confirmation of his faith in the cause of Spanish liberalism. Throughout the ebbs and flows of the peninsular campaign, he remained in touch with the leading figures in the provisional government. With Jovellanos he corresponded regularly on the subject of a proposed Spanish constitution, ideally bicameral (in order to link the Spanish grandees to the system) and of course along Foxite lines. He was also the power behind a new journal, *L'Espagnol*, under the editorship of Joseph Blanco White, a former priest and adviser to the Central Junta, who had fled to England when the provisional government was forced to leave Seville in 1810. Intended to influence English opinion in favour of the Spanish liberals, *L'Espagnol* was generally regarded as a mouthpiece for the views of Holland House, and as such distrusted by the British government.

The Hollands returned home to find the Whigs still in the doldrums. The departure of Grey (Lord Howick) to the Lords on the death of his father in 1807 had deprived the party of an effective leader in the Commons, which was now led by George Ponsonby, a worthy but uninspiring figure. For the time being, in the words of Macaulay, the Whigs ceased to be of any consequence.

In these circumstances the role of Holland House, as an alternative centre of the opposition, took on a different aspect. There might be few opportunities for political action, but the prestige of the Whig aristocracy and the growing importance of the *Edinburgh Review*, whose chief writers regarded Holland House as their natural London habitat, gave it a social and intellectual power that outweighed its lack of influence in Parliament. And even though it was not directly involved, the fast-changing events of the Peninsular War, and the constant flow of literary, political and social gossip feeding into it, made it a hugely exciting place to be.

For Lady Bessborough, perhaps Lady Holland's closest friend, the end of 1809 brought heartbreak when Lord Granville Leveson-Gower, her lover of 16 years' standing, married her niece, Lady Harriet Cavendish. The daughter of Lady Bessborough's beloved sister, the Duchess of Devonshire, Harriet had always been dear to her aunt. Lady Bessborough was now 48; at 37, it was time that Lord Granville settled down. He married with Lady Bessborough's blessing, and Harriet's full understanding, and the old affectionate correspondence between them carried on. The only person who seemed to take the matter badly was the Prince of Wales who, calling on Lady Bessborough, launched a violent tirade against her faithless lover, then flung himself upon his knees, and clasped her round the waist with such a string of vows, entreaties and promises of eternal love that 'really G.,' she wrote, 'had not my heart been breaking I must have laugh'd.'[8]

Lady Holland was too discreet to discuss her friend's misfortunes in her journal. They had had their differences, and in the privacy of her letters to Lord Granville, Lady Bessborough enjoyed making fun of her caprices. But they had known each other since their early days in Italy and had supported each other through love affairs and family dramas ever since. The Bessboroughs' children had the run of Holland House, and Caroline, Lady Bessborough's daughter, had recently married William Lamb, son of the Hollands' old friend Lady Melbourne. Clever, indolent and charming, Lamb was a recent recruit to the Foxite Whigs and one of the younger stars of Holland House. So too was Lady Caroline, a brilliant, butterfly-like figure who could be relied on to show off and amuse. She loved dressing up, at one point disguising herself as a schoolboy, at another emerging from behind a curtain dressed up like Sydney Smith. But after three years of marriage, she was already showing signs of the instability that was the reverse side of her charm and, in the autumn of 1809, with the return of Sir Godfrey Webster's regiment from Spain, she embarked on a violent flirtation with Lady Holland's son.

Lady Holland had seen very little of her eldest son; since their father's death he had virtually broken off relations with her. But she strongly objected to Caroline's intrigue. Caroline reacted violently, vowing she would never set foot in Holland House again if her conduct was to be criticized, and furiously reminding Lady Holland of her own: 'No human power,' she declared,

> shall ever dissolve the friendship or [dis]allow the sentiments I feel for your son. But you do well to renounce a Mother's name and to leave him to the false friends and bad company your neglect of him has early brought him to... it might be deemed no greater impertinence

in me to remind you of the Duties of a Mother than in you to taunt me with those of a wife.[9]

In the end it was Sir Godfrey – a brash, heavy-drinking young man – who got out of the entanglement. Long before this Caroline had written effusively to Lady Holland begging her forgiveness for her outburst. Lady Holland seems to have taken it in her stride. She was used to Caroline's attention-seeking ways, though she could not foresee what dramas lay in store two years later when Caroline first met Lord Byron at Holland House.

Lady Caroline's affair with Byron belongs to another chapter. Meanwhile, the autumn of 1810 saw the final collapse of George III into insanity. He had long been teetering on the brink; the death of his favourite daughter Amelia in November pushed him over the edge. An immediate crisis sprang up with Holland House of course in the midst of the plotting. Lady Holland, reported Lady Bessborough, 'seems already to have the cares of office upon her. Two such large packets arriv'd to both of them during the short time I saw them, that it only wanted a red box to make me think our old Administration in again.'[10] The press took up the theme: a cartoon in the *Satirist* entitled 'Sketch for a PRIME Minister, or how to purchase a PEACE' showed Holland in skirts and his wife in breeches knocking at the door of the Treasury while Napoleon slyly offers them a bag of gold.

The Prince of Wales had always been a supporter of the Whigs, and here at last, it seemed, was a chance of their return to power. But the prince disliked their leaders, Grey and Grenville – Grey for his haughty manner and for having cut him out with the Duchess of Devonshire years ago, Grenville because he had supported Pitt against him in the regency crisis of 1788. He was also under pressure from the queen who warned him that a change of government might have fatal effects on his father's reason. In the end he decided to take the line of least resistance, and to accept a restricted regency for a year, leaving Spencer Perceval, who had succeeded the Duke of Portland as Tory prime minister, in power.

The Whigs were furious, but they still had hopes that at the end of the year, if the king did not recover, the prince would turn to them to make a government. But the prince was growing out of sympathy with many of the Whigs' objectives. He knew how unpopular the idea of Catholic Emancipation was in the country, and was unwilling to raise the subject at that stage. He supported the Tories too in their energetic pursuit of the war; the Whigs' calls for peace and constant carping at the government's policies were increasingly perceived as unpatriotic. On a personal front, he was grateful to Perceval for piloting a bill to increase his income through the House of Commons – in view of his reckless extravagance at a time when the country was suffering severe economic hardship, this was no mean feat.

Even though he was warming to Perceval, however, the regent still felt some loyalty to his former Foxite friends. He made one last gesture to the opposition by offering Grey and Grenville places in a coalition government, an offer almost bound to be rejected since they would be joining an administration whose policies they strongly opposed. Predictably the two refused to accept unless there was an understanding that Catholic Emancipation would be granted. It was a pledge which, as they well knew, the prince was no longer prepared to make. He let them go with few regrets, and the Tories were con-firmed in office.

Not unnaturally there was a howl of protest from opposition journalists and writers at this betrayal of the Whigs. The stream of lampoons and epigrams against the prince in the press was only matched by the 'personal asperity', as Holland put it, with which his name was mentioned in private company, not least in such favourite former haunts as Holland House. 'Those who had early opportunities of studying the character of the Prince,' wrote Holland, 'should have known that personal slights were more deeply felt and more certainly resented by him than real injustices, injuries or ill-usage.'[11] Maddened by the criticisms of his erstwhile friends, the prince turned violently against them, and on 22 February, at a banquet at Carlton House, launched into such a furious attack on them that the young Princess Charlotte, who was present, burst into tears.

The incident gave rise to an anonymous poem, 'Sympathetic Address to a Young Lady':

> Weep daughter of a royal line,
> A sire's disgrace, a realm's decay;
> Ah! happy if each tear of thine
> Could wash a father's fault away...

The poem, published in the *Morning Chronicle* two weeks later, caused an enormous stir, confirming the rift between the Prince Regent and the Whigs, and winning its quickly discovered author, the young Lord Byron, a favoured place in the aristocratic and intellectual salon he had long aspired to, Holland House.

8

Enter Byron

B yron's relationship with Holland House had got off to a
bad start. In 1807 his first published volume of poems, *Hours
of Idleness*, had been unfavourably reviewed by Brougham in the
Edinburgh Review. Byron's riposte, *English Bards and Scots Reviewers*,
published the following year, was a swingeing satire on his poetic
contemporaries, on the *Edinburgh* reviewers ('Holland's hirelings'),
and on the Hollands themselves, whom he believed, mistakenly, to
have inspired the hostile criticism. His lines on the Hollands, with
their dig at Lady Holland's virtue, were especially offensive:

> Blest be the banquets spread at Holland House,
> Where Scotsmen feed, and critics may carouse...
> They write for food – and feed because they write:
> And lest, when heated with the grape,
> Some glowing thoughts should to the press escape,
> And tinge with red the female reader's cheek,
> My lady skims the cream of each critique,
> Breathes o'er the page her purity of soul,
> Reforms each error, and refines the whole.

It was typical of the Hollands' good nature – or carelessness of criticism – that they did not hold Byron's lines too much against him, and when, four years later, using his fellow poet Samuel Rogers as a go-between, Byron asked Holland's help in preparing his maiden speech in the House of Lords, he willingly agreed. The speech, delivered on 27 February 1812, was a protest against a frame-breaking bill, directed at Luddite weavers in Nottinghamshire (Byron's home county), making the smashing of machinery punishable by death. Holland, who had recently been appointed Recorder of Nottingham, was naturally against such a barbaric measure, and though Byron's speech failed to sway the House of Lords, it was warmly greeted by the opposition peers. (The bill, in fact, was never put into effect.)

In retrospect Holland doubted that Byron would ever have made a good politician: 'His fastidious and artificial taste and his over-irritable temper would, I think, have prevented him from ever excelling in Parliament.'[1] But he was happy to welcome a new recruit to the opposition, and invited him to dine at Holland House that evening. It was a gathering of the Foxite inner circle: the dukes of Devonshire and Bedford, the Marquess of Lansdowne (the second son of the first marquess, his elder brother having died the year before), lords Grey, Lauderdale and Cowper. In this intimate setting, with its easy flow of conversation, Byron could be himself in a way he could never be in public. Relaxed and delightful, the evening confirmed his arrival on the political scene; the publication of his lines on Princess Charlotte shortly after set the seal on his Whig credentials.

By now Byron had realized his mistake in attributing the hostile notice in the *Edinburgh Review* to the Hollands and, largely to please them, had suppressed the next edition of *English Bards and Scots Reviewers*. He was pinning all his hopes on his forthcoming poem, *Childe Harold's Pilgrimage*, the product of his four years of wandering in Greece and the Near East. He sent an advance copy to Lord Holland, deliberately making light of it in his accompanying note: 'Your lordship, I am sorry to observe today, is troubled with the gout; if my book can produce a *laugh* against itself or the author, it will be of some service. If it can set you to *sleep* the benefit will be yet greater.'[2]

Byron's pretended insouciance, as we know, was unnecessary. The publication of *Childe Harold's Pilgrimage* on 10 March 1812 made him famous overnight. Feted in society, a star in the salons of the Whig aristocracy, he preserved a particular fondness for Holland House, and regarded Holland as his political guide and mentor. At Holland House too, there was a literary mix he found particularly attractive, poets and writers mingling naturally with diplomats, politicians and grandees.

Holland's literary tastes had been very much set by Fox. Like his uncle he loved the classics, and in English poetry, Chaucer and Shakespeare apart, he preferred the poets of the eighteenth century; he loved Cowper, Swift and Pope, and was never without a book of Dryden's poems by his bedside. He had a few contemporary favourites: Walter Scott, though not his Tory politics; George Crabbe, whose low-keyed poems of country life had been much appreciated by Fox as well; Tom Moore, famed for his romantic *Irish Melodies* and his daring verse satires against the government; and the banker poet Samuel Rogers, best known for his long and now largely forgotten poem *The Pleasures of Memory*. Scott, living in Scotland, and Crabbe, a country rector, seldom came to London, but both Moore and Rogers were frequent visitors to Holland House. Moore, a Dublin grocer's son, had won his way into the strongholds of Whig society as much by his sparkling conversation as by his talents. 'I have known a dull man live on a bon mot of Moore's for a week,'[3] wrote Byron. Rogers, by contrast, was dour and cadaverous, with a bitingly sarcastic tongue. (His voice was so weak, he explained, that people only listened when he said unkind things.) But he could be generous to friends in trouble, and his literary breakfasts at his house in St James's Street, with its red-silk hangings and fine Renaissance paintings, were famous: Holland, Sheridan, Moore and Byron, as well as Coleridge and Wordsworth, were among the stars that gathered there.

Interestingly, the Hollands, like their friends on the *Edinburgh Review*, had a blind spot where the Lake Poets were concerned. 'This will never do,' was Jeffrey's comment when *Lyrical Ballads* first appeared, while Fox, when presented with a copy by Wordsworth, had politely remarked that he was not of the poet's faction. The Hollands themselves had met Wordsworth on a journey to the north in 1807, Lady Holland finding his conversation 'much superior to his writings'. Essentially Augustan in their tastes, they could not agree with his celebration of the rural poor, unlettered cottagers and labourers to whom he ascribed philosophic sentiments more suited, surely, to the educated classes. As for Coleridge, he was so much talked about that Lady Holland was curious to meet him, though she had heard that his conversation was 'often obscure, a mystical species of Platonic philosophy, which he dresses up according to his own metaphysical taste and calls the *mind*',[4] and she had no time for his poetry.

Byron would have joined with the Hollands in disliking the 'pond poets', as he called them, though he owed far more to Wordsworth than he cared to admit. But he delighted in the literary company at Holland House. Rogers and Moore were friends already, but Sheridan was a new acquaintance. Battered by life – he had recently lost his seat in Parliament – and frequently drunk, Sheridan still retained much of his charm: even his dregs, as Byron remarked, were better than 'the first sprightly runnings'[5] of others. The Hollands were always remarkably kind to Sheridan, who had been financially ruined in 1809, when the Theatre Royal, Drury Lane, his only capital asset, had been burnt to the ground. He frequently stayed the night at Holland House, when he would always take a bottle and a book to bed with him, 'the *former* alone,' remarked Lady Holland, 'intended for use.'[6] On his way back to London the next day, he would stop for a dram at the Adam and Eve public house at the foot of the park, running up long bills which Holland had to pay.

Byron hugely admired Sheridan, and the two men, one at the outset of his fame, the other already a figure of the past, met frequently at Holland House, where Sheridan, undeterred by poverty and failure, still took on all comers. 'He was superb!' wrote Byron later.

> ...he had a sort of liking for me – and never attacked me – at least to my face, and he did everybody else – high names & wits and orators, some of them poets also – I have seen [him] cut up Whitbread – quiz Me de Staël – annihilate Colman – and do little less by some others (whose names as friends I set not down) of good fame and abilities.[7]

Lady Holland was in her element amid such conversational fireworks, orchestrating and animating and adding the occasional caustic comment. 'I am sorry to hear you are going to publish a poem,' she remarked to one unfortunate writer. 'Can't you suppress it?'[8] To Rogers, who was writing a book on his travels, she said: 'Your poetry is bad enough, so pray be sparing of your prose.'[9] Her husband, however, took most of the sting from her attacks, bathing all in the sunshine of his genial nature. Witty, well informed and questioning, he guided the conversation with the lightest of touches, and was especially kind to timid younger guests. Like his uncle, he was sympathetic to the 'young ones'.

Byron, titled and a poet, spanned the two main elements at Holland House – the aristocratic Whigs and the writers and intellectuals who gravitated there. The two mixed happily at table but were well aware of their separate status. 'Talents in literature,' wrote Tom Moore ruefully, '...may lead to association with the great but not equality.'[10]

Caroline Fox was a case in point; as a young woman at Bowood she had been loved by the great political philosopher Jeremy Bentham. He had never dared to tell his love, and when, years later, shortly before his death in 1832, he wrote her a playful letter mentioning his early feelings, she responded so frostily that he was deeply hurt. Bentham might be the leading thinker of the age, but Caroline had too great a sense of caste to consider someone who was only an attorney's son.

Lady Holland took the idea of class more lightly. She never had any doubts as to which category she belonged, but she was much too intellectually and socially adventurous to be constrained by it. Perhaps the fact that she was not fully accepted in society had a bearing on her attitude, but her very recklessness in marrying against convention proved how little she was bound by it. And the Foxes, from the first Lord Holland's runaway marriage onwards, had never paid much heed to conventional morality. Wit, talent and learning, far more than social status, were the keys to entry into Holland House, though the presence of the Whig nobility, their power backed by great possessions, gave it an authority it would otherwise have lacked.

Byron, of course, was delighted to be part of the company; after an impoverished and difficult youth it was a thrill to be accepted by his social and intellectual peers. Less happily, it was at Holland House that he first met Lady Caroline Lamb. He had seen her before at a party, when she, disgusted by the attention he was receiving, ostentatiously turned away when he was introduced. Now, arriving with his host at Holland House one afternoon, he found her, still muddied from her ride from Melbourne House in Piccadilly, sitting talking to Rogers and Moore. She jumped up on seeing him, and insisted on going to change before they were introduced. By the time the evening ended she had invited him to call on her next day.

From then on their romance took fire, Caroline dazzled by Byron's fame and air of moodily romantic mystery, Byron fascinated by her

boyish looks, her Devonshire House drawl, her wildness and original-
ity. There was nothing discreet about their affair and Caroline's exhi-
bitionism and courting of scandal were a sore trial to all her family:
the patient William, her mother Lady Bessborough, her mother-in-law
Lady Melbourne – even, eventually, to Byron himself. The Hollands
were unfussed by the affair, remaining tolerant and uncritical through
all its ups and downs. They had grown very fond of Byron, and he
of them. Still repentant for his insulting lines in *English Bards and
Scots Reviewers* – 'I wish I had not been in such a hurry with that
confounded satire,' he wrote – he dedicated his poem *The Bride of
Abydos* to Lord Holland, and was a constant visitor to Holland House.
Of all the circles he moved in, the Hollands', he thought, was 'the first
– everything *distingué* is welcome there', and Lady Holland, when in
a good humour, was *perfect*. 'No one more agreable, or perhaps so
much so, when she will.'[11]

Lady Holland, however, was not always in a good humour and
1812 was a particularly difficult year for her. In July she gave birth to
another daughter, her tenth child. The baby only lived a few hours,
and she herself took a long time to recover. She suffered from bouts of
depression and ill health for ever after, and often took it out on those
around her; even Holland was not immune from her sharp tongue.
This was nothing new. Lady Bessborough, an amused observer of their
life together, records a couple of angry scenes between them, in both
of which she was indirectly involved.

The first took place some years before when Lady Holland tried
to prevent her husband calling on the Bessboroughs on their way
home from Westminster one evening. When he attempted to stop
the coach and go on foot, she flew into a violent rage, forbidding the
footman to open the door, telling everyone in the coach that he had
lost his wits, and that they should call for Dr Willis, the king's doctor,
to shave and blister his head. 'As all this was done angrily and not in

joke, he was provok'd and in spite of all her commands to the contrary, jump'd out and came to C. Square [the Bessboroughs' house in
Cavendish Square]. When he return'd home he found a bed order'd
for him downstairs.'[12]

On a second occasion, when the Hollands and various friends had
called, and Lady Holland was busy talking to Lord Lauderdale in a
corner, Holland whispered to Lady Bessborough that if she could steal
a candle, they might slip away to play chess in the next room. They
proceeded to do so very quietly, enjoying the sense of playing truant.

> But, like most other concealments this was soon discovered, and we
> were made to pay for our amusement. She was seriously angry with
> us both – quite painfully so with him, and ended by saying she should
> come no more. He rebell'd a little and said he would come when she
> went to the Opera, but she said she would forbid it.[13]

Lady Bessborough does not tell us how this second episode concluded,
but Holland was good at sidestepping and usually more amused than
otherwise by his wife's tempestuous ways. He was still as much in love
with her as ever, as a poem he wrote soon after makes clear:

> The morning dawned and by my side
> Spite of impending day
> In sleep, that night and care defied
> My sweet enchantress lay
>
> Closed were indeed those sparkling eyes
> That set my soul on fire
> But other charms in slumber rise
> To kindle fierce desire

The grace of her reclining head
That even heaving breast
And limbs so carelessly outspread
Ten thousand thoughts suggest.

Yet passion in my bosom strove
Unruly at the sight
And fain my rude and boisterous love
Had wakened her to delight

No, let the thought, I cried, be check't
The sacrilege forbear
Love shall those tender looks respect
That heavenly slumber spare.

I said then bending o'er her charms
With fondness I explore
How soft how fair a spirit warms
The being I adore

For oh her lovely smiles express
The image of her mind
She looks, and sure she lives no less
Calm innocent, and kind—[14]

Perhaps there was an element of poetic licence in the final line, but Lady Holland, for all her tantrums and caprices, was often genuinely kind. We see her, for instance, offering an anonymous loan to the impoverished poet Thomas Campbell, arranging to do so through a friend in order not to humiliate him by offering it herself, and she brought the same surprising delicacy to many other unsung acts of generosity. She also used her influence, as we have seen in the case of Sydney Smith, to help her friends, and to intimates, like Lady Bessborough and her wayward daughter Caroline, she was endlessly loyal and uncensorious. And even though a London pharmacist claimed to have invented a pill for people who had been frightened at Holland House, those who knew it best enjoyed the extra zest her sharp tongue gave it, and were well able to hold their own. 'Ring the bell, Sydney,' she once commanded Smith. 'Oh yes,' he replied, 'and shall I sweep the floor as well?'[15] No one knew better than Smith how to handle her, and his letters, with their teasingly affectionate tone, struck the perfect note. 'How very odd, dear Lady Holl,' he writes on one occasion,

> to ask me to dine with you on Sunday, the 9th when I am coming to stay with you from the 5th to the 11th! It is like giving a gentleman an assignation for Wednesday when you are going to marry him on the Sunday preceding – an attempt to combine the stimulus of gallantry with the security of connubial relations. I do not propose to be guilty of the slightest infidelity to you while I am at H H except you dine in town, and then it will not be infidelity but spirited recrimination,
>
> Ever the sincere and affectionate friend of Lady Holland,
>
> Sydney Smith[16]

9

Towards Waterloo

O N 11 May 1812, Holland was talking to Lord Spencer in the House of Lords when he heard the report of a pistol and a scream of horror following it. 'I recollect exclaiming, "What is that?", he wrote in his memoirs,

> and being told after a short interval that it was a madman who thought himself the Duke of Norfolk and frequently molested the Courts of Justice with his pretensions. It was not long however before a figure, pale and breathless, rushed into the House, and, leaning on the bar, repeated twice or thrice, 'He is murdered; I saw him dead.'[1]

The prime minister, Spencer Perceval, had been assassinated by a ruined businessman called Bellingham, who blamed his troubles on Perceval's conduct of the war. In the consternation that followed, the future of the government was once more in the balance and the hopes of the Whigs were briefly raised again. But the regent's attitude towards the Whigs had hardened, and the Whig leaders in their turn were not prepared to make the necessary concessions to form a coalition government. After over a month of frenzied negotiations, Lord

Liverpool, the Minister of War, became prime minister, with much the same administration as before.

Although the new ministry, 'huddled up from the cast rags and tatters of the old,'[2] in Holland's words, seemed too weak and ill assorted to last, it proved unexpectedly successful thanks to the changing fortunes of the war. In July 1812, Wellington defeated the French at Salamanca and advanced to Madrid. In the event he did not hold the capital but his victory gave the promise of ultimate success in Spain and provided the government with the perfect opportunity to call a general election. They were returned with a majority of two to one, leaving the Whigs in greater disarray than ever.

Sidelined in politics, though stalwart in his interventions where Catholic Emancipation or civil liberties were concerned, Holland turned his attention to the affairs of Drury Lane. Following the destruction of the theatre, he had joined the committee led by the Whig MP Samuel Whitbread responsible for its rebuilding. (Poor Sheridan, crippled by debts, had been excluded from it.) The theatre was due to reopen in December 1812. A competition for a poetical address to be spoken on the opening night had failed to produce a suitable entry, and Holland asked Byron to produce one. Byron was dubious at first – 'prologuing is not my forte' – but he promised that he would do his best. His letters to Holland about the poem, 18 in all, cast a fascinating light on his painstaking processes of composition, and his respect for his friend's judgement. Lady Holland obviously had her say as well: 'Tell Ly. H I have had sad work to keep out the Phenix,'[3] he writes in one letter; apparently 69 of the competitors had invoked the phoenix in their entries, and he studiously avoided doing so. But his poem went through endless redrafts and corrections before he was finally satisfied with it, Holland perceptively commenting on them all.

The poem was delivered on the theatre's opening night. Byron had taken special trouble to include a couplet praising Sheridan's achievements:

> Dear are the days which made our annals bright,
> Ere Garrick fled or Brinsley ceased to write.

But Sheridan was bitterly offended by his treatment by the committee and refused to set foot in the theatre. It was typical of Holland's tact and charm that the playwright did not include him in his general resentment. Memories of Fox were still a powerful link between them and there is a delightful picture in one of Sheridan's letters of 'the joyous dear manner in which *he* [Lord Holland] seeing me come up Berkeley Square yesterday, *ran* like a schoolboy, lame as he was, to catch me by the hand.'[4]

In June 1812, leaving the command of his armies in Spain in the hands of his lieutenants, Napoleon had invaded Russia with an army of 480,000 men, setting in motion the train of events that would lead to his downfall. By the end of the year, all but 20,000 of his huge army had perished in the snow during the retreat from Moscow. In March 1813, Prussia rose up against him, but Napoleon, who had abandoned the remnants of his army in December, had gathered up new troops from France to fight the Prussians and the Russians on German soil. Initially successful at Dresden, he was defeated by the combined armies of Russia, Austria, Prussia, Sweden and Britain at Leipzig in October, and forced to withdraw to the Rhine. Meanwhile, in July, the Anglo-Spanish army had broken the French hold on Spain at the Battle of Vittoria and four months later reached Bayonne, on the French side of the Pyrenees.

Lady Holland's second son, Henry Webster, now serving in the peninsula, was wounded in the neck by a musket ball at Vittoria. (Sir

Godfrey had left the army to take over his father's parliamentary seat in Sussex three years earlier.) Lady Holland had been overcome by the news, Holland told his sister. Fortunately Henry made a quick recovery, going on eventually to fight at Waterloo.

The Hollands' reaction to Napoleon's setbacks had been ambivalent. On the one hand they welcomed his defeat in Spain, where the provisional government was nationalist and liberal; on the other they were lukewarm about the allied victories in Germany, opening up the possibility of his downfall and the restoration of the monarchy in France. 'I cannot make out the consistency of their views,' wrote Lady Bessborough to Lord Granville; 'they would defeat Buonaparte in Spain, and let him defeat the Allies in Germany. This is beyond my Politicks.'[5] For the Hollands who saw France's return to Bourbon rule as the worst of all possible outcomes, their attitude was perfectly logical. For most Whigs, however, it was hard to argue with the government in their successful prosecution of the war.

With little to oppose on the war front, the Whigs – or at least some of them – found their best weapon against the government at home in the quarrels of the Prince Regent and his estranged wife, Princess Caroline of Brunswick. It had been a miserable match from the start; having married her to please his father and to induce him to pay off his debts, the prince had taken an immediate aversion to his wife and had soon broken off matrimonial relations. But they had had one daughter, Charlotte, and though Caroline's indiscretions had led to her being censured by a commission of inquiry in 1806, the kindly George III had always insisted that she should not be separated from her daughter. No sooner had the power passed from his hands than the Prince Regent, still vindictive towards his wife, refused to allow her to see her daughter more than once a fortnight. Despite Caroline's protests, the government supported him and it was left to Brougham – out of Parliament but eager to return there – to offer his services as her legal adviser and defender. By exciting public sympathy for the princess, he hoped to throw odium on the regent and his ministers, and make political capital from her wrongs.

Once again the Hollands were ambivalent in their attitude. Lady Holland, who had never been received at court by George III, had hopes of regularizing her position when the Prince Regent became king, and therefore refrained from taking sides. In any case the Hollands remained on relatively friendly terms with the prince: the memory of Fox was still dear to him, and though he had broken with them politically, he privately conceded that the Whigs made much the best company. As for Holland, he was disgusted by the public's fascination with the royal squabbles, which, true to the Foxite creed, he regarded as a severe reflection on the institution of the monarchy. 'Strange indeed,' he remarked in his memoirs, 'that neither war nor peace, laws nor liberties, could excite so much anxiety in a free and civilized nation as the personal character and comfort of two individuals, who had nothing but their rank about them to raise interest or even curiosity!'[6]

More interesting to the Holland House circle than the Prince Regent's affairs were the tempestuous goings-on of Lady Caroline Lamb in the death throes of her love affair with Byron. Her scene-making reached its climax at a party in July 1813 when, feeling herself rebuffed by Byron, she seized a knife, and either deliberately or inadvertently slashed her hand; it bled on her dress and she collapsed. Byron had not even been in the room when her 'cursed scarification,' as he called it, took place and only heard of it the next day. But the episode caused a major scandal and Caroline's husband William Lamb carried her off to the country to escape the worst of it. From there she sent a hysterical note to Lady Holland.

Lady Holland, hear me – you can add to the agonizing tortures I endure, you may serve me. I have never harmed you – it is cruel to trample upon one so wholly ruined as completely fallen as I am... I do implore you as you hope for mercy, show it – and do not speak of this horrid scene more than you can help, and when you must speak of it for the sake of better than I am, make light of it – or deny it...[7]

But there was little enough that Lady Holland or anyone else could do to silence gossip. The Caroline affair was on every lip, and even the newest arrival in London, Madame de Staël, the celebrated author of *Corinne*, had her opinion on the matter. 'The Staël last night attacked me most furiously,' wrote Byron to Tom Moore, 'said that I had "no right to make love" – that I had used [Caroline] barbarously – that I had no feeling and was totally *in*sensible to *la belle passion*, and *had* been all my life. I am very glad to hear it, but did not know before.'[8]

Madame de Staël had arrived like a tornado in London in June, where within four days of installing herself at her hotel more than 300 visitors had called to sign their name. 'The great wonder of the time is Madame de Staël,' wrote Lady Holland to her friend Mrs Creevey. 'She is surrounded by all the curious and every sentence she utters is caught and repeated with various commentaries.'[9]

Like every distinguished foreign visitor to London, Madame de Staël had gravitated naturally to Holland House; not for her the stuffy attitude of the English aristocracy towards Lady Holland's past. Her own private life was turbulent, and she was accompanied by her lover John Rocca (whom she had secretly married two years before), a dazzlingly good-looking young man 22 years her junior. She herself was far from beautiful: stocky and coarse-featured, her best points were her fine eyes and bosom, the latter always lavishly displayed. But Lady Holland was agreeably surprised. 'She is much less ugly than I expected,' she wrote to Mrs Creevey; all the same it was amusing to hear her 'flummering' Sheridan, a byword for duplicity, 'upon the excellence of his heart and moral principles, and he in return upon her beauty and grace.'[10]

Rocca, who did not shine in company – 'speech is not his language,' said Madame de Staël – was soon packed off to Bath to take the waters, while she pursued her triumphant way in London. Exiled by Napoleon, who feared the influence of her literary salon, Madame de Staël had been a one-man opposition to his government. 'She is violent against the Emperor, whom she says is not a man,' wrote Lady Holland; '"ce n'est point un homme, c'est un système" – an incarnation of the Revolution. Women he considers as only useful "pour produire des conscrits", otherwise "c'est une classe qu'il voudrait supprimer".'[11]

Not surprisingly Madame de Staël had strong opinions on English politics as well. 'She harangued, she lectured, she preached English politics to the first of our Whig politicians, the day after she arrived in England,' wrote Byron,

and (if I am not misinformed) preached politics no less to our Tory politicians the day after. The sovereign himself, if I am not in error, was not exempt from this flow of eloquence. As Napoleon had been lectured on the destinies of France, the Prince Regent of England was asked 'what he meant to do with America.'[12]

Lady Holland was not best pleased to be outshone by such a rival, and one detects a hint of pique. 'She is certainly very clever, but also very tiresome,' she told Lord Lansdowne, describing an evening at Holland House at which Madame de Staël's 'political queries and flowery harangues' had been wittily turned against her by the former Foreign Secretary, Lord Wellesley. 'Congreve could not have written a better scene.'[13] Some years later, when the merits of women writers were being discussed, and Madame de Staël was mentioned, with

Madame de Sévigné and Sappho, as among the three greatest, Lady Holland disagreed so strongly that the subject had to be changed.

Holland was more charitable. He admired Madame de Staël and knew how heroically she had rescued friends from the Terror, and how generously she had supported those, like Talleyrand, left destitute at the time of the Revolution. With all her occasional absurdities, she was, he thought, 'a very good-hearted woman, and everyone knows, a very clever one'.[14] Throughout her stay, she was a frequent visitor to Holland House, where her name is entered in the library's loans book (she borrowed a life of Robert Walpole) and where, as she knew, she could find the best society in London.

Meanwhile the tide of war had turned in Europe. On 30 March 1814 the allied armies entered Paris. On 6 April, Napoleon abdicated; he was exiled to Elba shortly after. The elderly Louis XVIII, brother of Louis XVI, was proclaimed king. Passing through London, on his way to take the boat to France from Dover, he was greeted by crowds of carriages and attendants, all wearing, in Holland's words, 'that ancient badge of pure hereditary despotism, the white cockade'. The Prince Regent ceremoniously presented him with the Order of the Garter, but the two actors, wrote Holland, 'were too old, too unwieldy and above all too well known to excite any great interest on that flat and insipid exhibition'.[15]

Much as he loathed Napoleon's lust for war, it was impossible for Holland to show any enthusiasm for the restoration of the Bourbons. But peace was signed in Paris, and the whole of the Continent was open to English travellers once more. Madame de Staël, of course, had left for France at the first possible moment; the Hollands planned to follow in July. It was to be a family party, including their eldest son Charles, aged 18 and studying to go to Oxford, Henry Edward, 12, Mary, eight and Georgiana, nearly five, as well as the indispensable Dr Allen and Lady Affleck, now once more a widow. Two of the children, Henry and Mary, were delicate, and Lady Holland herself was often in poor health. From his rectory in Yorkshire Sydney Smith wrote to remonstrate:

> I am uneasy, dear Lady Holland, at your going abroad. Consider what it is to be well. If I were you, I would not stir from H.H. for 2 years; and then as many jolts and frights as you please, which at present you are not equal to. I should think you less to blame if the world had anything new to show you; but you have seen the Parthian, the Mede, the Elamite and the dweller in Mesopotamia... and the roads upon the earth are as well known to you as the wrinkles in Rogers's face.
>
> Be wise my dear lady and re-establish your health in that gilded room [the Gilt Room] which furnishes better and pleasanter society than all the wheels in the world can whirl you to...[16]

But the Hollands' appetite for foreign travel was as strong as ever. By 10 August the family and their usual retinue of servants were installed at a hotel on the Île Saint-Louis and they were soon receiving and calling on the leading figures of the new regime. Even though circumstances had changed, the cast of characters was much the same. They dined with Talleyrand, now the Minister of Foreign Affairs for Louis XVIII. Holland, who had known him in all his incarnations, as moderate reformer, penniless exile and Napoleon's right-hand man, was agreeably surprised by his welcome. The prince, he told his sister, 'received me, and yet more emphatically Lady Holland, with a franchise and cordiality, even a kindness which I hardly thought were in his character.'[17] Also present at the dinner was Fouché, Minister of the Interior. One of the worst monsters of the Terror, he had risen under Napoleon, who created him Duke of Otranto, to become his chief of police; he had now switched allegiance to the Bourbons. Holland, who had first met him in 1802, when his countenance, he recalled, exhibited all the profligacy and ferocity one would expect from a revolutionary, mentions him without comment on this occasion.

Visiting Fontainebleau soon after, Lady Holland, impelled by 'a morbid feeling of curiosity' made her way into the 'fatal room' where Napoleon had signed his abdication. 'Alas! Alas! Why did he go to Russia and why was he so headstrong?'[18] Two months later from Florence, the next stage of their journey, she persuaded Colonel Campbell, the British commissioner in Elba, who was on leave in Florence, to take back a bundle of English newspapers for the emperor. Napoleon, knowing of her interest in mineralogy, sent her some samples of iron ore from the island in return.

These polite exchanges were more important than they seemed. It was on reading a paragraph in one of the papers Lady Holland sent him that Napoleon first learnt that the allies were planning to move him to a safer place of exile, possibly St Helena, after the Congress of Vienna. The news, which apparently made a great impression on him, may well have been a factor in the desperate gamble of his escape from Elba two months later.

Meanwhile the Hollands were continuing their tour through Italy, stopping in Rome, where they saw a great deal of Napoleon's brother Lucien Bonaparte, and where they commissioned a bust of the former emperor from the Venetian sculptor Antonio Canova. They had just arrived in Naples, where they were entertained 'very civilly' by the king and queen (Joachim Murat and Napoleon's sister Caroline), when they heard the dramatic news of Napoleon's flight from Elba. 'Here's a job,' wrote Holland to his sister.

> Bonaparte escaped from his gaol! Where is he going? What are his chances of success? Whatever the results I think it a misfortune. If he fails he must be sacrificed and who can contemplate the extinction

of such genius and activity with thorough indifference? If he succeeds we must have twenty more years of war... We are preparing
for an excursion to Paestum but the escape of the *hero* has set Lady
Holland's spirits in such a flurry of agitation that I suspect she will
not be calm and sedate enough to enjoy the improving gravity of
Dorick architecture.[19]

The immediate result for the Hollands was to make their journey home
more dangerous and uncertain, though astonishingly they contrived to
obtain a passport, granted by Napoleon, enabling them free entrance
into any part of France, in order to embark from Calais. The passport
was never used. They were travelling towards their crossing point on
the Rhine at Coblenz, their way much impeded by advancing Russian
troops, when they heard the news of Napoleon's defeat at Waterloo.
The Hollands wept at his downfall but the coachman whom Charles
was sitting next to on the box spoke the voice of common sense. 'Don't
mind, Mr Charles, it's all right. I think it a very good thing that Boney
has been beaten.'[20]

Of course the Hollands had to agree. Whatever their sympathy
for the fallen emperor, they could only rejoice at England's victory.
'Lord Wellington's glories have opened our road,' wrote Holland to
his sister. 'The English have raised themselves in the estimation of
mankind for courage heroism and all the virtues which give a nation
superiority over others but I wish in a better cause.'[21] Even though the
restoration of the Bourbons brought peace to Europe, he continued
to regard them as agents of reaction: 'I am in opinion to the full as
violent perhaps more so than in 1793.'[22]

Passing through Brussels on the way home he visited the battlefield,
'horrible even beyond any description Ld Byron's verses can give of
it,'[23] he told his sister, and was moved by the gallantry of the French
wounded, who when needing amputation insisted that 'Messrs Les

Anglais' had the right to be treated first. The news that Henry Webster had survived the battle unharmed was an immense relief.

By the end of July the family was safely back at Holland House where Lady Harriet Leveson-Gower (wife of Lady Bessborough's beloved Lord Granville) called to find Lady Holland 'seated on the grass with Allen and a plate of Baba, very cross and absurd about Bonaparte, "poor dear Man" as she called him.'[24]

10

Defenders of Napoleon

T HE Hollands had landed in England at the very moment that Napoleon, on board the warship *Bellerophon*, was waiting outside Plymouth to hear the government's decision on his fate. He never set foot on British soil. After 11 days of uncertainty he was transferred to the *Northumberland* in preparation for the voyage to St Helena: a five-month journey lay ahead. The Hollands deplored the government's 'ungenerous decision' but knew that public opinion was on its side. All they could do was to try to mitigate the conditions of Napoleon's imprisonment, and if possible influence opinion in his favour.

Their first task was to win the sympathies of Sir Hudson Lowe, who had just been nominated as governor of St Helena. Within a fortnight of their return the Hollands had launched a charm offensive. Between 18 August, when he first dined there, and 23 January, when he sailed for St Helena, Lowe was invited to dinner at Holland House eight times, the guests including the regent's brother the Duke of York, Byron, still at the height of his celebrity, the ever-present Samuel Rogers, Lord Lansdowne, Lord John Russell, who had actually visited Napoleon on Elba, and, to add a touch of patriotic colour, Lady Holland's son Henry Webster, who had fought at Waterloo.

How could Lowe fail to be charmed by such distinguished company, and by the flattering attentions of his hosts? But there were important counter-influences. Lord Bathurst, the Secretary of State for War, in charge of Napoleon's fate, was a hard-headed Tory and not above making jokes about the Hollands. The government's instructions for Lowe were clear. Napoleon was to be treated as a prisoner of war, not a former emperor. He was to be addressed as General Bonaparte; no letters or parcels should be sent to him except through the Secretary of State. Lowe was a stickler for the rules; he was also mindful that Napoleon had escaped from Elba through the laxness of the governor, Colonel Campbell. Lady Holland's tactful pleas that some informal arrangement might be made to send minor comforts to Napoleon 'in the interests of humanity' fell on stony ground.

There were further complications when Lowe, encouraged by Bathurst, who felt that a wife would be an asset to the governor, married a colonel's widow, Mrs Johnson. He knew he must either offend the court by taking her to Holland House, or Lady Holland by not doing so. Fortunately the marriage took place not long before they sailed, and when, in a last attempt to win Lowe round, Lady Holland asked them both to dinner, Lady Lowe was able to decline politely, on the grounds that she was overwhelmed with preparations for the voyage. Sir Hudson came alone. His manner was reserved, as well it might be. Only a few days before he had co-signed a letter with the Lord Chancellor to the Undersecretary at War, Sir Henry Bunbury, advocating a bill to outlaw Napoleon for life. It was clear that the Holland House attempt to win his sympathies had failed.

Lady Holland hid her chagrin. It was essential to remain on good terms with Lowe, if only as a future channel of communication. Her husband moved to the attack in Parliament. On 8 April 1816, during the debates on the bill for 'the more effective detaining in custody of

Bonaparte' he entered a vigorous protest against Napoleon's treatment in the Journal of the House of Lords:

> To consign to distant exile and imprisonment a foreign and captive chief who after the abdication of his authority, relying on British generosity, had surrendered himself to us in preference to his other enemies, is unworthy the magnanimity of a great country – and the treaties by which, after his captivity, we bound ourselves to retain him in custody at the will of sovereigns to whom he had never surrendered himself, appear to me to be repugnant to the principles of equity, and utterly uncalled for by expedience.[1]

It was a solitary protest which he knew would make him unpopular with both the court and the country; to the vast majority of the public the name of Napoleon was anathema. Knowing the state of public opinion, the rest of the Whig party made no comment on the bill, though to the great annoyance of the Prince Regent, his eccentric brother the Duke of Sussex, an ardent Whig supporter, added his signature to Holland's entry.

Meanwhile news was beginning to come through from St Helena. In September 1816, Dr Warden, the surgeon of the *Northumberland*, arrived in England and dined at Holland House. It may have been through him that Count Montholon's *Remonstrance* (in fact written by Napoleon) complaining of the harsh conditions of the emperor's captivity, reached England. It was published amid wide publicity early in 1817, and echoed soon after, though in far milder terms, when Holland called for an inquiry on the matter in the House of Lords on 8 March. He knew he must tread delicately in order not to embarrass his fellow Whigs, and he was not, as he said, such a 'coxcomb' as to think the decision on Napoleon's exile could be reversed. But reports seemed to show that the restrictions on Napoleon – on his freedom of movement, by confining him to the unhealthy high ground of the island, on his finances, by forcing him to sell his plate to provide essentials for his entourage, and on his right to communicate and receive letters and newspapers – were unnecessarily severe. The blame, if it existed, lay with the government, not Lowe, 'the gallant officer... with many of whose good qualities he had the good fortune to be personally acquainted'.[2]

It was a tactful and moderate speech, and though it was shot down by Bathurst, it may well have helped to improve the terms of Napoleon's imprisonment. Several members of his family, including Napoleon's mother, wrote grateful letters to thank Holland for his intervention. Lord Bathurst's office began to be more flexible in allowing parcels and letters to go through, and Lady Holland took full advantage of the change in mood. Over the next four years of Napoleon's exile she sent him more than 1,000 books and periodicals, among them regular copies of the *Edinburgh Review*, which Napoleon followed eagerly. (For some time he hoped that a change of government and the return of the Whigs to power might put an end to his captivity.) There were other comforts from Holland House – food, eau de Cologne, a microscope, even seeds for the garden of his residence at Longwood. A special gift of sugared plums, '*les pruneaux de Lady Holland*', was almost the last thing he asked for. Meanwhile Canova's bronze bust of Napoleon had arrived from Rome and had been set up on a column of Scotch granite in the garden of Holland House. Four lines in Greek from the *Odyssey* were inscribed on the column beneath; Holland would translate them as follows:

> He is not dead, he breathes the air
> In lands beyond the deep,
> Some distant sea-girt island where
> Harsh men the hero keep.

The Hollands' sympathy for Napoleon extended to his supporters. Holland did his best to save the life of Marshal Ney, sponsoring a desperate appeal for clemency from Ney's wife to the Prince Regent (who 'did not feel called to intervene'), and writing to his kinsman Lord Kinnaird in Paris asking him to intercede with Wellington on Ney's behalf. This letter, arriving the day after Ney's execution, was indiscreetly shown to Wellington, who took grave offence at a passage which, according to Holland, he mistakenly thought to be 'an imputation upon him as jealous or fearful of the military superiority of Marshal Ney'.[3] Two years later, in Paris, Wellington cut Holland dead.

These initiatives, and the fact that Holland House continued to be a refuge for exiled Bonapartists, were enough to make even Holland's friends uneasy. In 1817, when there was a suggestion that Grey might be retiring as leader of the opposition, Holland was not in the running to replace him. 'Lord Holland is here,' wrote the Whig politician John Wishaw, discussing possible alternatives, 'but he is considered too violent and an outcry has been attempted against him with some success as a friend of Bonaparte and France.'[4]

Byron had shared the Hollands' sympathy for Napoleon. 'I am damned sorry to hear it,'[5] had been his response to the news of Waterloo. During their wooing of Lowe in the autumn of 1815, he and his new wife Annabella had twice dined with the Hollands to meet him. It was a new departure for Annabella. Three years before, when her cousin Caroline Lamb had invited her to a party where Lady Holland would be present, she had been dubious whether to accept. 'If I am asked to be introduced to Lady Holland's acquaintance I shall certainly decline,' she told her mother, 'but I think you will agree with me that no one will regard me as being corrupted by being in *the same room* as her.'[6]

Since then her attitude had changed. Had her marriage lasted she too might have become a familiar figure at Holland House. As it was, it was to Holland that her adviser Dr Lushington turned as an intermediary, when the question of her separation from Byron first arose in January 1816. Reluctant to be involved at first, Holland good-naturedly agreed to write to Byron. He had the very best opinion, he assured him, of Lushington's head and heart: 'I am persuaded that his motives are most honourable both to his client and to you.'[7]

'There can be no subject – however unpleasant – which would not become less so – by you taking the trouble to be the organ of communication,'[8] wrote Byron gratefully. But neither Holland's interventions nor those of anyone else could prevent the separation or divert the storm of scandal which broke round Byron's head as rumours and speculations about his conduct multiplied. The British public, as Macaulay put it, was undergoing one of its periodic fits of morality. Shunned by the society that had idolized him, execrated by a vengeful Tory press, Byron left England on 25 April, never to return.

Throughout the painful months leading up to the judicial separation the Hollands had been consistently kind to Byron, refusing to join the outcry against him. Byron had always been devoted to them. Before his departure he presented Lady Holland with a collection of miniatures of subjects from his poems by the well-known illustrator and artist Thomas Stothard. She was reluctant to accept them at first, feeling he should give them to his wife, but Byron would not do so, insisting that they would only be seized by the bailiffs if she did not take them. Thereafter they hung in her private drawing room at Holland House, where favoured visitors would be taken to see them.

Some of Byron's happiest times in London had been spent at Holland House, and he would look back on them fondly in his years of exile. 'It is not my plan to be very long abroad...' he wrote to Lady Holland in a farewell note, 'and it does not much matter – in all times and all places I shall remember the kindness of you and your Lord.'[9]

Not usually sentimental, Lady Holland kept a soft spot in her heart for Byron. 'He was such a loveable person,' she once told Moore. 'I can remember him sitting there [in the library at Holland House] with the light upon him, looking so beautiful.'[10]

It was not to be expected that Caroline Lamb would refrain from joining in the clamour against Byron. She was generous with dark hints – of Byron's incest with his half-sister, of his homosexual entanglements – and her confidences to Annabella, under the guise of female solidarity, had done much to harden his wife's attitude towards him. Ever since the end of her own affair with Byron Caroline had been working on a novel, *Glenarvon*, in which she would take her revenge on him. Its publication in May 1816 unleashed a fresh burst of scandal. A wild extravaganza, almost unreadable today, it succeeded as a 'kiss and tell' – or, as Byron put it rudely, 'F— and publish' – account of her affair, combining gothic romance, complete with ghosts and skeletons, with a satire on the Whig society in which she had been brought up. Byron, the fiendish but irresistible hero, is Glenarvon, a rebel Irish leader who betrays his country's cause; Calantha, the doomed heroine, is Caroline herself. Among the supporting characters, Lady Holland is savagely caricatured as the Princess of Madagascar, the wife of the Nabob of that name.

Lady Holland, as we have seen, had always been tolerant of Caroline's goings-on. But a few weeks before the book was published Caroline was involved in a new drama when she lost her temper with her pageboy and narrowly missed killing him by flinging a cricket ball at his head. The news of the incident naturally spread and Caroline was hustled off to the country in disgrace. Lady Holland had done her best to quieten gossip, but when Caroline, in one of her usual incoherent letters, wrote to thank her, she crisply replied that the less she spoke about 'this unpleasant subject' the better. 'The anxiety your mother, William, and the Melbournes must feel should in my judgement occupy your thoughts much more than anything that I… or anybody else may say or think about you.'[11]

Caroline was furious; stung by Lady Holland's letter, she no longer felt any compunction at wounding one of her mother's oldest friends. We first meet the Princess of Madagascar in the novel when the ingenuous heroine, Calantha, is invited to dine at Barbary House, 'an old-fashioned gothic building… three miles beyond the turnpike.'

> Calantha now, for the first time, conversed with the learned of the land – she heard new opinions stated and old ones refuted, and she gazed, unhurt but not unawed, upon reviewers, poets, critics and politicians. At the end of a long gallery [the library] two thick wax tapers rendering 'darkness visible' the princess was seated. Few events, if any, were ever known to move her from her position… A poet of emaciated and sallow complexion [Samuel Rogers] stood beside her.

The princess receives Calantha graciously, charming her with sugared phrases, 'nodding at intervals and dropping short epigrammatic sentences, when necessary, to such as were in attendance round her.'

'Is she acting?' says Calantha at length, in a whisper to the poet. 'Is she acting or is this reality?'

'It is the only reality you will ever find in the princess,' he returns. 'She acts the Princess of Madagascar from morning to night.'

'But why,' asks Calantha, 'do the great Nabob and all the other Lords in waiting, with that black horde of savages—'

'Reviewers, you mean, and men of talents.'

'Well whatever they are tell me quickly why they wear collars and chains at Barbary House… I would die sooner than be thus enchained.'

'The great Nabob,' she is told, 'is the best, the kindest, the cleverest man I know, but like some philosophers he would sacrifice much for a peaceable life. The princess is fond of inflicting these lesser tyrannies, she is so hopelessly attached to these trifles... that it were a pity to thwart her. For my own part I could willingly bend to the yoke, provided the duration were not eternal; for observe that the chains are well gilded, that the tables are well stored, and that those who bend the lowest are the best received.'

'And if I also bow my neck,' asks Calantha, 'will she be grateful? May I depend upon her seeming kindness?'

The poet's naturally pale complexion turns bluish-green at this enquiry.

So far the portrait, if unkind, has its elements of truth. But the story takes off into fantasy when the princess is revealed as a monster of deceit and treachery who leads the attack on Calantha when society turns against her.

> Cold princess!... You taught Calantha to love you by every pretty art of which your sex is mistress... You laughed at her follies, courted her confidence and flattered her into a belief that you loved her. Loved her! – it is a feeling you never felt. She fell into the mire; the arrows of your precious crew were shot at her – like hissing snakes hot and sharpened with malice and venomed fire, and you – yes – you were the first to scorn her... aye and the fawning multitude which still crowd your door and laugh at you and despise you... The sun may fairly shine again on her: but never, never whilst existence is prolonged will she set foot in the gates of the palace of the Grand Nabob or trust to the smiles and professions of the Princess of Madagascar.'[12]

Glenarvon was published anonymously, but everyone knew who had written it; its thinly disguised portraits of her family, friends and lover (even including some of Byron's letters) completed Caroline's social ruin. Holland was so indignant at her depiction of his wife that he turned his back on her when he next saw her. Lady Holland was deeply hurt by her ingratitude. 'Every ridicule, every folly and infirmity (my not being able from malady to move about much) is portrayed,' she told Mrs Creevey. 'The charge against more essential qualities is, I trust and believe, a fiction; at least an uninterrupted friendship of 25 years with herself and family might leave me to suppose it... The work has a prodigious sale, as all libellous matters have.'[13]

It was Caroline's husband who suffered most. Miserably he wrote to Holland:

It must have seemed strange to you that I have not been to see you. And you may perhaps put a wrong construction on it – it is nothing but the embarrassment which the late events have not unnaturally revived. They have given me great trouble and embarrassment and produced an unwillingness to see anybody and more particularly those who have been objects of so wanton and unprofitable an attack. I did not write, because what could I say... I am sure you will feel for my situation.[14]

Chivalrously Lamb refused to desert his wife, but no one held him responsible for her sins. Before long he was back at Holland House, as cheerful and clubbable as ever. Caroline, drink-sodden and unstable – but still capable of writing three more novels – remained in the country. She never went to Holland House again.

11

At Home at Holland House

A PART from his interventions on behalf of Napoleon, most of Holland's political activities in 1816 and 1817 took place behind the scenes. Thanks to the *Edinburgh Review* and liberal papers like the *Times* and *Morning Chronicle*, Whig opinions were becoming widely read and the name of Charles James Fox was still a rallying cry at Whig clubs across the country. In London, 'Fox Club' dinners to celebrate Fox's birthday took place yearly, sometimes at Brooks's Club, sometimes at Holland House, with Holland usually presiding. Elsewhere the clubs were fairly transient, often dying out after a few years, but they helped to form a body of opinion outside Parliament. Since the regent still refused to contemplate a Whig government, the Whigs' best hope lay in changing the system altogether. The idea of electoral reform was once more in the air. William Cobbett's radical paper the *Weekly Register* called for universal suffrage and annual parliaments. The Whigs had more limited aims, but for the first time since the 1790s they began to take them seriously.

In 1816 and 1817, however, the most immediate questions before Parliament were those of taxation and domestic unrest. The Liverpool government's attempt to continue the unpopular wartime property tax was roundly defeated by a combination of the Whigs and its own supporters. But the Whigs were less successful in preventing the suspension of habeas corpus in February 1817, a measure, thought Holland, which would lead to 'a complete surrender and extinction of our laws and liberties'.[1] After the first post-war euphoria, bad harvests and economic distress had led to widespread disturbances, the government responding to what Holland called its 'silly alarms of revolution' by increased repression. Although the Foxite Whigs, among them Lord John Russell in a notable maiden speech, opposed the suspension vigorously, Grenville and his followers voted with the government. The 12-year alliance between Grey and Grenville was unravelling.

Holland was in the midst of the party's discussions. Grey, the leader, unwell and threatening resignation, was hard to prise away from his home and family in Northumberland and it often fell to Holland to be his go-between in London. His loyalty to Grey as Fox's successor and leader of the party was absolute; modesty and perhaps a certain indolence kept him from any ambition to replace him. But Holland House, in Grey's absence, was an essential meeting place, not only for the Foxite Whigs but for those of kindred sympathies, liberal Tories and the less extreme among the radicals in Parliament. Consensus might not be achieved, but at least some form of opposition was kept alive.

Since 1815 the Whigs had suffered two major losses. The first, a few weeks after Waterloo, had been the suicide of Samuel Whitbread, triggered, it was hinted, by the news of Napoleon's defeat, though the official explanation was that it was due to overwork in untangling the affairs of Drury Lane. A fervent admirer of Napoleon, Whitbread had been one of the most radical and energetic of the Foxite MPs, and like Grey (whose sister he had married) was a founder member of the Society of the Friends of the People. But his origins as the son of a wealthy brewer and the sneers they aroused in Parliament and the

press had been stumbling blocks in his career; an element of para-
noia, not altogether unjustified, may have lain behind his death. Its
shocking circumstances – he cut his throat – left his parliamentary
colleagues reeling.

With the death of Sheridan the following year, the last of Fox's great
contemporaries left the scene. Though often annoying the Foxites by
his insistence on following his own line, he had shared their political
ideals of Catholic Emancipation and parliamentary reform, and had
fought untiringly for civil liberties by Fox's side. For all his faults, his
debts, his drunkenness, he had been, as Holland put it, 'the wonder of
the age', unrivalled as a playwright, an orator and a wit. Holland was
a pall-bearer at his funeral at Westminster Abbey; the magnificence
of the occasion, with the mourners led by two royal dukes, was in
painful contrast to the misery and poverty of Sheridan's final days.

In June 1817, as soon as Parliament stopped sitting, the Hollands
set out on their travels again. It was a good moment for a change of
scene; the last two years in politics had been unproductive and frus-
trating. They travelled in style, taking five coaches and nine servants,
including a cook and a confectioner, as well as their three younger
children (Charles, the eldest, was stationed in Corfu), a tutor and the
inevitable Dr Allen. The size of their party when they travelled, wrote
Caroline Lamb, was enough to start rumours of an invasion.

After touring the newly united Kingdom of the Netherlands – 'there
is too much water in this country for a nervous person,'[2] wrote Lady
Holland from Amsterdam – they installed themselves in Paris for
an extended stay. 'The soirées at Lady Holland's are very agreeable',
wrote Harriet Cavendish, now Lady Granville – her husband Granville
Leveson-Gower had been made Viscount Granville in 1815. At one
point the two families took separate floors at the Hôtel de Paris, where
Lady Granville found Lady Holland, 'enthroned in a room of green
and gold', complaining vociferously because the proprietor would

not allow her cook to enter the kitchen. Lord Holland, 'a great love and a great grig', was as adorable as ever: 'There is something so very delightful in the artless, almost childish simplicity of his character, when united to a mind and understanding like his.'[3]

Paris was full of English friends, presided over by the British ambassador Sir Charles Stuart. Caroline Fox and Elizabeth Vernon came over to join the fun. The two ladies, wrote Holland, 'spend all their mornings at Milliners, haberdashers, feather makers and upholsterers, then they dine at Ambassadors and Ministers, and go to one or even two spectacles in the evenings.'[4] For the Hollands it was a chance to take the temperature of French politics. Madame de Staël had died a few weeks before their arrival, but her former lover, Benjamin Constant, creator of the constitution during Napoleon's brief return from Elba and now a liberal deputy, was one of their most frequent contacts. So too were Lafayette, who had recently emerged from retirement to become a liberal deputy, and Talleyrand, who, having saved France's frontiers at the Congress of Vienna, had been forced out of politics after Waterloo but remained a shrewd observer from the sidelines. The great question of the day was the continuing presence of the allied troops in Paris (which the Foxites had strongly opposed) but in the long term it was the future of the monarchy which raised most doubts. Holland's distrust of the Bourbons was instinctive. 'I am more than ever persuaded,' he told Charles, 'the Bourbons will not last unless they can do one of two things: wage a successful war or give themselves the air of reigning by the revolution and not in spite of it.'[5]

The Hollands returned to England on 18 November to the news of the death in childbirth of the Prince Regent's only daughter, Princess Charlotte, three days before. Everyone they met on the road from Dover to London, including post boys and turnpike men, was wearing some kind of mourning. But the outburst of grief produced by her death, thought Holland, was more an indication of the unpopularity of the Prince Regent and his brothers 'than of the childish affection for Royalty, which the people of England so frequently display'.[6] The regent's heir was now the Duke of York, and since he had no children there was a flurry among his younger brothers to marry and produce an heir. The Duke of Clarence (later William IV) abandoned his long-term mistress, Mrs Jordan, to marry a German princess, and the Duke of Kent was forced to do the same.

Meanwhile the Hollands settled back in at Holland House. It was now 20 years since they had moved there, and there had been many additions and improvements. The library, numbering some 10,000 volumes, was constantly being added to: Holland's Spanish collection, in particular, was said to be the best in England. The portraits of past friends and statesmen, collected by the first Lord Holland, had been joined by those of their own friends: Grey, Lansdowne, Tierney, Lord John Russell, Rogers, Moore and many others. Most notable of all was a seated statue of Fox in classical dress in the entrance hall, a cast of the original by Sir Richard Westmacott erected by the Duke of Bedford in Bloomsbury Square.

The house's foundations, which had been threatened by underground springs, had been stabilized by a new system of drainage but not before alarming rents – 'i nostri cracks' as the Italian supervisor Serafino Bonaiuti described them – had appeared in the west wing, and the library fireplace had begun to move. A few years later the construction of a corner addition at the south end of the library wall helped support the building further, as well as providing a small inner library on the first floor.

In 1810 Bonaiuti, who seems to have been a man of many talents, designed the Portuguese garden, on the west side of the house; now known as the Dutch garden, its formal layout with zigzagging paths and box-edged flower beds is still virtually unchanged. Unchanged too is the inscription in the little arbour, set into the long espaliered wall beside the formal garden, which was Samuel Rogers's favourite retreat at Holland House:

> Here Rogers sat, and here forever dwell
> With thee the pleasures that he knew so well.

'The Pleasures of Memory', as we know, was Rogers's most famous poem; the two lines are by Holland.

Lady Holland took great pleasure in the gardens at Holland House, returning with delight to 'the fresh air, verdure and singing birds... after the dense vapours, gaslights and din'[7] of city life. In summer its borders were bright with dahlias, a flower she is credited for having introduced into England, bringing back the seeds from Spain, where they had recently arrived from Mexico, after her visit there in 1804. Her husband celebrated her initiative in verse:

> The Dahlia you brought to our isle
> Your praises forever should speak:
> Mid gardens as sweet as your smile,
> And in colour as bright as your cheek.[8]

Like his wife, Holland loved the house's gardens and the woods and fields surrounding them. But he took only the mildest interest in running the estate. He introduced a flock of merino sheep, which he had purchased in Spain in 1809, to Kensington but on the whole left farming to his manager. It was just as well. As far as sheep, 'that particular animal by whose destruction mutton is obtained', were concerned, Sydney Smith once told him, he betrayed the most profound and ludicrous ignorance. 'You are a statesman, a scholar and a wit, but not a butcher.'[9]

On the east side of the park was Little Holland House. Formerly a farm, its land had been added to the demesne by Holland's father. In 1803, the house was leased to Caroline Fox and their step-aunt, Elizabeth Vernon, 'Aunt Ebey', as they called her. The two women lived there together for 25 years, their presence providing a comforting backdrop for the Holland children when their parents were away. Lady Holland, despite occasional moments of irritation, got on well with Caroline and some of her best and most interesting letters from abroad were written to her sister-in-law.

In February 1818, Holland's maternal uncle and former guardian, the Earl of Upper Ossory, died. Having amply provided for his daughters and two illegitimate children, he left his estate of Ampthill to Holland – a bequest, wrote Holland, 'munificent enough in itself, and to me beyond all value, from recollection of those who had inhabited it, and of the happy hours, days, months and years I had spent in their society.'[10] In the long run the expense of keeping up the estate would prove a heavy burden, but the unexpected legacy was a further tribute – if one were needed – to the affection he inspired.

The following year brought a still more painful loss. In September 1819 the Holland's youngest daughter Georgiana, aged ten, became seriously ill with what turned out to be tubercular peritonitis. Lady Holland, who feared the worst, was driven almost beyond endurance by the well-meant cheerfulness of the ladies of Little Holland House, who pooh-poohed her anxieties, and seemed to laugh at her 'folly of feeling and fearing'. For the first time since she had known them, she told her son Henry, she was glad to hear their carriage leave. 'I cannot bear up when my heart is almost broken to hear fine strung phrases, and talk, upon talk, upon such disciplined minds and feelings. When I am wretched I have no control, and I like those best who fluctuate in my hopes & fears.'[11]

Georgiana died on 1 November. She was ten years old.

'Lord and Lady Holland are in very great affliction,' wrote Allen to the Whig MP Thomas Creevey, 'and you who know the dear little girl they have lost and how much they were attached to her, will not wonder at their sorrow. At present Lady Holland bears the loss with greater firmness, but she will feel it through her whole life.'[12]

Allen had adored Georgiana, his favourite in the family, and had been with her throughout her illness. She was buried at Millbrook, near Holland's childhood home at Ampthill, and a marble bust of her by Westmacott, the small head crowned with snowdrops, was erected in her memory in the church. Allen kept a replica of it in his study at Holland House.

In the midst of the family's distress there was a further bitter twist for Lady Holland. 'I have received an anonymous letter,' she told Henry,

> full of triumph at my misfortune denouncing the vengeance of God that my darling being [taken] was a judgement on me for being a worthless mother and tyrant wife... and foretelling that my husband will be snatched from me and you all... I am at a loss to conjecture who could bear such malice towards me, or indeed be so full of malice against any human being at such a moment.[13]

No one ever discovered the author of the letter, but it may well be that Caroline Lamb's cruel portrait of her in *Glenarvon* helped create the hostile climate which made its writing possible. In some sections of society she had never been forgiven for her divorce; there were also those, her eldest son Webby among them, who felt it had driven her husband Sir Godfrey to suicide. She put on a bold face to the world, but she had had much to suffer from its slights. The Holland House salon was in its way her recompense; the more successful it became the more she denied her exclusion elsewhere. And her husband's devotion never wavered, the tragedy, if anything, bringing them still closer. Breaking the news of Georgiana's death to Charles in Corfu, Holland paid fresh tribute to her qualities: 'Much as I have always thought of your Mama's goodness of heart & strength of mind her conduct to me & all of us on this heart-breaking occasion has raised my opinion of it & I adore her more than ever I did.'[14]

12

The Trial of Queen Caroline

S OME hint of Lady Holland's irritation with her sister-in-law during Georgiana's last days must have filtered through to Caroline, for we find her, in a letter to her brother, declaring that she would not think of coming to Holland House unless he invited her personally. Holland was quick to smooth her ruffled feathers – 'Lady Holland feels it must appear awkward neither to see nor write to you when so near'[1] – and the old familiar intercourse between the two households was gradually resumed. Caroline Fox shared many of her brother's qualities. Like him she loved reading and, though neither a beauty nor a wit, she had acquired a poise and breadth of information from her upbringing amidst the intellectual circle surrounding her uncle, the first Lord Lansdowne, which stood her in good stead at Holland House. Her brother trusted her political judgement; from his earliest days, when travelling on his grand tour, he had been accustomed to share his views with her. Less extreme in her likes and dislikes than Lady Holland but still a fervent Foxite, she was in many ways a more reliable sounding board than his wife.

The Hollands had returned from France to new problems and divisions amongst the Whigs. The repeal of the suspension of habeas corpus in January 1818 removed one main subject of contention with the government, but the Whig attempts to oppose an Indemnity Bill, indemnifying those who had misused their powers during the suspension, were easily defeated. During the debates on the subject, noted Holland with characteristic modesty, 'I acquired by practice more fluency in speaking than I had hitherto possessed, and got the ear of the House in a degree that placed me higher in the rank of speakers than I had hitherto aspired to be or perhaps could ever really deserve.'[2]

At the age of 45, Holland was growing into the role of elder states-man. He was also a benevolent figure. He was not in touch with the great changes in society which the industrial revolution was bring-ing about; like Fox, who confessed he could not get through Adam Smith's *The Wealth of Nations*, he was not much interested in trade or economic questions. But his hatred of injustice and oppression, perhaps born of his sufferings as a schoolboy, was a consistent theme throughout his career. His private charities were numerous, often to those of very different opinions from his own, whether French priests who had fled to England during the Revolution or impoverished radi-cal writers like William Godwin. In Parliament he steadily pursued a liberal course. 'It is certain,' wrote Brougham in his *Statesmen in the Time of George III*, 'that whenever any occasion arose of peril to the great cause of toleration the alarmed eye first turned to him as the refuge of the persecuted.'[3]

As well as supporting the Whigs' main policies on Catholic Emancipation and electoral reform, Holland made a number of interventions of his own. His repeated petitions on behalf of debtors who were held in prison indefinitely, often in appalling conditions, did much to secure the Act of 1812 which put a limit to their punishment. He campaigned against the game laws allowing the use of lethal man-traps and spring guns against poachers, and served as commissioner when the bill to remove them went through the Lords. He moved the second reading of a bill to abolish the death penalty for stealing, a motion which failed at the time but which subsequently passed into law. During the war he protested against the government's failure to exchange prisoners of war; in 1811, because of his 'generous and compassionate spirit',[4] he was petitioned directly by the crew of a French ship, *La Baleine*, who had been prisoners for over seven years. He called for the limitation of *ex officio* (or government) evidence, whereby the Attorney General could hold a suspected person for an indefinite period without giving his reasons, or applying to the courts. And in 1818, when the Alien Bill, allowing political exiles to be expelled without notice, was revived, he managed to prevent the closing of a loophole – whereby, under Scottish law, foreigners who had shares in the Bank of Scotland became naturalized subjects – by prolonging the debate in the House of Lords till it was too late to include it.

Holland had a special interest in this last measure: Talleyrand's illegitimate son, the Comte de Flahaut, Napoleon's ADC at Waterloo, who had fled to Britain after Napoleon's defeat, had availed himself of the Scottish anomaly to stay there. Saved from expulsion by Holland's delaying tactics, he would be forever grateful to Holland House, where his Napoleonic connections made him a special favourite with Lady Holland. Others might find her difficult, but for Flahaut she was a guardian angel, adored for her goodness by all 'true and generous hearts'.

Meanwhile public affairs took a dramatic new turn when, in August 1819, a mass meeting demanding electoral reform at St Peter's Fields in Manchester was broken up by a cavalry charge, which killed 11 people and injured hundreds more. The Peterloo massacre, as it became known, was widely condemned, and the general indignation was increased when the government, within a day of receiving the news, sent a letter signed by the regent, congratulating the magistrates who had ordered it. 'The Parliament, however, as then constituted,' wrote Holland in his memoirs, 'had no sympathy with the sufferers; and when convened in November passed several angry and restrictive laws without repugnance or even the formality of inquiry.'[5]

The laws in question were the controversial Six Acts, the most important of which forbade the publication of 'seditious libels' (in principle, anti-government opinions) and severely restricted the right of public assembly. The Foxite Whigs protested vigorously, but the Grenvillites, fearful of the breakdown of law and order, supported the government's measures. The long alliance with Grenville was at an end, though Holland remained good friends with him in private. He had always admired his integrity, and quoted his uncle's opinion of him in his memoirs. 'I like Grenville very much,' said Fox in 1805. 'He is a *direct* man.'[6]

Holland had been one of the most effective speakers against the Six Acts. Public meetings, he contended, were a useful vent for popular feeling; by stifling all expressions of dissent, discontents would be driven underground, leading to the far more serious danger of secret cabals and conspiracies. How far his views were prophetic was shown only two months later, with the shocking discovery, on 24 February 1819, of the so-called Cato Street Conspiracy. Its leader, the radical speaker Arthur Thistlewood, angered and frustrated by the new laws, had plotted to murder Lord Liverpool and all his Cabinet, and set up a revolutionary regime. Thistlewood and three other plotters were hanged, the rest sentenced to transportation for life, a sufficient example, in the government's view, to scare off other troublemakers. Cobbett had fled to the United States, other leading radicals were in prison and the Whig grandee Lord Fitzwilliam had been dismissed as a Lord Lieutenant of the West Riding in Yorkshire for allowing a public meeting in protest at Peterloo. For the time being the policy of repression seemed successful.

But other forces were at work, this time of an unexpected kind, to prove that popular opinion could not always be denied. On 30 January 1820, George III had died, after a twilight life of almost ten years. The first important question when George IV succeeded to the throne was his proposed divorce of his detested wife, Queen Caroline, on the grounds of her misconduct and adultery. The blatant hypocrisy of the charges against her, in view of his own notorious profligacy, aroused furious indignation across the country and for a moment the monarchy itself seemed threatened.

Caroline, who had been living abroad since 1814, had arrived in London to claim her rights in June and was immediately welcomed as a heroine. Having failed to buy her off with an offer of £50,000 a year to live abroad and renounce her title, the king had persuaded a reluctant government to bring divorce proceedings against her in the House of Lords. The outcry against him was terrific. The press, supposedly muzzled under the Six Acts, outdid itself in scurrility; the authorities, faced with the possibility of widespread disorder, dared not use the law against it.

The Whigs, remembering their cavalier treatment by the regent in 1811–12 were quite happy to harass the king, and Brougham, who had been out of politics for the last three years, constituted himself the queen's great champion. Holland had been privately approached by Liverpool to ask if he would take part in a committee to examine the evidence against her. 'I declined,' he wrote in his memoirs, '...on private rather than public grounds, thinking my name by no means an advantageous one to be selected for a judicial inquiry on a matter connected with divorce.'[7]

True to this decision Holland stayed aloof from the hurly-burly of the trial, instead amusing himself as a spectator by writing nonsensical puns and epigrams on the various indecencies which occurred in the evidence, and tossing them across the table for the diversion of the Chancellor, Lord Eldon. 'I believe,' he wrote later, 'I was the only Lord practised in public speaking who asked not a single question during the enquiry.'[8]

Despite the salacious nature of the evidence against her – in particular her relations with her equerry Bartolomeo Pergami – the injured queen would sometimes nod off during her trial. For Holland it was the excuse for an epigram:

> Here her conduct no proof of the charges affords,
> She sleeps with no menials, she sleeps with the Lords.[9]

Like most of his fellow Whigs, he was mildly sympathetic to the queen. Lady Holland, who still hoped to be received at court, took the side of the king. This led to strained relations with her husband, as Creevey reported to his wife:

> Holland set off at *four* in the morning for Oxford to help Lord Jersey at his county meeting [in support of Queen Caroline]. It was with the greatest difficulty my lady let him go, and he begged me not to mention it before her as it was a *very sore subject.*[10]

In the end the clamour against the bill was so great that after the third reading the government announced that it would be postponed. In the eyes of the public it was an acquittal. There was a general illumination in London (with the natural exception of Carlton House), ships on the river were lit up, and thousands of people, accompanied by bands and music, surged through the streets carrying torches and busts of the queen. Two months later, when Caroline drove to St Paul's for a service of thanksgiving for her acquittal, the *Times* described the crowds as bigger than any ever seen in history.

Public opinion had triumphed but the queen's own story would end in tragedy. Over the next few months there was a gradual reaction against her as the Tory papers moved to the attack. There were satirical songs and rhymes about her; a series of grotesque cartoons showed her gambolling with her lover, or lolling beside a pile of empty brandy bottles; even her supporters began to feel embarrassed by her indiscretions. On 29 July 1821, the day of the king's coronation, the queen, who had announced her intention of attending the ceremony, was forcibly turned away at the door of Westminster Abbey. This last humiliation was a death blow; already unwell, she died from an inflammation of the stomach a few weeks later.

It was a sorry end to an unedifying saga. For Holland the whole affair had been a dangerous farce, which reflected no credit on anyone concerned, least of all the institution of the monarchy. But his memoirs provide an amusing coda to the story. On 21 May 1821, Napoleon died on St Helena. The news, which reached England before the queen fell ill, was announced to the king in ambiguous terms: 'I have, sir, to congratulate you. Your greatest enemy is dead.' 'Is she, by God?' the king exclaimed, thus unguardedly betraying where his real priorities lay.[11]

The Hollands had been spending the summer months in Paris when on 4 July an anonymous note to Lady Holland was left on their doorstep with a five-word message: *'Le grand homme est mort.'* The official news of Napoleon's death, which came out a few hours later, provoked surprisingly little reaction from the public at large. 'The perfect Apathy of everyone high and low here upon such an event as Napoleon's death astonishes and puzzles me', wrote Lady Bessborough from Paris,

> it seems to me a mixture of ingratitude and stupidity. It was cried about the streets and the affiche describing it sold with ballads and accounts of the Process, and for the most part no notice taken or even many of the papers bought. Except by Ly Holland, who closed

her door one eve. & is really quite low spirited with it, no one seems to think about it.[12]

In his will Napoleon left Lady Holland a gold snuffbox, with an antique Greek cameo on the lid, which had been given to him by Pope Pius VI; the card inside was inscribed in his own hand: '*L'empereur Napoléon à Lady Holland, témoignage de satisfaction et d'estime*.'[13] On 14 September, the day after the Hollands returned to Holland House from Paris, Bertrand and Montholon, the leaders of Napoleon's entourage on St Helena, arrived there in full Napoleonic uniform to deliver the emperor's gift in person.

It was a controversial legacy, and one which gave rise to much critical publicity. One Whig writer, Lord Carlisle, published a seven-verse poem in the weekly magazine *John Bull*, urging her to throw it in the Thames. The first verse read as follows:

> Lady, reject the gift, 'tis tinged with gore
> Those crimson spots a dreadful tale relate;
> It has been grasp'd by an infernal power;
> And by the hand that seal'd young Enghien's fate.[14]

Byron, living in Italy, but an avid reader of the English newspapers, was quick to spring to her defence:

> Lady, accept the box a hero wore
> In spite of all this elegiac stuff
> Let not seven stanzas written by a bore
> Prevent Your Ladyship from taking snuff.[15]

Throughout his stay in St Helena, in order to make sure her gifts to Napoleon got through to him, Lady Holland had been in friendly

correspondence with Sir Hudson Lowe. Lowe might have been forgiven for thinking that he and Lady Holland were on the best of terms.
However, there had already been complaints from Montholon and
others about his rigid and unsympathetic attitude to his prisoner.
Among other petty restrictions, he had made a habit of holding
back newspaper articles and caricatures which were favourable to
Napoleon. Two months before Napoleon's death he had written to
Lady Holland apologizing to her for withholding two caricatures
she had sent and hoping he had not aroused her 'reprehension'. His
motives, he explained, were humane; he did not want to excite false
hopes in Napoleon by showing him the views of those who found
'talents to admire' in him.

Soon after his return to England Lowe came to call at Holland
House. The door, which had once opened so easily, was closed to
him; when he gave his name and asked for Lady Holland, he was told
she was not at home. A day or two later he received a note from her:

> I was in London when you were good enough to call at Holland House,
> but am not sorry at an opportunity of acknowledging your attentions
> by writing, as I confess I should have some difficulty in conversing
> with you on subjects connected with them, being one of that numer-
> ous class you describe in your letter of 5th March as seeing in the late
> great man chiefly, if not exclusively, 'talents to admire'.[16]

Lady Holland had five copies of her letter made, perhaps intending to
publish it. She never did so, but now Sir Hudson could no longer be
of use to her, she could at least express her anger at his treatment of
Napoleon by delivering a crushing snub. The unfortunate governor,
conscientious and upright but totally unsuited for his near impossible
task, has been badly treated by posterity. He would fare no better at
Holland House.

13

'A House of All Europe'

T H E popular reaction to the trial of Queen Caroline had shown that whatever the repressive intentions of the Six Acts, public opinion could not be ignored. Meanwhile the government itself was beginning to undergo a transformation. Lord Liverpool, after presiding for ten years over what Macaulay described as 'the most reactionary team of ministers ever assembled for the direction of public affairs' was turning to new men. Robert Peel replaced Lord Sidmouth (as Addington had become) as Home Secretary and began a massive reform of criminal law; the suicide of Castlereagh in 1822 left the way open for the more liberal Canning to become Foreign Secretary; Canning's chief supporter William Huskisson became President of the Board of Trade and set about dismantling the cumbersome system of tariffs and duties which were hampering free trade.

It seemed as though the liberal Tories had stolen the Whigs' clothes. Only the issues of Catholic Emancipation and parliamentary reform remained unsolved. On the subject of Catholic Emancipation the ministry had agreed to differ, some like Canning supporting it, others like Peel and Wellington strongly opposed to any change. But since George IV was now as much against it as his father, and would not allow it to be raised in Cabinet, the question was left in abeyance.

The last chance of conciliating the Irish before they took matters into their own hands was rapidly slipping away.

The issue of parliamentary reform offered better opportunities for the Whigs. With just a handful of radical members in the Commons and none in the Lords, they were able to present themselves as the only party which could channel the growing demands for reform through Parliament. By making electoral reform a condition of their taking office (unlikely while George IV was alive) they could take the credit for being reformers and at the same time keep the movement under control. 'However small the quantum of reform you propose,' wrote Holland to Grey in November 1820, 'if proposed directly and made a *sine qua non* it gives you should it be resisted all the advantages of having proposed reform to the fullest extent with the public, and it gives the country the advantage of enlisting the popular cry under the banner of moderate, practical and useful reform.'[1] In other words the Whigs could make the running either way.

Holland House as usual played its role in keeping up morale. 'The meeting of Parliament and a few Holland House dinners may perhaps put some life into us,'[2] wrote Tierney, now leader of the Whigs in the Commons, to Grey at one low moment. Of course it was not the only centre for Whig politics. There were meetings and discussions in many places: at Brooks's Club, where Fox's portrait by Reynolds presided in the entrance hall; at Devonshire House, where the bachelor Duke of Devonshire kept up the traditions of his mother Georgiana, and lent his support though not his voice – for he never spoke in the Lords – to the Whig cause; at Lansdowne House and Bowood in Wiltshire, where the third Marquess of Lansdowne, an intellectual like his father the first marquess, had gathered a coterie of savants and political economists; in the palatial country houses of Whig magnates like the Duke of Bedford and Lord Fitzwilliam, who held whole counties under their sway. But nowhere had quite the glamour of Holland House. There were even some MPs, wrote Tierney, who would not vote unless they had been asked to dinner there.

Since the end of the war Holland House had expanded its European horizons too. Just as Fox had been a European figure, a symbol of free speech in a reactionary age, so Holland House had become a rallying point for European liberalism, 'a house of all Europe', as the diarist Charles Greville described it. In part this was due to the cosmopolitan outlook of the Hollands themselves: they shared a gift for languages and love of foreign travel and in their many journeys abroad had got to know the leading political and intellectual figures of the countries they visited. Opinionated but immensely well informed, they almost ran a separate foreign policy from Holland House.

At times their influence was entirely benevolent. For instance, when the Hollands were staying in Verona during the Hundred Days, they had renewed their acquaintance with the former Spanish prime minister Godoy, who was living under the protection of the exiled Charles IV of Spain. The Hollands had always liked Godoy and when he lamented to Holland that his position in Italy would be very precarious if Charles IV died and asked if there might be a chance of asylum in England, Holland promised he would try to help. Four years later, when Charles IV died, Holland approached the prime minister, Lord Liverpool, on Godoy's behalf, and obtained permission for him to come to England as a private citizen. Godoy's response, wrote Holland in his *Foreign Reminiscences*, was as follows:

> He had for many years disposed of the resources of one of the richest kingdoms in Europe, he had made the fortunes of thousands and thousands, but I was the only mortal who since his fall, had expressed or shown recollection of any service, great or small, received from him. I might therefore judge of the pleasure my letter had given him.[3]

In the event Godoy was allowed to stay in Italy but the episode showed Holland – and Liverpool – at his best. Other foreign interventions were less happy. Holland, as we have seen, had taken a close interest in the creation of the Spanish constitution in the years between 1809 and 1812, and he and Allen, who had made himself an expert on the matter, had been in frequent correspondence with the leading Spanish liberals. In April 1815, when the future constitution of Naples was in question Holland and Allen sketched out a series of similar proposals for Joachim Murat, who was still in charge. Unfortunately their courier was stopped by the Austrian authorities in Lucca and the draft constitution ended up in Vienna. Since Murat was shortly afterwards overthrown by Austrian forces in favour of the legitimate king, Ferdinand IV, Holland's attempts to interfere not only embarrassed the British government at a difficult point in their relations with Austria, but scandalized political allies like the Grenvillites for whom, in the words of Grenville's brother, Thomas, this 'scrawling out [of] Italian constitutions'[4] was totally unacceptable.

In 1823 Naples was once more at the centre of a controversy, one in which, though unintentionally, Holland caused further offence. Revolution had broken out in Naples and its twin kingdom of Sicily, and Ferdinand IV had been forced to agree to a liberal constitution. Fearing that the revolutionary contagion might spread, the three leading powers of the so-called Holy Alliance – Russia, Austria and Prussia – met Ferdinand at the Congress of Laibach and agreed to send Austrian troops to support him. Promptly rescinding his promise of a constitution, Ferdinand made the most of the Austrian presence to embark on a savage purge of the liberals who had opposed him.

The British had never joined the Holy Alliance, regarding it as visionary and impractical, and though the British ambassador Lord Stewart attended the congress he refused to support its decisions. Holland went further in the House of Lords, where he played, he admitted, perhaps an 'imprudent and intemperate' role in denouncing the policies of the Holy Alliance. In particular, he pointed out the inconsistency of Tsar Alexander I, who owed his own throne to a revolution, in condemning the risings in Italy. (In 1801 Alexander had been staying in the palace where his father, the mad Tsar Paul I, was assassinated; he had known of the plot to depose him but not, apparently, of his intended murder.) The subject was so sensitive that Holland was called to order by the President of the Council before he had time to finish his sentence. What he meant to say, he claimed, was

> that it ill became him [the Tsar] to charge those who derived their power from insurrection or mutiny with being necessarily accessories after the fact to the preparation of a crime when he himself was sitting on a throne reeking with the blood of his father, and would by a parity of reasoning, be exposed to the unfounded or, at least, questionable imputation of being cognizant and responsible for the murder.[5]

Cut short before the qualifying final clause, the sentence implied that Alexander had been privy to his father's death. It was a saying of the unsayable that caused a diplomatic uproar. Pozzo di Borgo, the Russian ambassador in Paris and an old friend of Holland's, announced that he could no longer receive him or accept his invitations; Prince Lieven, the Russian ambassador in London, was said to be considering challenging him to a duel; Princess Lieven, till then a frequent visitor, cut off all further intercourse with Holland House. Lady Holland was beside herself; she had not slept since it happened, reported Creevey two days later. Holland did his best to smooth things over by publishing an anonymous explanation of the misunderstanding in the *Times* – 'a peace offering to the Emperor of all the Russias, the Lievens and the Princess of Madagascar,'[6] as Creevey put it. But in private he was unrepentant. 'Whether Alexander knew of Paul's murder or not', he wrote to Lord William Russell some months later,

> I think he has done much worse things than that lately... Madame de Lieven who is a sensible woman and not a Russian [she was a Baltic German] knows very well that the Czar and his subjects when they mix with Europeans *ne font que jouer la comédie* and that even the anger of being accused of murder is but an affectation of sentiment to which they are [as] utterly strangers, as the religious horrors or devotion of Talma [the actor] in Oedipe or Hippolytus.[7]

It was not until after Alexander's death in 1826 that the Lievens felt able to see the Hollands again. Prince Lieven was no great loss. He was a colourless man whose favourite expression (and nickname in London) was 'Vraiment'. His wife, however, was a clever and fascinating woman, a former mistress of Metternich, who loved dabbling in English affairs and whose confidants ranged from Grey to Wellington and George IV. Holland House, with its cosmopolitan and political mix was a perfect setting for her talents and she must have been delighted when the time came to return.

There were always defections from Holland House as visitors took offence for one reason or another, though few of them stayed away for ever. Brougham, a favourite in the first days of the *Edinburgh Review*, had suddenly stopped going there in 1810, returning just as suddenly six years later on the condition that no one ask the reason for his absence. Holland, who had helped him find a seat in Parliament, had been wounded at his defection, but the estrangement was probably due to a quarrel with his wife. Brougham objected to her political interference; the idea of 'carrying on the party by a *coterie* at Lady Holland's elbow', he once told Creevey, 'cannot be submitted to for a moment.'[8]

Canning was another friend of Holland's who fell by the wayside. Excluded by his birth, he felt, from high office under the Whigs, he had chosen to follow Pitt instead while continuing to share the Whig aims of Catholic Emancipation and the abolition of slavery. His intimacy with Holland dated back to their days at Eton and Oxford and though their political paths had diverged, they retained a fondness for each other. It was one which Lady Holland did not share; she was jealous of their early friendship and regarded Canning as a traitor to the Foxite cause. Holland's feelings were more complex. He had too much goodwill towards Canning, he once explained, to be 'a fair and impartial judge of the propriety of attacking him'[9] in debate. But it was only very seldom that Canning came to Holland House.

Even Creevey, whose gossipy letters and diaries give us some of our most amusing glimpses of Holland House, was sometimes driven to rebel. In 1820, for instance, he had stayed away for several months in protest at Lady Holland's attitude of 'virtuous indignation' against Queen Caroline. He had needed some persuading to return. 'Lord Holland came up to me in Brooks's yesterday and reproached me for never coming near my lady,' he reported to his stepdaughter; 'and after saying many civil things to me in his pretty manner, said I should go and see her with him. So I did, and she was all civility and *humility*.'[10]

It was only a temporary victory. Humility was not Lady Holland's style. But her sharp tongue and domineering ways, the source of endless anecdotes, were as much the spice of Holland House as her husband's learning and delightful conversation. Familiars loved complaining of their hostess. For instance, wrote Creevey,

> In addition to all her further insults on the town, she has set up a huge *cat* which is never permitted to be out of her sight, and to whose vagaries she requires unqualified submission. Rogers, it seems, has already sustained considerable injury in a personal affair with this

1 The third Lord Holland in 1795, painted in Florence by François-Xavier Fabre.

2 Lady Webster (later Holland) in 1793, painted in Naples by Sir Robert Fagan.

3 Lady Webster (later
Holland) in fancy dress as a
Virgin of the Sun, by George
Romney, 1796.

4 Charles James Fox, Lord
Holland's beloved uncle, by
Karl Anton Hickel, 1794.

5 Dr John Allen, the librarian
at Holland House, by Sir Edwin
Landseer, 1830.

6 'Introduction of Citizen Volpone and his suite at Paris' by James Gillray, 1802. Fox and his wife are presented to the First Consul; Lord and Lady Holland are on the right.

7 The Reverend Sydney Smith by Henry Perronet Briggs, 1830. The witty clergyman was one of the stars of Holland House.

8 Lady Caroline Lamb in page's costume, *c.*1813, by Thomas Phillips.

9 Lord Byron at the height of his fame: engraving by Harlow of the portrait by Henry Hoppner Meyer, 1816.

10 Madame de Staël, after a portrait by Gérard, 1812.

11 'Sketch for a Prime Minister', published in *The Satirist*, 1 February, 1811. The Hollands knock at the door of the Treasury; Napoleon slyly offers them a bag of gold.

12 The Portuguese Garden (later the Dutch Garden) at Holland House, with the bust of Napoleon by Canova in the foreground.

13 The poet Samuel Rogers, sketched at Holland House, c.1835, by Sir Edwin Landseer.

14 The third Lord Holland by Sir George Hayter, 1820.

15 'A tête à tête', Lord Holland and Talleyrand, by the political cartoonist, HB (John Doyle), 1831.

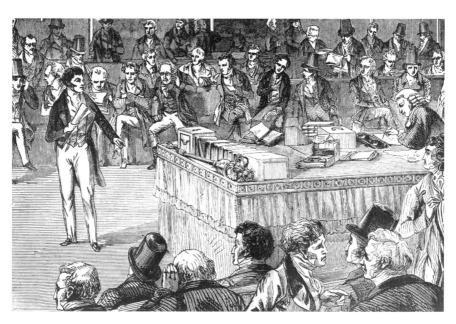

16 Lord John Russell introducing the Reform Bill in the House of Commons, 1 March, 1831.

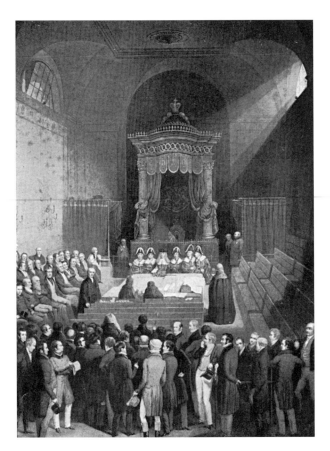

17 The Reform Bill receiving the Royal Assent in the House of Lords on 8 June, 1832, after the painting by Samuel W. Reynolds. Lord Holland is the second figure on the left in front of the throne; Brougham is presiding.

18 The second Earl Grey, 'Lord Grey of the Reform Bill', after the portrait by Sir Thomas Lawrence.

19 Sketch of William Lamb, later Lord Melbourne, by his wife Lady Caroline Lamb, c.1814.

20 The library at Holland House painted by C.R. Leslie, 1838 Left to right: Lord Holland, Dr Allen, Lady Holland, and the page, William Doggett.

21 The library at Holland House after the air raid, 28 September 1940.

animal, Brougham only keeps *him* or *her* at arm's length by snuff, and Luttrell has sent in his formal resignation of all further visits till this odious favourite is dismissed from the Cabinet.[11]

The old familiars did not change, spreading out from the inner circle of Whig relations and grandees: Allen of course, the witty dilettante Henry Luttrell, Samuel Rogers, Sydney Smith, Francis Jeffrey and Tom Moore. But the company was constantly being replenished. Men of science like Sir Humphry Davy and Alexander von Humboldt; the political economist Thomas Malthus; painters like David Wilkie, Edwin Landseer and Thomas Lawrence; Byron's friend John Cam Hobhouse; the American writer Washington Irving; the Scottish historian Sir James Mackintosh; the great Shakespearean actor John Philip Kemble; foreign diplomats; Spanish liberals; French intellectuals; exiled royalty; rising politicians – all passed through Holland House at one time or another, their names neatly entered in the dinner book by Allen. Music was the only exception in the array of talents represented there. Holland, like Fox before him, was decidedly unmusical, and his wife went along with his tastes.

There was one great gap in the circle. In November 1821 Lady Bessborough died suddenly in Florence, where she had been nursing a dying grandchild. Ten years older than Lady Holland, she had been her most intimate friend, not above making fun of her absurdities, but always witty, loving and supportive. Even her daughter Caroline's behaviour had done nothing to make a rift between them. 'I have been dreadfully shocked by the acct. which arrived [by] this post from Florence,' Lady Holland wrote to her son Henry. 'I feel her great kindness rush upon my recollection.'[12] It was the end of a friendship that went back to the carefree days in Italy nearly 30 years earlier when she and Holland had first fallen in love, and something of their youth died with her.

14

Reforming Campaigns

F ROM his vantage point of Holland House, closely in touch with many of its leading figures but without great personal ambition, Holland was ideally placed to observe and record the politics of his day. His two-volume *Memoirs of the Whig Party During My Time*, covering the period from his entry into Parliament in 1797 till 1809, his *Foreign Reminiscences*, describing his encounters with European royalty and politicians before and during the Napoleonic wars, and his *Further Memoirs of the Whig Party*, ending in 1823, have always been a mine of information for historians and biographers. Their Whig bias – pro-Fox, anti-royalty – was only to be expected, but his closeness to events and first-hand knowledge of the characters involved made them an invaluable source. They did not appear till after his death, the first three volumes mentioned being edited by his son Henry, but he had always intended them for publication. They were, he admitted, 'rambling, desultory and imperfect', but they were true, and related to subjects which, 'having afforded amusement and instruction to the writer in the course of his life', might be of possible interest 'to some reader of similar habits and tastes after its close'.[1]

Holland's model for his reminiscences, he tells us, was Horace Walpole, whose *Memoirs of the Last Ten Years of the Reign of George II* he edited and published in 1822; we must assume he began his own soon afterwards. Walpole had bequeathed his memoirs, together with a chest of papers, to the sixth Earl Waldegrave, who was not allowed to take possession of his legacy till he reached the age of 25. This had happened in 1810 and Holland had agreed to edit the memoirs – 'ill written but entertaining, and from the dearth of all good histories of the period 1751–1760, very readable'[2] – as well as editing those of the previous Earl Waldegrave, whose memoirs covered the same time span.

Walpole had died when Holland was 20. 'I had from earliest youth,' wrote Holland in his memoirs, 'great curiosity about men remarkable for their literary attainments,' and he had been flattered by the notice Walpole had taken of him on his occasional visits to London or Strawberry Hill. 'In person,' wrote Holland, 'he was slender and prim, in his manners extremely artificial, and in his temper somewhat susceptible about trifles,' and he quoted George Selwyn's observation that the master of Strawberry Hill was the one of the best-preserved mummies in its collection of antiquities. But whatever the peculiarities of Walpole's taste and character, his writing abounded in fascinating historical and literary material, the fruit of a long life spent in the company of statesmen, artists and wits. 'No one employed as I have been in editing, and as I now am, in imitating his labours,' wrote Holland, 'can seriously wish to disparage one whom he shows himself willing and perhaps unequal to emulating.'[3]

Such literary and historical activities were always part of Holland's life. As well as his political memoirs, there were translations from Ariosto, Calderón and Lope de Vega; unfinished notes on Fox's life and correspondence, later completed by Lord John Russell; a number of pamphlets on political issues; a journal of his time in office from 1831 to 1840 (not intended for publication and thus less formal than his memoirs); an extensive correspondence and a stream of occasional verse. Of course, by the standards of his friends from the *Edinburgh*

Review he was an amateur, and he never pretended to be more. His greatest contribution lay in the way he animated others, in his passion for literature and history and in the breadth of his information. 'I don't suppose there is any Englishman living who covers so much ground as he does – biographical, historical and anecdotal,'[4] wrote Creevey, while Greville, returning home after an evening at Holland House, could only lament the inadequacies of his education:

> I felt as if a language was spoken before me which I understood, but not enough to talk it myself. There was nothing discussed of which I was altogether ignorant, and when the merits of Wordsworth, Coleridge and Crabbe were brought into comparison and Lord Holland cut jokes upon Allen for his enthusiastic admiration of the 'De Moribus Germanorum', it was not that I had not read the poets or the historian, but that I felt I had not read them with profit. I have not that familiarity with either which enables me to discuss their merits, and a painful sense came over me of the difference between one who has superficially read and studied, and one who has laid a solid foundation in early youth... He who wastes his early years in horse racing and all sorts of idleness, figuring away among the dissolute and foolish, must be content to play an inferior part among the learned and the wise.[5]

Central to the intellectual life at Holland House, and regarded as an oracle on literary matters, was John Allen, or 'Jack' as he was known in the family. Since he first joined the family in 1801, he had become an essential part of the household, his medical qualifications secondary as he grew into the role of librarian, comptroller and inseparable friend. It was he who organized the lists of dinner guests, assigned rooms to people who were staying and at dinner sat at the foot of the table to do the carving. (Lady Holland's frequent criticisms from the other end of the table once led him to tell her to carve herself.) Although he contributed a number of learned articles to the *Edinburgh Review*, and thanks to the Hollands' influence was appointed Master of Dulwich College in 1820, he was too devoted to the family, and perhaps too unambitious, to stray very far from their orbit. For Holland he was an invaluable adviser, whether in acquiring books or pictures or providing references for his speeches in the House of Lords, and he shared to the full his political ideals. Some of his ideas – for instance, the creation of life peers – were far ahead of his time and his views on Ireland, as expressed in the *Edinburgh Review* a few years after the Act of Union, would echo down the century:

> She [England] has added about five millions to her population by her union with Ireland; and would to heaven we could say, that she had by that instance added in the same proportion to her strength and security; and that a blind and bigoted attachment to ancient prejudices, and a callous and disgusting indifference to the feelings and interests of so large a portion of her subjects, had not converted that which ought to have been her pride and strength, into her chief source of weakness and apprehension.[6]

The problems of Ireland, where coercion seemed the only way to keep the peace, showed no signs of going away. One of the initiatives of which Holland was proudest was a bill which gave the Irish the same rights as the rest of the United Kingdom when accused of 'overt acts of treason': in Britain two witnesses were required to substantiate such a charge, in Ireland only one. Since treason was a capital offence, the difference could be a matter of life and death. In the summer of 1821, taking advantage of an admission by the Lord Chancellor, Lord Eldon, that the law should be the same in all parts of the United Kingdom, Holland obtained his promise that he would not oppose a bill to amend it. The bill, which he introduced himself, 'glided almost imperceptibly' through both houses of Parliament to Holland's intense satisfaction. 'Is it vanity to say,' he wrote, 'that when one has succeeded in making such an amendment one feels that one has not lived in vain?'[7]

Meanwhile the central issue of Catholic disabilities remained unresolved. In 1821 a bill for Catholic Emancipation was passed by a small majority in the House of Commons but was thrown out by the Lords. It was the first time that the Commons had voted in favour of such a measure but with the Lords and the king still strongly opposed to it, the prospect of its becoming law seemed as far away as ever. What made matters worse were the false hopes that had been aroused when George IV made a state visit to Ireland earlier that year. He had been received with wild enthusiasm by the populace and by Catholic leaders like Daniel O'Connell, who had knelt down in the surf to offer him a laurel wreath on his departure. It was soon clear that nothing had changed; though in the case of George IV, as Holland recorded in his memoirs, there was more than mere bigotry behind his opposition to Catholic Emancipation:

> The Duke of Orléans (Louis Philippe) told me that in the year 1814 or 1815, I forget which, he distinctly avowed his hostility to all concession whatsoever, and explained the nature of his repugnance to it and of his scruples by saying that if catholics could be lawfully admitted to political power they could not lawfully be excluded from the Crown and the title of his family would in that case cease to be legitimate.[8]

Like every monarch since the expulsion of James II, George IV owed his crown to the principle of the Protestant succession. For the Irish, frustrated by years of waiting, such historical quibbles were neither here nor there. Despairing of obtaining justice from the British government, they set about getting it for themselves. A year of famine in

1822, bringing fresh misery to the rural population, was the trigger for concerted action. Political divisions between the different branches of the Catholic movement were put aside and in the summer of 1823, under the leadership of Daniel O'Connell, they united to form the Catholic Association.

To the Irish, Catholic Emancipation meant much more than the right to sit in Parliament and hold high office. (Catholics were still barred from top positions in the law, the civil service and the armed services.) The Catholic Church was part of their national identity and their fidelity to it had been maintained through more than two centuries of oppression. The Catholic Association quickly turned into a mass movement, backed by the Church and funded by a vast number of small subscriptions, the 'Catholic rent' as it was called. O'Connell, a lawyer, made certain that the association remained within the law and when two years later the government legislated against Irish associations (on the grounds that they were usurping the role of Parliament) he neatly sidestepped the new restrictions by forming a second Catholic Association. Ostensibly created for the purposes of education and other permitted activities, it in fact carried on the work of the old one.

The year 1823, a turning point in the struggle for Catholic Emancipation, was also a key date for another of Holland House's cherished causes, the abolition of slavery. In 1806 Fox had died happy in the knowledge that the slave trade was about to be abolished; the hope had been that with the ending of the slave trade the institution of slavery would gradually wither away. By the early 1820s the abolitionists realized that this was not going to happen by itself and in 1823 the Society for the Mitigation and Gradual Abolition of Slavery (later the Anti-Slavery Society) was formed. In May the same year the MP Thomas Fowell Buxton, who had taken over the leadership of the campaign from the ageing William Wilberforce, introduced a motion 'That the state of slavery is repugnant to the principles of the British and the Christian religion' and called for its gradual eradication in the British colonies. The motion was accepted in principle by the government, though it was indignantly rejected by the colonial authorities, and it would take another decade before abolition was achieved.

Holland shared Fox's abhorrence of slavery but his own situation was complicated by the fact that, thanks to Lady Holland's inheritance from her father, he was himself the owner of large plantations in Jamaica. At the time of her divorce from Webster, Holland had been relieved that Webster had taken over the West Indian properties as part of the settlement, but they had reverted to his wife on Webster's death. It had been a condition of her inheritance that her husband should add her maiden name of Vassall to his own. Webster had done so on their marriage. In order to establish his claim on the property, Holland was obliged to do the same when Webster died. He changed his family name to Vassall Fox in 1801.

But he was always a reluctant slave owner and his first move on taking over was to refuse to allow the purchase of any more slaves on his estates, the only exception being when two groups of slaves already working there, who had been owned by Webster or his agent, would have otherwise been sold to other masters and torn from their families. For the rest he seems to have been a humane and conscientious employer, issuing orders for extra holidays, forbidding the beating of field workers or any derogatory reference to their servile state, and building churches and schools on his estates. Unlike Jane Austen's Sir Thomas Bertram he never actually visited his West Indian properties, but he kept in close touch with his agent and others on the spot, among them his friend Matthew 'Monk' Lewis (author of the gothic bestseller *The Monk*), a plantation owner who shared his moral scruples about slavery. Their example, they hoped, would help to encourage other planters to improve conditions as a first step towards abolition.

Like many others, Holland had practical reservations about the timing of abolition – too sudden a transition might lead to the bloodshed that had followed the emancipation of the slaves in the French island of Saint-Domingue in 1790 – and the welfare, employment and civil rights of former slaves as well as the degree of compensation required to satisfy the planters needed careful working out. Without being directly involved in their negotiations, Holland played a key role as an intermediary between both sides, though his claims to special knowledge could sometimes irritate his colleagues. 'I cannot allow,' complained the Colonial Undersecretary Lord Howick, 'that we are as ignorant as you seem to suppose of the state of society in the colonies.'[9]

The abolitionists always regarded Holland as an important ally. Among the Holland House papers are letters from many of the leading figures in the movement, including Thomas Clarkson and Zachary Macaulay – the father of the historian – as well as Wilberforce himself. There could hardly be a greater contrast between the two men: Wilberforce driven by his Christian faith, Holland a sceptic, Wilberforce a Tory, who had been Pitt's greatest friend, Holland the heir to Charles James Fox. But the sympathy between the two was genuine. 'If it were only the zeal you have always manifested as an abolitionist I should consider you as entitled to my eternal gratitude,' wrote Wilberforce in 1820,

> and if I may without impropriety open my heart to yr Lordship I can truly declare, and strange as it may seem to you considering how much I was opposed to the late Mr Fox in politics, ye case was the same with him also, the simplicity, good nature and frankness I have remarked in you, have impressed me with feelings of regard for you wholly disproportionate to the degree in which I have the pleasure of your acquaintance.[10]

Later there would be disagreements between them on the speed of abolition but Wilberforce had no doubt of Holland's fidelity to his 'warm-hearted uncle's' ideals. 'I am scarcely more convinced that I myself am an honest abolitionist,' he told him, 'than that you are and ever have been such.'[11] The bill to abolish slavery was finally passed in 1833 – a few days before the death of Wilberforce. Holland had been more cautious than Wilberforce in his approach, but he had never allowed his interests as an owner to divert him from the central cause. In his chapter on Holland in his *Statesmen in the Time of George III*, Brougham makes special mention of his 'extraordinary disinterestedness':

> In the right of Lady Holland, a great Jamaica heiress, he was the owner of extensive plantations cultivated by slave labour; but there was no more strenuous advocate of the abolition both of the slave trade and slavery; and Lady Holland herself, the person most immediately interested in the continuance of these enormous abuses, had too much wisdom and too much virtue ever to interpose the least difference of opinion on this important subject.[12]

Since Brougham, as we know, was no lover of Lady Holland, we can be sure that his tribute was unbiased.

15

Family Matters

L ONG before the abolition of slavery the Hollands' estates in Jamaica had ceased to pay their way. Already in 1822 the properties had failed to produce an income, and Lady Holland talked of cutting down on entertaining – 'open doors bring open mouths'[1] – and of closing Holland House entirely when they went away. (As well as their usual foreign trips they took a rented house in London when Parliament was sitting.) But it does not seem to have cramped her style too much, and, though they took place less frequently, her big dinners were larger than ever. In a letter to her son Henry Fox, she writes of the dining room being 'pressed and jammed, in consequence of an *unaccounted* number rushing in to dinner'.[2] On another occasion an unexpected guest arrived when the company was seated at an already overcrowded table. 'Luttrell, make room,' she cried in her most imperious voice. 'It must certainly be *made*,' he replied, 'for it does not *exist*.'[3]

One person who seldom appeared at the evening gatherings at Holland House was the Hollands' daughter Mary. With her brothers away, she had led a lonely and secluded life, looked after by a governess and seemingly rather neglected by her parents. Caroline Fox, who always took the part of her nephews and nieces, complained that Mary was never allowed to appear when there was company at the house. In 1823, however, when she was 17, it was time for her to 'come out' in society, to be presented at court and go to balls. Since her mother was still not accepted at court, Lady Lansdowne (married to Holland's first cousin) took her under her kindly wing, and chaperoned her to her first ball, which took place at Devonshire House that April. Caroline Fox, Miss Vernon (Aunt Ebey) and Mrs Brown, the housekeeper, together 'manufactured' her dress, and though she was terrified beforehand, she found herself thoroughly enjoying her evening. Lady Lansdowne stayed up till five but could not feel tired, she said: looking at Mary's happy countenance was reward enough.

Mary had been due to be presented at court on the preceding day, but the ceremony was put off as the king was laid low with gout, and the event did not take place till June the following year, when she was again accompanied by Lady Lansdowne. Caroline Fox recounted the scene to Henry Fox:

> The toilet of the Royal person, I fancy, is so laborious and fatiguing, and so laced up is he, that it is impossible for him to stoop low enough to come in contact with the cheek of the young beauties below a certain stature; in consequence of which, such are suddenly lifted up by the attendants behind them to the level with the Kingly cheek. Mary was one of these, and I daresay she will describe to you her dismay, surprise and confusion, when she felt a hand under each arm raising her up and letting her down again.[4]

Once Mary was launched her mother was eager to find her a husband, even enlisting Henry Fox's help: 'As Mary is *out,* I think it will be better policy to keep her in the eye of the batchelors... and I wish for your assistance to introduce some good *épouseurs* to her notice.'[5]

Mary, a sweet, good-natured girl, pretty but shy, was embarrassed by her mother's too obvious ambitions. Like many racy ladies turned respectable, Lady Holland was excessively strict where her own offspring were concerned. Charles Fox, now a captain in the 15th Regiment of the Line, was stationed in Malta, and Henry, after leaving Oxford, spent most of his time abroad, so Mary bore the brunt of her controlling instincts. The poor girl, wrote Lady Granville, 'is so tied by the leg, so watched by the eye, so regulated, so tamed, so told to say this, not to do that… that she has lost all effect in society but that of being *gênéd* herself and a *gêne* to others… I never saw so many natural advantages thrown away.'[6]

It seems strange that Lady Holland, who had suffered so much at the loss of her daughter Georgiana, should not have been more considerate of Mary's feelings. But her character had hardened from years of defying the world, and her husband's unfailing devotion had shielded her from criticism at home. Later, her children would accuse her of keeping their father from them; kindly though he was, he was content to follow his wife's lead in family matters. With all of her children now grown up there was plenty to concern her.

Godfrey Webster, her eldest son, was a lost cause. Now MP for his father's constituency in Sussex, and married with a family of four sons, he still refused to see his mother. With Henry Webster, she was on good terms and he was encouraged to treat Holland House as his home. But he was always jealous of his half-brother Charles. A professional soldier himself, he felt that Charles had benefited from his parents' wire-pulling in a way that he had not, and at one point wrote furiously to his mother, accusing her (wrongly) of blocking his chances of promotion. He later apologized but the violence of his invective brought back memories of the irrational rages to which his father Sir Godfrey had been prone. 'Pray advise him when he feels angry not to put pen to paper,' wrote Holland to Charles, 'for he brandishes his pen as a drunken dragoon does his sword and scarcely knows the things he says.'[7] Harriet Webster, the daughter Lady Holland had tried to hide away, had been brought up by her guardians the Chaplins, and denied any access to her mother; when she got married in 1816 to Fleetwood Pellew, son of Lord Exmouth, she did not ask Lady Holland to her wedding or attempt to meet her afterwards. Henry Webster and Charles Fox both got married in 1824: Henry to Grace Boddington, the daughter of a rich cotton merchant, Charles Boddington MP, 'the Cotton King', as Lady Holland called him; and Charles, after various amorous adventures, to Mary Fitzclarence, the natural daughter of the Duke of Clarence by his mistress, the celebrated actress Mrs Jordan – no beauty in Lady Holland's opinion but 'handsome is as handsome does'.

Henry Fox, Holland's heir since Charles was illegitimate, was Lady Holland's favourite son, perhaps because he most resembled his father in his cheerfulness and sweet nature. The lameness which had afflicted him since childhood made a military career impossible, and after an undistinguished two years at Oxford he had settled happily in Italy, refusing all attempts to involve him in Whig politics. In Genoa he fell in with Byron, who was delighted to be reminded of his pleasant hours at Holland House. 'I have seen... Henry Fox, Lord Holland's son, whom I had not looked upon since I left, a pretty mild boy', Byron wrote to Tom Moore in April 1823. 'I have always liked that boy – perhaps from some resemblance in the less fortunate part of our destinies – I mean to avoid mistakes, his lameness. But there is this difference, that *he* appears a halting angel, who has tripped against a star; whilst I am *Le Diable Boiteux*.'[8]

Moore, who was dining at Holland House soon after, showed the letter to Lady Holland. 'Lord Byron has written to Mr Moore an account of you, very pretty and complimentary', she told Henry; 'you shall see it, as I could not resist taking a copy, tho' the alliance with such a man is not desirable & creditable beyond distant admiration.'[9]

It was a far cry from the days when Byron had been the star of London drawing rooms. Fond though she was of him, Lady Holland's caution reflected her feeling that the storm-tossed poet was not an ideal associate for her son. Three months later, Byron left for Greece to fight in the Greek War of Independence. In November that year, when a delegation of Greek deputies was travelling to London to raise a government loan, he gave them a letter of introduction to Holland, who he knew was a warm supporter of their cause.

> I think it probable that their acquaintance may be interesting to you – and am very sure that *Yours* will be useful to them and their Country – They will inform you of all that is worth knowing here – and (what is little worth knowing unless you should enquire after a former acquaintance) of the '*whereabouts*' and '*whatabouts*' of yrs ever and truly, Noel Byron.[10]

It was, as it turned out, Byron's last communication with Holland House. On 19 April 1824, he died at Missolonghi. The news ran through London like wildfire, the press and public who had once reviled him now uniting to hail him as a martyr in the cause of Greek freedom. Among the Holland House papers are some elegiac lines in Holland's hand, never published but reflective of his feelings at the time:

> Short tho' thy course oh Byron and the date
> Of our strange friendship shorter – yet a throng
> Of thoughts press on me if I read thy song
> Hear but thy name or ponder on thy fate
> Marvellous youth! In fame thou wilt be great
> In genius wert so – and the random tongue
> Of praise and censure does thy memory wrong.[11]

Byron's sister, Augusta Leigh, was his heiress. She knew how much her brother had valued the friendship of the Hollands and she sent them both mementoes from his belongings. 'I am almost ashamed of the shabby appearance of what I have selected for you from the very few articles I have yet received from my brother,' she wrote to Lady Holland,

and it is really only as being valued by him that I can ask you to accept it. There are more things coming to England and I hope amongst them I may find something more worthy of your acceptance. All you so kindly say of him is most gratifying to me – more so than I am able to express.

And to Holland, to whom she had sent a ring: 'It will be a great consolation to me to know that my dear Brother's character and feelings were so well understood by one whose friendship and regard he so highly valued.'[12]

The news of Byron's death had scarcely reached London before a new controversy arose. In 1819 Tom Moore had fled to Europe to avoid imprisonment for debt, and had visited Byron in Venice. Byron, who sympathized with Moore's plight, had presented him with the manuscript of his memoirs, which were not be published till after his death, but which could be shown to anyone Moore thought fit and used, if he wished, as security for a loan. Moore had taken liberal advantage of this permission on his return to England, and had shown the manuscript to a number of friends, among them the Hollands. This was tactless, since the memoirs included a disobliging reference to Lady Holland's past – unrecorded, since the memoirs were later destroyed. Lady Holland took it in good part. 'Such things give me no uneasiness...' she told Moore. 'As long as the few friends that I am *really* sure of speak kindly of me (and I would not believe the contrary if I saw it in black and white) all that the rest of the world can say is a matter of complete indifference to me.'[13] But she thought that Byron's veiled reference to his half-sister as his 'love of loves' might cause trouble, while the fact that Moore had raised a loan of £2,000 on the memoirs from Byron's publisher John Murray struck Holland as unwise. He wished that he could have raised the money in some other way, he told Moore; it was like 'depositing a sort of quiver of poisoned arrows... for a future warfare upon private character,'[14] and he advised Moore to retrieve the book from Murray if he could.

Moore took these words to heart – the Hollands were two of his most powerful patrons – and he was in the throes of buying back the memoirs from Murray by taking out a loan from his own publishers, Longman's, when the news of Byron's death reached London. From then on events moved inexorably towards the destruction of the memoirs. Byron's wife and sister, fearful of scandal, abetted by Byron's executor Hobhouse, jealous of Moore's friendship with Byron, were insistent that they should be destroyed. Despite Moore's agonized protests, the memoirs were burnt in the fireplace of Murray's drawing room, and the luckless Moore, too proud and touchy to accept payment from the Byron family, was left with a debt of £2,000 to Murray.

Holland had always been sympathetic to Moore, and though concerned about the publication of the memoirs, would never have agreed to such an act of vandalism. 'Sam Rogers & I suspect the Hollands do not like the share they suppose me to have in the business,'[15] wrote Hobhouse uneasily. Later, when Moore, in an attempt to retrieve his money, embarked on a biography of Byron, the Hollands were generous with their help, allowing him to use his letters to them, and filling in the background of his brief political career. (Hobhouse, by contrast, refused to let Moore see any of Byron's letters to him.)

A piquant footnote to the story of Byron and the Hollands comes from the journal of Henry Fox, who eight months after Byron's death embarked on a short-lived affair with Byron's last love Teresa Guiccioli. 'I was not prepared for the extreme facility of the conquest,' he confessed, 'which (such is the perverseness of one's nature) scarcely gave me pleasure...' Within a few weeks he had grown thoroughly disgusted: 'With T.G. I had various quarrels and hysterics; she is jealous and exigeante and troublesome. Poor Ld. Byron! I do not wonder at his going to Greece.'[16]

16

A Surrogate Son

H ENRY Fox's refusal to follow family tradition by entering Whig politics was a grave disappointment to his parents. For Holland it was a betrayal of all that the Foxes had stood for. 'I must say,' he wrote to Henry in 1820, 'it ill becomes one of our name who have derived so much of our consideration and our existence in the world from such connexions to speak of them as not worth having… We Foxes owe as much to party as party owes to us.'[1]

By 1824 it seemed that the case was hopeless. 'I do not think he will do anything in public,' wrote Lord John Russell to Lady Holland. 'He has not any feeling for it and still less *Whig* feelings.'[2] Stubbornly Holland persisted, and at the end of 1825, without telling Henry, he accepted the offer of a vacant seat for him at Horsham, made by the Duke of Norfolk. Henry arrived in Paris the following March to find that he was an MP despite himself. But the arrangement made him so unhappy that after nine months of toing and froing, he wrote to the Duke of Norfolk resigning his seat, without ever having taken the necessary oath.

A career in diplomacy was the second-best choice as far as Henry's parents were concerned, but Henry was in no hurry to take up an official post, and spent the next couple of years abroad, falling in and out of love, even briefly getting engaged, but showing no signs of settling down. It was not a satisfactory state of affairs and the fact that both the Hollands' sons seemed to prefer living abroad to taking their place in English society was perhaps a reflection on their relationship with their parents.

Fortunately an ideal replacement was at hand. Ever since he had travelled with the Hollands in Spain and Portugal in 1808 and 1809, Lord John Russell had been almost a member of the family, beloved by parents and children alike. The third son of the Duke of Bedford, he had been born into the Whig tradition, and his politics were coloured from the first by a feeling for the underdog. He was barely 14 when he wrote in his diary, 'What a pity that a man who steals a penny loaf should be hung, whilst he who steals thousands of the public money should be acquitted.'[3] Having entered the House of Commons in 1813, a few weeks before he came of age, he made his first major speech when he opposed the suspension of the Habeas Corpus Act in 1817. But his chief aim in politics was the achievement of parliamentary reform, and from 1820 onwards he devoted his energies to pressing for it in the House of Commons, where he was regarded as the leader of the reforming wing among the Whigs. His father had been a member of the Society of the Friends of the People nearly 30 years earlier, and he was acting, he felt, in a spirit which would have won the approval of his hero, Charles James Fox.

For the Hollands he was like a surrogate son, and his freedom of speech with Lady Holland, over 20 years his senior, must have been the wonder of more timid guests at Holland House. Here he is, for instance, reproving her for spreading despondency among the Whigs, and setting out his terms for peace:

1. Lady Holland shall be allowed to prefer vacillating, shabby and adverse politicians if agreeable, to dull, thick and thin voters. Granted.

2. Lady H. shall be permitted to take no part in discussions of Currency, Taxation and Law of Nations. Answer. Granted.

3. Lady H. shall be entitled to prefer persons who sell their talents for a sum of money to all other politicians whatsoever. Answer. Refused.

4. Lady H. shall be at liberty to impute the worst motives of malignity and selfishness to all persons who support Ld. Holland's politics. Answer. Refused.

5. Lady H. shall be at liberty to stop political conversation when it becomes tiresome.

Answer. This question shall be referred to Commissioners – John Allen on one side and Lady Cowper [William Lamb's sister Emily] on the other.

'So much for nonsense,' he concludes.[4]

The mid 1820s were difficult years for the politics of Holland House and of the Whigs in general. To some extent this was because the liberal Tories were pursuing many of the same aims, and rather than maintaining a united front the party split as different members supported one policy or another in the House of Commons. There was no question of the Whigs allying themselves to the liberal Tories; Grey and Canning detested one another, while the king, whose hatred of the Whigs had become almost obsessional, declared he would rather have the Devil than the Whigs in the administration. But opposition lost much of its sting in this atmosphere, and though Liverpool kept an uneasy balance between the two sides, there was more division between the 'Ultra'-Tories, opposed to Catholic Emancipation, and those like Canning who supported it, than there was between the liberal Tories and the Whigs. On this, above all other issues, the king remained a force to be reckoned with. And despite the growing agitation for the measure in Ireland, he continued to block all Cabinet discussion of the subject. It was as if he hoped that by doing nothing the whole problem would go away.

For the Foxite Whigs opposition to the Crown was nothing new. But public opinion was now flowing with them, and even though the king could drive his ministers to distraction, he was not as powerful as his father and, except where Catholic Emancipation was concerned, could be overawed by talk of popular protest. Canning's aim, in Holland's view, was to conciliate both the Whigs and public opinion and though the Whigs parted company with him on the question of parliamentary reform – to which, remembering the horrors of the French Revolution, Canning was strongly opposed – they broadly supported him on foreign policy.

With the Irish question in abeyance, the Whigs' main interest at this time was in the affairs of Spain, a subject specially dear to Holland's heart. The return of the exiled king Ferdinand VII at the end of the Peninsular War had put paid to the liberal constitution established there in 1812, and a period of extreme reaction had followed. In 1820, a military uprising leading to revolution forced Ferdinand to restore the constitution of 1812. But the quarrels between different factions, and the growing disorder in the country, gave the king the excuse to call for foreign intervention, and in April 1823 the French army, backed by the Holy Alliance, marched into Spain. Grey had assumed a warlike stance at the news that invasion was threatened: the Holy Alliance, he wrote to Holland in January, should be warned that Britain was the ally of Spain, and that any outside interference would be resisted. However, he did not come to London to press his case, and though Holland and Brougham agreed with taking a strong line the rest of the party was divided. 'As a result,' wrote Lord John Russell, 'we do nothing but abuse one another – the violent laugh at the moderate and the moderate look grave at the violent.'[5]

Canning cut through these doubts and indecisions by pursuing a policy of strict neutrality. He refused to admit that Britain had a moral obligation to support the Holy Alliance; he also refused to help the Spanish liberals when the king was restored to power by the French army in October 1823. But French ambitions could only be allowed to go so far, and in 1825 Canning took the initiative in recognizing the independence of the rebellious Spanish colonies in South America. 'I resolved,' he declared in the most famous of his speeches, 'that if France had Spain, it should not be Spain "with the Indies". I called the New World into existence to redress the balance of the Old.'[6]

The Whigs could not realistically criticize the government's policy over France's invasion of Spain, for as Holland pointed out to Grey, 'this must practically imply a censure on ministers for not making war or an exhortation now to make it, and public opinion would certainly not support, perhaps the case could hardly bear, either of these measures.'[7] But at least they could claim a share of the credit for recognizing the independence of the Spanish colonies, a measure first suggested by Lansdowne in the House of Lords nine months earlier, and Canning's speech on the subject in the House of Commons was greeted with cheers from the opposition side.

For the Hollands the immediate result of Ferdinand's reinstatement was an influx of Spanish refugees to Holland House. Lady Holland was in two minds about receiving them. She still had lingering hopes of being received at court, and she knew that the king would always support a fellow monarch. 'Would you believe it,' wrote Creevey to his step-daughter,

> Lady H. wd. not let Holland dine with Lord Lansdowne last week – a
> dinner made purposely for Mina [a liberal Spanish general and hero of
> the Peninsular War], merely because she thought it might not please
> the King if he heard about it. Nor will she let Mina or any Spaniard
> approach Holland House for the same reason. Was there ever such
> a ——?[8]

But Holland, easy-going on most matters, was not going to let his wife direct him where his political beliefs were concerned, and she was quickly made to change her tune. Mina and the radical politician Don Agustin Argüelles were guests of honour at a banquet at Holland House in March 1824, and, together with other leading Spanish liberals, were frequent visitors thereafter. Two years later, the Duke of Wellington, now reconciled with Holland after the misunderstanding over Ney, agreed to dine at Holland House to meet another distinguished Spanish liberal, General Álava, who had served under him in Spain.

As well as welcoming exiled Spanish liberals, Holland did his best, with influence and money, to mitigate penalties for those trapped in Spain, where Ferdinand had instituted a savage programme of reprisals, and to see that their families were provided for. This was despite the financial problems which the Hollands were still experiencing. Their West Indian properties were running at a loss, they had been forced to borrow from Caroline Fox and Lady Affleck in order to buy their son Charles's commission as a major, and were contemplating letting Ampthill. From 1823 they had begun letting or selling off outlying areas of the Holland House estate for building; the first houses to go up were on the west side of the park, on what is now Addison Road.

Whether in the interests of economy or because there was little to be done in politics, the Hollands set out for an extended stay in Paris in September 1825. They travelled by steamboat for the first time, with Mary, Allen, Lady Affleck and a retinue of 21 people. Lady Granville, whose husband had been appointed ambassador in Paris the previous year, kept a sharp eye on their doings. 'The Hollands have a good apartment and an excellent cook,' she wrote to her sister, Lady Carlisle.

She [Lady Holland] is very well and to me all smiles, but to her alentours rather more in the termagant line than common. To the awestruck world who frequent her house (the most strict, undivorced and ultra-duchesses now go there), she appears encompassed by solemnity and a state of fan and elbow chair and shaded light which make them suppose themselves in the presence of Maria Theresa at least.[9]

One unexpected bonus of the Hollands' visit, according to Lady Granville, was Mary's success in Parisian society. 'Dearest, what an odd thing life is and how it ups and downs, and ebbs and flows, rises and sinks, for human beings in general and Mary Fox in particular,' she told her sister.

> You know in England she has short legs, looks a little gummy, is taken out as a good work, and Lansdowne and you find her rather a heavy shuttlecock... Here she is a Venus – she is 'la plus belle, la plus magnifique, la plus piquante, l'esprit brille dans ses yeux, son âme se voit dans sa charmante figure'... In short she is a sort of sky rocket in Paris.[10]

For the first time Lady Holland began to regard Mary as a social asset, no longer to be banished behind the scenes when there were important dinners. But there were no signs of an acceptable suitor coming forward. 'Mary has the ill luck of always captivating royalties, which is rather troublesome leading to nothing but talk,' her mother complained to Henry. And, a little later, 'Mary has been a great expense. I wish she had an admirer... You must try not to set her against people, as she is getting on, no longer the youngest among the belles.'[11] It is pleasing to relate that Mary found an ideal husband, Lord Lilford, with no help from her mother, five years later.

Both the Hollands had bouts of ill health during their stay in Paris. Lady Holland suffered from arthritis and was sometimes so lame that she had to use a wheelchair; Holland had frequent attacks of gout.

But they managed to enjoy a busy social life, Holland seeing much of the Duke of Orléans (later Louis Philippe I), with whom he had long political discussions. Her husband was received 'quite dans l'intérieur en famille with the Duke of Orléans', Lady Holland told Allen proudly.[12]

Belonging to the junior branch of the Bourbons (his father Philippe Égalité had signed the death warrant of Louis XVI, and had himself been executed a year later), Orléans had returned to Paris and the goodwill of his elder cousins in 1815, after a picaresque career in exile including four years in the United States. He had learnt to tread delicately in politics, but his sympathies were far more with the constitutional monarchy enjoyed in Britain than with the ultra-royalist views of Charles X, who had inherited the throne, but none of his moderation, from his elder brother Louis XVIII the previous year. Obstinately insisting on his divine right to rule, Charles had had himself crowned with medieval ceremony, passed laws condemning sacrilege and increased the privileges of the Church and aristocracy. In 1825, with a royalist majority in the Chamber of Deputies, his throne still seemed secure. But a revolution was preparing in the shadows, though neither Holland nor Orléans himself were yet aware of it.

Well received in French society, particularly by those of liberal views, the Hollands were also visited by their English friends. Rogers and Luttrell, the old '*affidés*' ('accomplices'), as Lady Granville called them, joined them in Paris, as did Sydney Smith on his first visit to France. Thanks to introductions from the Hollands he enjoyed a busy social life, attending a ball at the British embassy, mixing with a 'profusion of French duchesses' and frequently dining with the Hollands at their apartment in the Rue de la Grange-Batelière. On one of these occasions, he told his wife,

there was at the table Barras, the ex-Director, in whose countenance I immediately discovered all the signs of cruelty which distinguished his conduct. I found out at the end of dinner, that it was not Barras, but M. de Barante, an historian and man of letters, who, I believe, never killed anything greater than a flea.[13]

The Hollands spent nine months in Paris, returning to Holland House in June 1826. Little had changed during their absence. The Tory government was still divided, the liberals, led by Canning, far closer to the Whigs than to their hardline colleagues. 'We are certainly to all intents and purposes a branch of His Majesty's Government,'[14] Tierney had reported to Holland three months earlier. 'Its proceedings for some time past have proved that, though the gentlemen opposite are in office, we are in power. The measures are ours, but all the emoluments are theirs.'

The old party system was falling apart though the likelihood of a new one, with Tory and Whig liberals lined up against the Tory diehards, was remote. As long as Liverpool held the two sides of the party together, there was no chance of a formal accommodation with the Whigs, nor was Grey in favour of such an arrangement. But in February 1827, Liverpool suffered a massive stroke, which left him, in the words of the *Times*, 'if not actually, at least politically dead', and with his departure from the scene, a whole new set of possibilities opened up.

17

Party Confusions

L IVERPOOL had not been a charismatic figure, and during the early years of his government his domestic policies had often been reactionary and repressive. But he had held the Tory party together for a decade and a half, and his last few years of government had seen a number of major reforms. With his removal from politics, the coalition between the 'Ultra'-Tories, opposed to Catholic Emancipation, and the liberals became unsustainable. On 10 April 1827, after much prevaricating, the king appointed Canning prime minister. For the right wing of the party, Canning had always been a suspect figure; they disliked his foreign policy, and distrusted him as an adventurer and a parvenu. Seven members of the Cabinet, led by Peel and Wellington, resigned, and Canning reluctantly turned to the Whigs for support.

The Whigs themselves were divided. Grey, who detested Canning, held aloof. He knew that the new prime minister was not in a position to force through Catholic Emancipation, and he was not prepared to join him otherwise. Lansdowne, on the other hand, felt that by taking office under Canning he would block the return of the Ultra-Tories and he, William Lamb and several others joined the government in May, Lansdowne becoming Home Secretary and Lamb Chief Secretary for Ireland. Holland would not come in without Grey, and refused to accept a government post, though he promised support from outside. Perhaps it was just as well. George IV had found it hard enough to accept the idea of a coalition with the Whigs and according to Creevey had exploded when Holland's name was suggested. He would have no minister, he declared, who had insulted all the crowned heads of Europe.

Lady Holland was bitterly disappointed by her husband's decision. 'She told me,' wrote Hobhouse, after dining at Holland House that May, 'that she had wished Lord Holland to take office; and that he had requested her to leave him alone and not give advice either one way or another.'[1]

'This was very strong language,' commented Hobhouse, 'from the mildest of men and the most submissive of husbands.'

To Henry in Italy, Holland explained the reasons for his refusal to take office. He had been much blamed by some persons, he wrote, 'and I fear particularly your Mama.'[2] But he would not have felt comfortable in acting without Grey, or with the compromises he would have had to make:

> The truth is that in a Government which can do so little immediately either for the measures it approves or for the friends on whom it depends and which is obliged to submit to so many compliances with the Court I should have been an impatient unruly unhappy & inconvenient colleague.[3]

It was on the issue of Catholic Emancipation, above all, that Canning had been forced to give way. As before, the king had agreed that it should be an open question among his ministers, but in defiance of the growing discontent in Ireland, he would not allow it to be a Cabinet measure.

In this way, Grey complained to Holland,

the question, of all others most immediately affecting the peace and
safety of the country, is excluded from the deliberations of the Cabinet,
and left to be perpetually agitated and perpetually debated between
members of the same government professing different opinions. I
declare most seriously and conscientiously my firm conviction that
an administration decidedly anti-catholic would be infinitely less
mischievous than such a state of things.[4]

In the midst of these crosscurrents Holland House remained a place
where all shades of opinion could meet. Lansdowne, William Lamb
and others who had followed Canning were as much at home there
as before. Even Canning came to dine. Lady Holland may have had
her reservations but Holland had no fault to find with him. 'Canning
has, I am quite satisfied, behaved fairly and openly to us all,' he told
Henry; 'but his power is not equal to his inclination.'[5]

Holland enjoyed discussing politics with his son. He had learnt to
accept his refusal to take his place as an MP, though his withdrawal
had involved him in some embarrassment. (Caroline Fox had been
very much a peacemaker over this.) But he was much too fond of him
to quarrel. 'Your retreat from Parliament which if you liked Politicks,
would be vexatious, is under the circumstances of the case & with your
foolish dislike of it quite right,' Holland wrote to his son pacifically.

Long absence from England, I confess I contemplate with more pain
than abandonment of Parliament and dislike of politicks. I long to have
the comfort during my remaining years of my children's society & as
much as any of them of yours – However I trust to your affections of
which I have much already – God bless you dear Boy.[6]

Over the next few months Holland's letters to Henry followed the state of play. The king was as stubborn as ever over Catholic Emancipation, but there was now a long-term ray of hope. The death of the king's brother, the Duke of York, at the beginning of the year, had made his next brother, the bluff and boisterous Duke of Clarence, the heir to the throne. York had been violently anti-Catholic; Clarence on the other hand was sympathetic to the Whigs and the Catholic cause. His daughter, as we have seen, was married to Holland's son Charles, and he was on the best of terms with Holland House. 'He has become very prudent and is much improved,'[7] reported Lady Holland.

In the meantime, as Holland wrote to Henry in July, there were two distinct parties in opposition, 'the Tory intolerant ex-ministers' and the 'dissatisfied Whigs', led by Grey. The latter, he wrote, were very small in number,

> but Grey's character and talents make them of importance & the
> [Ultra] Londonderry faction, very active and violent in their enmity to
> Canning, forms a better link than I could wish for occasional concert
> for co-operation between them and the Tories – the latter play hard
> for Ld Grey and would sacrifice everything but their fundamental big-
> otry to procure him for their leader – They are loud in their excessive
> admiration of his oratory, elevation of character &c & a little flattery,
> always I am afraid agreeable to publick men, is relished wonderfully
> in that quarter, especially when administered by certain fair ladies.[8]

Grey had always been a ladies' man, though the idea that he could be won over by the Ultra-Tories' blandishments was probably far-fetched. But the two parties were united in their hatred of Canning and the prime minister was furiously attacked from both sides. In his first months of office Canning succeeded in steering the difficult path between them. He managed to win round the king, who saw him as an ally in fighting the aristocratic cliques, both Whig and Tory, who threatened the power of the Crown; and even though he was opposed to parliamentary reform himself, he kept the reformers on his side: their leader in the Commons, Lord John Russell, had agreed to waive the question for the time being. But the stresses and strains of office proved too much for Canning. His health had been failing for some time and towards the end of July he fell seriously ill. The kindly Duke of Devonshire offered him Chiswick House as a place to rest. 'Do not go there,' Lady Holland begged him when she heard this. 'I have a presentiment; you know Mr Fox died there.'[9] Canning laughed at her fears, but her superstition was well founded. He died at Chiswick House on 8 August. There were many who thought that his opponents had hounded him to death.

Holland, who had never joined Grey in attacking Canning, was stricken by the loss of his old friend. 'Your Papa has been confined some days and suffering from pain in his hand & wrist and occasionally shifting to his foot,' Lady Holland told Henry. 'His illness was much aggravated by the sad tragedy at Chiswick. Indeed it has overwhelmed and affected everybody, as you can imagine.'[10]

After a brief period of indecision the king appointed Lord Goderich, the Leader of the House of Lords, as prime minister, on the understanding that he make as few changes as possible, and above all no further Whig appointments. When Lansdowne urged the admission of Holland as Lord Privy Seal the king was able to refuse him on those grounds.

Holland, who had refused office earlier, was quite unfazed by this. Nor did he accept the tentative suggestion of a promotion in the peerage; it was certainly of no object to him, he declared indignantly, and if offered it would have been refused. Lady Holland made no secret of her annoyance at his unambitious attitude, proclaiming it to all and sundry. However, she met her match in Russell, as Hobhouse noted in his diary: 'There has been a fracas between Lady Holland and Lord J. Russell. The former asked the latter why Lord Holland had been excluded from office. "If you must know," said Lord John Russell, "it is because no man will act in cabinet with a person whose wife opens his letters."'[11]

Only a favourite could get away with such *lèse-majesté*.

Goderich's ministry lasted for only four months. Weak and irresolute – Grey nicknamed him 'Lady Goderich' – he was unable to hold the government together, and resigned in despair in January 1828. At the last moment he had attempted to strengthen his Cabinet by including Holland, but had been stymied by the king's reluctance to accept him. Holland would probably have refused it anyway: 'So much has been said of a project of offering me office that I must believe it has been in contemplation,' he wrote to Henry at New Year.

> *Alors comme alors*, but I hope it may be without Goderich at head of
> Government. With no hostility, nay with much predilection for him,
> I do not think I could prudently or creditably accept, and I am sure,
> if I refused, my refusal would in the present state of things injure the
> Ministry most materially, which I should be very sorry to do. He,
> Goderich, has behaved with irresolution, levity and *pour trancher le
> mot* incapacity, but with no bad design to any body.[12]

Goderich's resignation, a week later, put the matter out of the question. On 9 January 1828 the king called on Wellington to form a government.

'Lady Holland is the only dissatisfied Minister out of office,' wrote the witty lawyer Joseph Jekyll.

> She counted on sailing down daily with her long tailed blacks and
> ancient crane-necked chariot to sit with Holland at the Secretary's
> office, to administer the affairs of England and make Sydney Smith

a bishop. As for him, he never cared two pence about the whole job and the delightful fellow was quite right in treating it so.[13]

Wellington had taken power reluctantly. As a soldier of the Crown his one great object was to see that the government of the king was carried on, but the shifting state of parties made his task almost impossible. The king had made two stipulations: first that Catholic Emancipation remain an open question; second that his bugbear, Lord Grey, be excluded from the administration. Beyond this Wellington still hoped to have some kind of coalition, reinstating the Ultras, who had resigned on Canning taking office, but keeping on the Canningite Whigs as well as the liberal Tories. Lansdowne, however, was excluded, as leading too powerful a faction to be acceptable to the Ultras, and despite the pleas of George IV the Duke of Devonshire resigned in sympathy. Their joint departure brought back hopes that the Whigs might once more be united as an opposition party. With no firm leadership from Grey, Holland played his usual role as host and mediator between the different groupings. But the situation was too fluid, and the liberal Tories too close in sympathy to the Whigs, for any clear-cut policy to be established. The Tories themselves were hopelessly divided between 'Protestants' and 'Catholics', with Wellington and Peel leading the 'Protestant' side. At the beginning of 1828, as the problems of Ireland loomed ever larger, the party system seemed to have broken down.

18

Irish Affairs

S INCE her attack on Lady Holland in *Glenarvon*, Caroline Lamb had not been seen at Holland House. But her husband was there as often as before – nowhere, he thought, could you find better company – and Lady Holland's letters gave news of her from time to time. In 1824, after a drunken scene at Whitehall, in which she threatened to fight the sergeant on duty and tried to kill the servants who were restraining her, she was confined at the Melbourne family home, Brocket Hall in Hertfordshire, attended by two women from a mad doctor. 'She is kept low, which means being limited to one bottle of sherry daily,' wrote Lady Holland to Henry. 'There is something horrid in such a termination to a person one has known so intimately from infancy; but she never had a particle of good in her whole composition.'[1]

'Ly C. is again turned loose,' she reported a few weeks later. 'The physicians will not sign for her being mad enough to be confined. They say she is only wicked from temper and brandy.'[2]

In 1825, William Lamb, worn out by constant scenes and dramas, at last decided on a separation from his wife. She continued to live at Brocket, drunken and miserable, but in the autumn of 1827 she developed dropsy and it became clear that she was dying. Perhaps

Lady Holland sent some kindly message to her – she was after all the daughter of her oldest friend – for a letter from Caroline in the Holland House papers, dated January 1828, implies that she had been in touch.

> I can only write one line to thank you for your generous conduct. Will you accept from my heart my deep regret for the past – it makes me most unhappy now.
>
> I trust I may see you – if not believe me with every affectionate and grateful feeling,
>
> Yours
>
> Caroline Lamb[3]

Caroline died, aged 42, on 26 January 1828, having made her peace with Lamb, who had hurried over from Ireland at the last. Through her mother Lady Bessborough and her mother-in-law Lady Melbourne, she had belonged to the second generation of that intimate group, linked by politics and marriage, at the centre of Holland House society. Her story had ended tragically but others of this second generation were coming to the fore. Lamb, who inherited the title of Lord Melbourne that summer, was still in office as Chief Secretary for Ireland. His sister, Lady Cowper, was one of the younger beauties at Holland House; so too was Caroline's first cousin, Lady Granville, now ambassadress in Paris. Caroline's brother, Lord Duncannon, recently elected as MP for Kilkenny, had become a quietly effective figure in Whig councils; 'nothing could be done without Duncannon', commented the diarist Charles Greville. Above all Lord John Russell, the Hollands' beloved protégé, was forging ahead in the Commons as leader of the movement for parliamentary reform and a champion of religious liberties.

In February 1828, taking advantage of the confused state of the parties, Russell successfully pushed through a bill to repeal the so-called

Test and Corporation Acts, by which anyone belonging to a corporation or holding public office had to pass the 'sacramental test' of taking Communion in the Established Church. In effect dissenters – Baptists, Methodists and others – who refused to conform were protected by a legal indemnity, so they did not suffer the same disadvantages as Catholics, but the law was anachronistic and offensive to their beliefs. Backed by a powerful pressure group, the United Committee, the dissenters had long protested against the Acts and had naturally found a sympathetic ear at Holland House. At a meeting there the previous year, with Holland and Russell presiding, they had agreed that if the bill to remove their disabilities succeeded, they would support Catholic Emancipation – a major concession since, even more than the Anglicans, they abhorred the doctrines of the Church of Rome.

Holland introduced the bill, which had already passed the Commons, in the House of Lords on 18 April. 'Your Papa is reported on all sides to have made an admirable and impressive speech, full of knowledge, ability & talent,' Lady Holland told Henry the next day. 'He was even satisfied with himself. He was very nervous and afterwards could not sleep a wink... He is half afraid Ld Eldon, with his ingenuity & subtlety, will try to defeat the measure in Committee; and Newmarket on Monday carries off 12 or more votes.'[4]

Eldon, the former Lord Chancellor, indeed did all he could to scotch the bill, but despite his efforts (and the absence of some race-going peers) the bill was successful in the Lords. It was a great relief to Holland who according to his wife had been 'so dreadfully worried and anxious' about it that he could think of nothing else. Holland House meanwhile had been crowded with dissenters of all persuasions, and an amusing scene took place when the Archbishop of York arrived unexpectedly and had to be entertained by Mary in the library till her father could get them out of the way.

The repeal of the Test and Corporation Acts, as Russell had intended, brought Catholic Emancipation one step nearer. 'There is a general feeling that the Catholic Emancipation must ultimately be carried,' wrote Lady Holland to Henry, 'although the King works himself into a fury when the subject is named to him.'[5]

Among the comings and goings at Holland House that spring was a visit from Sir Walter Scott, up in London on a rare trip from Scotland. The Hollands were avid readers of his novels. 'Opinion?' said Holland, when he was asked what he thought of Scott's *Tales of My Landlord*. 'We did not one of us go to bed all night, and nothing slept but my gout.'[6] Scott in his turn thought Holland the most agreeable man he had ever met, remarkable for his critical judgement, and with a power of language which adorned his thoughts 'as light streaming through coloured glass heightens the brilliancy of the objects it falls upon.'[7] The fact that Scott was a diehard Tory, and Holland a Whig, made no difference to the liking between them.

Scott dined and slept at Holland House on 17 May, with Samuel Rogers as a fellow guest. The next morning the two men strolled around the grounds together. In a memorable passage from his journal Scott recorded his impressions:

The freshness of the air, the singing of the birds, the beautiful aspect of nature, the size of the venerable trees, all gave me a delightful feeling... It seemed there was pleasure even in living and breathing, without anything else. We (i.e. Rogers and I) wandered into a green lane bordered with fine trees, which might have been twenty miles from a town. It will be a great pity when this ancient house must come down and give way to brickworks and brick-houses. It is not that Holland House is fine as a building; on the contrary it has a tumbledown look; and although decorated with the bastard Gothic of James I's time, the front is heavy. But it resembles many respectable matrons, who having been ugly during youth, acquire by age a look of dignity – though one is chiefly affected by the air of deep seclusion round the domain.[8]

Scott's visit was a pleasant interlude in the midst of a dramatic spring and summer, in which Holland was once more a power behind the scenes. In February of that year the Marquess of Anglesey, a Tory with liberal inclinations, had been appointed as Lord Lieutenant in Ireland. A distinguished soldier, who had lost a leg at Waterloo, he was on close terms with Holland, and the correspondence between them casts a fascinating light on the run-up to Catholic Emancipation the following year. Although sympathetic to the Catholics, Anglesey was indignant at the menacing tone of O'Connell and his followers: he loathed the idea of truckling to 'overbearing catholic demagogues', however just their cause. Holland had been at pains to convert him. 'The longer this boon [Catholic Emancipation] is refused,' he wrote,

> the more offensive their manner of asking it is likely to become. If granted hereafter, it will probably have more the appearance and the reality too, of being extorted by force than it would now – In short we should make up our mind to grant it with as good a grace as we can even now, or be prepared for all the consequences of refusing it for ever... Surely Surely it would be hard on millions to suffer because their orators lacked judgment, taste, temper or honesty.[9]

Once arrived in Ireland, it did not take long for Anglesey to realize the good sense of Holland's view. Meanwhile the repeal of the Test and Corporation Acts had raised the hopes of the Catholic movement, and popular agitation had died down while they waited for the next move. On 8 May, a new motion in favour of Catholic Emancipation was passed by six votes in the Commons, and though it was rejected by the Lords, a statement by Wellington (who voted against it) that he was not against the measure in principle seemed a further step in the right direction. 'Nothing,' wrote Holland to Anglesey,

> could be better for our cause... I think the general intention and spirit of our great Commander's speech was good and he conveyed to my mind that he *wished at least* to bring the great question to some amicable adjustment... I do believe he wishes to occupy the high ground and is not without hope that by manoeuvre or by capitulation he may reach it.[10]

Whether Wellington's gradual approach would have succeeded was never put to the test, for within a few weeks a series of unexpected events brought matters to a head. A difference of opinion between Wellington and the Canningite Huskisson led to the latter's resignation at the end of May and a number of Canningites, including Lamb and Palmerston, resigned in sympathy. In reconstituting his Cabinet after their departure Wellington appointed a liberal Irish MP, William Vesey-Fitzgerald, to fill the vacancy at the Board of Trade. According to the rules of the time, new ministers were expected to resign and stand for re-election before taking office. However, since Fitzgerald had always been a staunch supporter of Catholic Emancipation, no one expected any trouble from his constituency of County Clare.

O'Connell saw his chance. Perceiving that while it was impossible for a Catholic to take his seat as an MP there was nothing to prevent him from standing for election, he came forward as a rival candidate. The Catholic Association threw its full weight behind him, Anglesey prudently stationed troops nearby, and the election took place in an atmosphere of perfect good order. On 5 July, to the wild elation of the crowds who had gathered there, O'Connell was returned by a large majority. 'I have made up my mind,' Anglesey told Holland, 'or very nearly made it up that this will be a very delightful determination to the odious question.'[11]

The government was stunned. O'Connell was elected, but there remained the question of whether he would be allowed to take his seat. If he was refused there would almost certainly be civil war in Ireland. Anglesey was convinced that immediate emancipation was the only answer. No power on earth, he told Lord Francis Gower, William Lamb's replacement as his Chief Secretary, could arrest the progress of the Catholics: 'There may be rebellion – you may put to death thousands – you may suppress it; but it will only be to put off the day of compromise.'[12]

But Wellington was not prepared to move so fast. Parliament was in recess, giving the government breathing space. Throughout the autumn, while Ireland seethed with discontent and anti-Catholic rallies were held in England, he gave no hint of his intentions. Left in the dark by Wellington, Anglesey did his best to keep the peace. He refused to launch prosecutions against Catholic leaders and held a private meeting with O'Connell in which, while stressing his determination to put down disorder, he advised him to conciliate the duke by refraining from personal attacks on him. O'Connell listened to his advice respectfully, and 'humbly offered his best assistance' in keeping the peace, but both he and Anglesey knew that matters might soon be out of their control.

In the absence of any guidance from Wellington, Anglesey turned to Holland for advice. He knew he could rely on his discretion, and had fed him copies of his confidential correspondence with the government, including the minutes of his meeting with O'Connell. 'I have no doubt that your view of O'Connel's character is the true one,' wrote Holland,

and as little that your language and tone with one of that character was well calculated to soothe and confirm him in all that was right and to do real good not only to the cause but to the Govt and the country. The Duke of Cumberland [the King's anti-Catholic brother] thinks you ought to be impeached for seeing him.[13]

It was the king, through his blind adherence to his coronation oath, who was still the greatest obstacle to Catholic Emancipation. Meanwhile Ireland was on the brink of anarchy. 'And Why,' demanded Holland.

> Merely My Dear Anglesey because one man has taken it into his head not to acquiesce in a measure which every man of sense has recommended for twenty-eight years – and which is as essential to his own character and happiness as to the interests of the Empire from which he derives his rank, station and enjoyments.[14]

Nothing, however, could be done without the king and only Wellington could bring him round. Till then, as the duke told Anglesey brusquely, it was his duty to refrain from discussing the matter, and Anglesey's to keep order in Ireland, leaving matters of policy to the government. Anglesey's hands were tied. Weighed down by the anxieties of his position, he seriously considered resigning and as so often sought advice from Holland. Holland was reassuring. No one else, he told him, could have managed to keep the Catholic question open for so long; he should only resign when it became impossible to continue. His advice reinforced Anglesey's feeling that he should soldier on as best he could. He would leave the odium of recalling him to the king and government.

He did not have long to wait. Two incidents sparked off the government's decision. First, after careful consultation with the Irish Lord

Chancellor, Anglesey decided not to remove two prominent members of the Irish Association from the magistracy, though requested to do so by Peel and Wellington; secondly he stayed with a well-known supporter of the Catholic cause, Lord Cloncurry, for the Curragh races. In both cases he had a perfectly reasonable explanation but Wellington had long been looking for an excuse to dismiss him. 'Lord Anglesey has gone mad,' declared the duke. 'He is bit by a mad Papist.'[15] On 30 December Anglesey was given notice of his dismissal. He told the members of his household that he would be leaving Ireland within the next few weeks.

Once dismissed, Anglesey saw no reason to hide his views. On 14 December the Catholic Primate of Ireland, Dr Curtis, had written to Wellington imploring him to come to a decision about Catholic Emancipation without further delay. In his reply the duke had told him that he saw no prospect of an immediate settlement, but that if he could bury the question 'in oblivion' for a time, he did not despair of finding one. Anglesey, who had seen the duke's reply, had already written to Curtis privately. On New Year's Day, two days after his dismissal, he published his letter in the *Dublin Evening Post*.

He had not been aware of the duke's precise sentiments before, he wrote. But he could not agree with him about burying the Catholic question 'in oblivion' – firstly because the thing was impossible and secondly because, even if it had been possible, the lull might be taken as an excuse to refuse emancipation altogether, and then all the miseries of the past few years in Ireland would be renewed. He was convinced that there would be no peace in Ireland till the question had been settled; meanwhile he urged the Catholics to continue to press their case by all lawful means, trusting in the justice of their cause and the growing strength of opinion in their favour. Brute force could achieve nothing:

It is the legislature that must decide this great question; and my greatest anxiety is that it should be met by Parliament, under the most favourable circumstances, and that the opposers of Catholic Emancipation shall be disarmed by the patient forbearance, as well as by the unwearied perseverance of its advocates.[16]

Conciliatory though it was in tone, the letter was a challenge to the party line. The duke was furious. Anglesey was ordered to leave Ireland on the spot, without waiting for the arrival of his successor. It was a public slap in the face. But Holland had nothing but praise for his initiative. 'The excellence of your letter to Curtis which rings [through] all England from side to side,' he wrote to Anglesey on 8 January,

would atone for a little want of caution, even if there were any... and I for one rejoice for your sake as well as for that of the country and the cause that you wrote it and it became publick at the moment when it was so well calculated to vindicate and raise you in the opinion of every sensible man and to allay the agitation into which your recal[l] had thrown the country.[17]

Anglesey's departure from Dublin two days later was a day of public mourning. A huge crowd, many of them weeping, gathered to bid him farewell. His dismissal seemed the end of any hopes for Catholic Emancipation in the next parliamentary session. Only Talleyrand, observing events from the other side of the Channel, was clever enough to read between the lines. 'When M. de Talleyrand heard that Lord Anglesey was recalled,' wrote Palmerston, 'he saw at once that the Duke had determined on conceding the Irish catholic claims and that he did not mean anyone else to have the credit of the concession.'[18]

19

The July Revolution

⁓

PARLIAMENT was due to open on 5 February. The king's speech would spell out what concessions, if any, would be made to the Catholics. Without revealing his hand in public, Wellington had already determined on full emancipation. Behind the scenes there were frenzied last-minute negotiations as his ministers, even those who had previously opposed the measure, did their best to persuade the king to agree. No one has been able to explain his resistance satisfactorily. He had been sympathetic to the Catholics as Prince of Wales, and the principle of Protestant supremacy had already been breached by the repeal of the Test and Corporation Acts. Perhaps he was driven by his loathing of the Whigs, perhaps he was merely too ill to cope with the idea of change. But finally, tearfully, resentfully, he had been forced to give in.

The king's speech was a grudging affair. It was agreed that the laws imposing civil disabilities for Catholics should be reviewed (a coded acceptance of Catholic Emancipation) but the measure would not be retrospective – to take his seat, O'Connell must stand for re-election – and the property qualification for voting would be raised from 40 shillings to £10 a year. Nonetheless the great point had been made. On 5 April 1829, after further obstructions from the king, who discovered new scruples about his coronation oath, the bill for Catholic Emancipation received the royal assent.

'Remember your Papa was the *first* man who moved C. Emancipation in the House of Lords when he was very young. It is a proud thing for him,'[1] Lady Holland wrote to Henry. It was indeed a proud moment for Holland, and for all those who had struggled for Catholic Emancipation so long. Writing to Henry while the bill was going through the Lords, Holland gave special praise to Anglesey who, as soon as the measure was announced, had flung himself wholeheartedly behind the government:

> To his wise, firm, good tempered and impartial administration, the Government and Empire owe the power of passing the measure as a boon and not as an article of capitulation... He comes home, full of just resentment and anxious to vindicate himself from the aspersions of having committed a breach of duty. But he finds the measure he had recommended, and for the promotion of which he was censured, and to all appearances punished, openly patronized by the government. He immediately suppresses his personal grievances [and] supports the measure with all his might and main... If this be not magnanimity and patriotism I know not the meaning of the words.[2]

Holland's tribute was well deserved. But the so-called boon, which might have won the hearts of the Irish a few years earlier, had come too late. They knew it had been offered under duress and they saw no reason to be grateful. For O'Connell and his followers Catholic Emancipation was merely a step on the road to Irish independence, and the bill had hardly been passed before they began campaigning for the repeal of the Act of Union. Far from ending discontent in Ireland, the reform would lead to a new round of demands.

Meanwhile the bill had split the Tory party. The Ultra-Tories were outraged. 'No popery' had been the slogan which united them and the vast majority of their fellow countrymen; they felt that the Church and constitution had been betrayed. Perhaps only a prime minister with the prestige and authority of Wellington could have seen the measure through, but it left his government much weakened, cut off from the Ultras on one side and the liberal, or Canningite, Tories on the other. The Whigs refrained from formal opposition; still divided among themselves, they were waiting to see what happened next.

Few of the intimates of Holland House had been more delighted by the news of Catholic Emancipation than Byron's friend Tom Moore. A Catholic himself, he had sung his country's sorrows unforgettably in his *Irish Melodies* and used his witty pen in a series of sparkling satires on the king and the Tory government. Even the king had been amused. 'Don't you remember Tom Moore's description of me at breakfast?' he once asked Walter Scott,

> The table spread with tea and toast,
> Death warrants and the *Morning Post*.[3]

Having recently published a two-volume biography of his fellow Irishman Richard Brinsley Sheridan – 'this will be a dull book, your Sheridan,' Lady Holland had forecast crushingly – Moore was now completing his researches for his life of Byron. Throughout the summer of 1829 he was a frequent visitor to Holland House – 'A good deal of talk about Byron' was a constant refrain in his diary – and his entries include some amusing glimpses of his hosts: 'To Holland House,' he writes on 14 June,

> where I copied out the passages of The Devil's Drive [an unfinished poem by Byron]... Found Rogers and Luttrell there; and all walked

out in the grounds with Lady H. who set off in her whiskey with Lord Ashburnham, while we remained with Lord Holland stock still on horseback and flattering himself he was taking exercise.[4]

'To Holland House,' he writes again on 23 September. 'As I was about to take my place next to Lord Holland at dinner, my Lady said, "No, come up here" ordering me into another seat. "So you have taken Moore from me", said Lord Holland with the air of a disappointed school boy.'[5]

On 1 January 1830 the first volume of Moore's *Life of Byron* appeared amidst a storm of controversy. Its references to Lady Byron were few and respectful but they did suggest that the outcry against Byron at the time of their separation had been largely undeserved. Lady Byron reacted furiously by privately printing a pamphlet, 'Remarks on Mr Moore's Life of Lord Byron'. Ostensibly a defence of her parents, whom Byron had criticized in letters quoted by Moore, it was in fact a work of self-justification, in which she hinted darkly at secrets too awful to be disclosed. She invoked the help of Holland, asking him to pass on a copy to Moore as if it had come directly from him. Holland declined politely; he would send Moore a copy if she wished, he told her, but he would not conceal that he had done so at her request. Moore, in his view, had dealt with the subject of the separation as kindly and discreetly as was compatible with justice to his friend; nor could it be denied that Byron's opinion of her parents had been as stated in his letters. He begged her, for her own sake, not to stir up further publicity by circulating the pamphlet. 'Lady Byron is getting into a silly controversy with Moore over some passages in his book,' Lady Holland told Henry. 'She will be the loser as many suppressed passages will now be disclosed, & she will not like it. Your Papa is doing his utmost to quell her restlessness but in vain. I am afraid she is a cold, obstinate woman, but do not mention this opinion.'[6]

Lady Byron, in fact, seemed bent on self-destruction, sending out so many copies of her pamphlet that they soon found their way into the bookshops, and inspired a wealth of prurient speculation in the papers. Wisely refusing to be drawn into an argument, Moore simply published the pamphlet as an appendix to his second volume, thus effectively taking the wind from her sails. He had dealt with the marriage as truthfully as he could in the prudish climate of the time; the facts have been raked over by biographers ever since.

Holland, who had listened to Lady Byron's confidences when she was contemplating divorce, had drawn his own conclusions about the reasons for the separation. They are revealed to us by Hobhouse in one of his marginal notes – some indignant, some reluctantly approving – in his copy of Moore's biography. Moore had suggested that Lady Byron might have overreacted by taking 'some hinted confession of undefined horrors' by her husband as sober truth. 'Something of the sort certainly,' agreed Hobhouse, 'unless, as Lord Holland told me, he tried to b—— her.'[7]

On 26 June 1830 George IV died, having reigned as regent and king for 19 years. In his resistance to Catholic Emancipation he had epitomized all the Hollands hated about the monarchy, but he had been the friend and admirer of Fox, and they both had kindly memories of his younger days. Lady Holland had failed to be received at court – the ban on divorcees was inexorable – 'yet personally,' as she told Henry not long before his death, 'I have good will to him, partly from old acquaintance & partly from believing there is more good in him than falls to the lot of most Princes: and had he not been one, he would, I am persuaded, have been a most amiable person.'[8]

The new king, William IV, as we know, was the father-in-law of the Hollands' son Charles, and the two families were on the best of terms. William IV loved having his children by Mrs Jordan around him – his wife, Queen Adelaide, was childless – and immediately appointed Charles, then serving in Halifax, as equerry to the queen. Holland, who was bidden to an audience at St James's Palace a week after George IV's death, was able to thank him in person. The king, he reported, had decided never to dine at private houses in London: 'There would be no end to it.' Perhaps he would make an exception in the case of the Duke of Wellington's Waterloo dinner. Holland House, however, was not in London, 'and *there* he should dine.'[9]

He did so for the first time as king on 30 July, when the guests included the Duke of Sussex (the king's brother), the Duke of Argyll, Nelson's friend Admiral Sir Thomas Hardy, the Granvilles, Melbourne, Luttrell, Lady Affleck and Miss Fox. Their names were entered in the dinner book as usual by Dr Allen, but, unusually, there was a footnote on the page: 'News arrived of the flight of the King of France to Compiègne. This news premature.'[10]

It must have been a dramatic interruption to the dinner party, and perhaps the Hollands' first intimation of the success of the July Revolution. Charles X's appointment of the arch-reactionary Prince de Polignac as his chief minister the previous summer had removed the last chance to come to terms with liberal opinion. On 25 July he issued the fatal ordinances that brought about his downfall, dissolving Parliament, reducing the franchise, above all suspending the freedom of the press. The last clause sparked revolution. On 26 July a group of journalists, led by Adolphe Thiers, issued a manifesto, denouncing the ordinances as unconstitutional and calling on France to resist. On the 27th, the presses of the opposition papers, published in defiance of the ordinances, were destroyed by the police. Angry crowds spilt onto the Paris streets; that evening, as garrison troops moved into position on the boulevards, the barricades began to go up. By 29 July, after three days of bitter street fighting, Paris was in the hands of the insurgents. The tricolour floated above the Tuileries, and the aged Talleyrand, watching the rout of the royalist troops from his window, turned to dictate a note to his secretary: 'On the 29th of July, at precisely five minutes past twelve, the elder branch of the Bourbon family ceased to reign over France.'[11]

But what of the younger branch? It was Charles X's cousin, the Duke of Orléans, to whom the deputies, alarmed by the popular fury and seeking to contain it, now turned. Son of Philippe Égalité, a soldier in the revolutionary army at the Battle of Jemappes, he had all the right credentials for a liberal monarch. On 30 July, flanked by Lafayette, and holding a tricolour in one hand, Louis Philippe was proclaimed 'Roi des Français' on the balcony of the Hôtel de Ville. The crowd, persuaded by the tricolour, dispersed. The three days of revolution, 'Les Trois Glorieuses', were over.

The Hollands were ecstatic at the news: 'We all foresaw that the ordonnances would be the ruin of the Ministry and the dynasty,' Holland told Henry,

> and for more than fifteen years many, and I among them have fore-boded that the French revolutions would end sooner or later in their natural euthanasia – a constitutional king of the House of Orléans. But who could have imagined that all would have been effected, and so heroically and happily effected, in three short days? And that the forbearance, magnanimity and wisdom of the people after victory should have been as great, glorious and perfect as the heroism during the contest. It makes one young again.[12]

It was only 14 months since Louis Philippe had dined at Holland House on a visit to England with his son, and his friendship with the Hollands went back many years. Holland had seriously considered going over to Paris immediately to congratulate the new king – he would have done son so '*con amore*', he told Brougham. Gout and etiquette forbade it, but he was gratified to receive a copy of the king's acceptance speech, and later a letter in the king's own hand – in impeccable English – thanking him for his good wishes:

> I am very thankful for Lady Holland's kind messages & for your very flattering expressions on the subject of the part I have acted in the new situation to which I have been called so suddenly. The task that has fallen to my lot is a laborious one & it is difficult after so great a convulsion to subdue the irritation & to re-establish public confidence. I am striving incessantly to maintain the peace within and the peace without. War, bad as it is at all times, would be in the present state of Nations, attended with miseries & misfortunes unparalleled in any former wars. [13]

Louis Philippe had come to power at a dangerous moment. The Holy Alliance – Russia, Austria and Prussia – had been formed to prevent the contagion of revolution spreading. It had only been the prompt recognition of the new regime by Wellington that dissuaded the other great powers from going to war to restore the Bourbon monarchy. But the French example inspired liberal and nationalist uprisings in other European countries. A revolution by the Belgians, demanding freedom from Dutch rule, broke out in Brussels a month later; it was followed that autumn by risings in Poland, Italy and Germany. The rebellions in the last three countries were ruthlessly suppressed. Only the Belgians succeeded in obtaining their independence, with the creation of Belgium as a separate state in December 1830 and its establishment as a constitutional monarchy under Leopold of Saxe-Coburg the following summer. The fact that this took place peacefully was largely thanks to Louis Philippe, to his ambassador in London, Talleyrand, and in a small but significant way to the influence of Holland House.

20

The Whigs in Power

I N 1815, the territory now known as Belgium, which had been annexed to France under Napoleon, had been added to the kingdom of the Netherlands, the idea being to create a buffer state on France's northern frontier. By driving out the Dutch garrisons in Brussels and the other Belgian cities in the late summer of 1830, the Belgians had effectively won their independence. But would they be allowed to keep it? The Holy Alliance, in accordance with its so-called obligations under the Treaty of Vienna, was preparing to put down the revolution in its usual way; the French, on the other hand, were determined to support the Belgians. The British meanwhile were adamant that Belgium, with its strategically important ports, should not return to French control.

It was in the midst of this complicated situation that Talleyrand arrived as French ambassador in England at the end of September. He soon established good relations with Wellington's Foreign Minister Lord Aberdeen, but this did not prevent him from frequenting Whig society or dining several times a week at Holland House.

Holland, who had known Talleyrand in so many roles, was delighted to see him in his new one as the ambassador of one constitutional monarchy to another. There were those who regarded him as a turncoat or worse – for Grey he was one of the three greatest rascals in Europe – but Holland would hear nothing against him. When Talleyrand was attacked in the House of Lords the following year, he sprang to his defence: 'Forty years acquaintance with the noble individual,' he declared, 'enabled him to bear testimony to the fact, that... there had been no man's character more shamefully traduced, and no man's public character more mistaken and misrepresented than the public and private character of Prince Talleyrand.'[1]

Holland House was Talleyrand's second home in London, and he made it his headquarters whenever his niece (and mistress) the Duchess of Dino, who acted as his ambassadress, was away. Now 76, with his thickly powdered curls and pallid wrinkled face, he looked, said one observer, like an aged lion. But the charm and fascination of his conversation were as great as ever. His bons mots were endlessly repeated. In his *Foreign Reminiscences* Holland quotes Talleyrand's humorous reproof to a young man who been boasting about his mother's beauty, and by implication that of her descendants. '*C'était donc*,' said Talleyrand, '*monsieur votre père qui n'était pas si bien.*'[2]

Lady Holland had mixed feelings about Talleyrand – she had never quite forgiven him for his betrayal of Napoleon – and he in his turn was not always charitable about her. '*Elle fait semblant de tout sçavoir, car cela lui donne de l'importance, et quand elle ne sçait pas elle invente,*'[3] he once remarked, and when someone asked why she had changed the time of her dinners to the inconveniently early hour of five, he said frankly, '*C'est pour gêner tout le monde.*'[4] To Holland, on the other hand, he was devoted. He addressed him in English as 'my dear friend', or sometimes 'dearest', in his letters, signing himself 'Talley', the nickname by which he was known in England. Holland regarded him as an honorary Foxite, a title first bestowed on him by Fox himself, and one he declared himself proud to accept.

Some people thought that Holland was taken in by Talleyrand: '[He goes] every evening late to Holland House, when everyone else is gone, and sucks Holland's brain for an hour or two before he goes to bed,'[5] reported the Duke of Bedford to his brother Lord William Russell. But Holland shared Talleyrand's aim of ensuring good relations between England and France, and their confidence was mutual. Neither was much bothered by the niceties of working through official channels, a fact that drove their Foreign Ministers to distraction. Talleyrand showed Holland confidential documents, Holland reported on Cabinet discussions. In their view Anglo-French co-operation was essential if the other great powers were to be kept from intervening over Belgium, and its establishment as a neutral and independent country was the only way to balance French and British interests. The fact that these aims were peacefully achieved, despite belligerent noises from all sides, owed much to the underlying trust between them. It was, as the historian Leslie Mitchell remarks, 'an extraordinary culmination of a 40-year friendship.'[6]

The problems of Belgium might not have been so easily resolved had the Tory government remained in power. When Parliament reassembled on 2 November 1830 the king's speech mentioned the revolution in Belgium with ominous disapproval. But the July Revolution in France, with its knock-on effect in Belgium, had speeded up demands for change in Britain too. The movement for electoral reform had been gaining momentum over the last few years, and with Catholic Emancipation out of the way, it had become the most important issue of the day. Wellington had been pragmatic over Catholic Emancipation. When Parliament opened that autumn most people expected that he would also introduce some measure of parliamentary reform, if only to silence more extreme demands. But the duke was not prepared to make concessions. His announcement in the opening debate that the British constitution was the most perfect yet devised by man, and that he would resist all attempts to change it, dismayed even his most loyal followers. The speech dealt a death blow to the ministry. The party was already weakened by the defection of the former Canningites and the Ultras, the latter still bent on revenge after their betrayal, as they saw it, over Catholic Emancipation. On 15 November the two groups combined with the Whigs and independents to defeat the government in the Commons. Wellington resigned and William IV, who unlike his brother had no objection to the Whigs, asked the 66-year-old Lord Grey to form a government.

After 23 years in opposition the Whigs were once more in power. With the prospect of office Grey discovered a new sense of energy and purpose. He had never wavered in his support for electoral reform though his aims were more moderate than they had been in 1792. Holland had done his utmost to keep his place as leader warm during Grey's years of semi-retirement in Northumberland; without the social and intellectual draw of Holland House, the Foxite Whigs who formed the core of his new Cabinet might have been scattered altogether. Now was the time when Holland could claim his reward. It had always been his dream to become Foreign Secretary, and Grey's first thought was to offer him the post. But Holland's health was no longer equal to it, and he was forced to refuse. The gout which had plagued him for years had become increasingly incapacitating, often confining him to bed for weeks on end. During one particularly severe attack that summer, Wellington had ridden out to Holland House on a night of pouring rain to ask after him: old friendship transcending the political differences between them.

Palmerston became Foreign Secretary, Holland taking the less onerous post of Chancellor of the Duchy of Lancaster. As a member of the Cabinet, he could still keep in touch with foreign affairs, often to the fury of Palmerston, though as we have seen with fruitful consequences for Franco-British understanding. The rest of the Cabinet, which included such Canningites as Melbourne, who became Home Secretary, was almost entirely aristocratic, 'not that I exclude a man of merit from another class,' Grey told his friend Princess Lieven, 'but between men of equal mind I would chose the aristocrat.'[7]

The wild card was Brougham. Not an aristocrat, but too popular with the public to be left out of the government, he had made his name as the defender of Queen Caroline and a vociferous advocate of legal and political reform. Rather than leave him in the Commons where his powerful and combative personality might cause trouble for the Leader of the House, Lord Althorp, Grey offered him the post of Lord Chancellor, with the title of Baron Brougham and Vaux. At first it was doubtful if he would accept – 'You can do more with him than anybody,'[8] wrote Grey to Holland anxiously – but it was the king who finally brought him round. 'You are all under great obligations to me,' he told Holland. 'I have settled Brougham. He will not be dangerous any more.'[9]

Grey's youthful championship of parliamentary reform had gone against the tide of the times; with the Terror raging across the Channel the Friends of the People had been seen as a dangerously subversive group. Now the whole force of public opinion was behind him. A rising middle class, rich and well educated, was demanding its share in government; lower down the scale workers' associations, suppressed since the Napoleonic wars, had begun to articulate their claims once more. Economic misery added to the sense of urgency; rick-burning under the auspices of the sinister 'Captain Swing' was spreading fear in the rural south, desperate workers were arming and training in the industrial north. The fear of revolution, which had once held back political change, had become the chief reason for bringing it about.

Grey set to work at once. No sooner had his Cabinet been approved by the king than he entrusted a committee of four – his son-in-law Lord

Durham, Lord John Russell, Lord Duncannon and the Cumberland baronet Sir James Graham – with the task of drawing up a Reform Bill. Their conclusions would be reached in conditions of the utmost secrecy, before being presented to the king at the beginning of the year.

Although the Whigs had always supported parliamentary reform, Holland himself was relatively lukewarm on the subject. 'For my part,' he wrote to Henry on the eve of Wellington's departure, 'I was never a very keen *reformer*, but I think reform now absolutely inevitable, and I am sure, if it be so, the sooner it is done the better.'[10] In this spirit he would take part in the parliamentary battles leading up to the passing of the Reform Bill, not so much as a maker of policy – he was far more interested in foreign affairs – but as a respected senior figure, whose tact and experience helped to reconcile differences in the Cabinet, and on whose discretion Grey could rely. Through his relationship by marriage he also had informal access to the king, and his daughter-in-law, now raised to the title of Lady Mary Fox, was a useful source of gossip on court life. The queen, a German princess of decidedly anti-democratic views, was fiercely opposed to reform. Holland's journal, which he began in July 1831, gives vivid glimpses of the domestic struggles – the queen frequently in tears – taking place behind the scenes.

The old Foxite doctrine of opposition to the Crown, steadfastly maintained through the reigns of George III and George IV, had now lost much of its relevance. Wellington, by overriding George IV's resistance to Catholic Emancipation, had proved that in the last analysis the will of Parliament must prevail. William IV was a very different character to his brother, sympathetic to the Whigs as we have seen, good-natured and anxious to do right. But he still had considerable power and Grey and Holland needed all their persuasive skills to win him round to the forthcoming bill; the alternative, Holland assured him, would be civil war and revolution.

Despite his wife's resistance, William IV accepted the proposed bill in its entirety, reassured by Grey's arguments that its provisions were essentially 'aristocratic': the stability of the country's institutions, including the throne, could only be ensured if the suffrage was extended. 'Never was there such a king,' wrote Holland joyfully to Anglesey; 'he not only acquiesces but espouses the measures deemed necessary by his ministers, however disagreeable to royal palates.'[11]

From the moment the bill was first in contemplation Grey had been convinced that there was no point nibbling at the question of reform. The only safe measure, he felt, was one that was broadly based and his committee had shared his view. When Lord John Russell introduced it in the House of Commons on 1 March 1831, it was considered so sweeping that not only the Tories but even the more timid Whigs were appalled. Had Peel, the Tory leader in the Commons, proposed to divide the House on its first reading, the bill – and the government – would probably have been defeated. But Peel was a cautious man who preferred to weigh things carefully, and the first reading of the bill, as was usual in the Commons, was allowed to pass without a division.

In fact the bill was far from revolutionary; less a democratic measure than a transfer of power from the upper to the middle classes, and the acceptance of an already existing situation. The working classes were excluded, and even the anomalies by which in a few boroughs they had been able to vote were abolished. Nonetheless it did much to impose some kind of order on a previously chaotic system: rotten boroughs (where the population had declined to below 2,000) and nomination boroughs (where the patron could name his own candidate) were abolished; the big industrial towns, like Manchester and Birmingham, were enfranchised; and a more equal system of representation was established between constituencies. The resounding welcome with which the public greeted the bill did much to persuade the waverers in Parliament. But the outcome of the vote, when it came up for its second reading, was uncertain to the last. The numbers were counted in an atmosphere of mounting excitement. When it finally became clear that the bill had been passed by one vote – 302 to 301 – a shout went up, wrote Macaulay, the new member for Calne, which could have been heard at Charing Cross.

The reformers' triumph was short-lived. Two weeks later the bill was defeated on an amendment in committee, and on 23 April Parliament was dissolved. In the election campaign that followed Lord John Russell, as the bill's proposer in the Commons, was the hero of the hour. When he went to Devonshire for re-election, huge crowds flocked to see him. 'The people along the road were very much disappointed by his smallness [Russell was only five feet tall],' reported Sydney Smith to Lady Holland. 'I told them that he was much larger before, but was reduced by excessive anxiety about the people. This brought tears to their eyes.'[12]

The Whigs were returned to office with a hugely increased majority – the Tories retaining little more than their nomination boroughs – and the Reform Bill, basically unchanged, was introduced into the new House of Commons on 24 June. This time it was passed by a majority of 136 votes on its second reading, but the struggle to get it through both houses would continue for another year and in the process bring the country to the brink of revolution. 'I am full twenty years too old,' sighed Grey to Holland in a moment of discouragement. 'In short I am miserable.'[13]

In Holland House at least he could be sure of friendship and support.

21

'The Bill, the Whole Bill and Nothing but the Bill'

O N 21 March 1831, Lady Holland reached the age of 60. Harking back to the days of their courtship, Holland concluded his birthday tribute on a touching note:

> I loved you much at twenty-four
> I love you better at three score. [1]

By now both the Hollands were semi-invalids, Holland largely confined to a wheelchair. He bore his sufferings with good humour, referring to himself jokingly as Lord Chalkstones (the chalky deposits formed by gout). Often, when his health was too bad to leave home the Cabinet would meet at Holland House (Lady Holland dining with her sister-in-law on these occasions) or in the London house they rented during parliamentary sessions.

Lady Holland took her aches and pains more seriously and kept a string of doctors – her 'host of leeches' as Holland called them – at her command. '*Malade et mourant lui semblent synonymes*,'[2] a French friend once remarked. But she had lost none of her zest for entertaining, and with her husband now in the government the influence of

Holland House was more powerful than ever. At a time when thrones were tottering elsewhere, Lady Holland, in the words of Lady Granville, was 'the only really undisputed monarchy in Europe'.[3]

It is interesting to see her at this period through the eyes of a new visitor, the young Thomas Babington Macaulay, already well known as a contributor to the *Edinburgh Review,* and a brilliant speaker in the debates on parliamentary reform. In May 1831 he was talking to Sir James Macdonald at a reception at Lansdowne House when he heard a voice behind him say, 'Sir James, introduce me to Mr Macaulay,' and, turning, 'beheld a large, bold-looking woman, with the remains of a fine person and the air of Queen Elizabeth.'[4] The introduction was followed by an invitation to dine at Holland House a few days later.

Macaulay was a rising man, but a visit to Holland House was an event. 'Well my dear,' he announced to his sister the day after, 'I have dined at Holland House.' The house, he wrote was delightful, 'the perfection of the old Elizabethan style', Lord Holland 'all kindness, simplicity and vivacity', and Lady Holland 'excessively gracious' to her new guest. But there was a haughtiness in her courtesy, he wrote, which, despite all he had heard about her, surprised him:

> The centurion did not keep his soldiers in better order than she kept her guests. It is to one, 'Go' and he goeth, and to another 'do this' and it is done. 'Ring the bell Mr Macaulay'. 'Lay down that screen Lord Russell; you will spoil it'; 'Mr Allen, take a candle and show Mr Cradock the picture of Bonaparte.'[5]

The first invitation quickly led to others and Macaulay was soon a familiar figure at Holland House, where the breadth of his knowledge and the brilliance of his conversation amazed his hearers. Once embarked on a topic, his flow of eloquence was almost unstoppable; 'he has occasional flashes of silence that make his conversation perfectly delightful,' remarked Sydney Smith. Lady Holland would call him to order with an imperious tapping of her fan: 'Now Macaulay, we have had enough of this; give us something else.'[6]

Macaulay, it was said, would talk to a fence post if no other audience was available, but this did not prevent him from being a shrewd observer of those around him and in his letters to his sister he gives us vivid sketches of his hosts.

With Holland, 'very lively; very intellectual; well read in politics and in the lighter literature both of ancient and modern times', he felt an immediate affinity:

> He sets me more at my ease than almost any person that I know, by a certain good-humoured way of contradicting that he has. He always begins by drawing down his shaggy eyebrows, making a face extremely like his uncle [Fox], wagging his head and saying: 'Now do you know, Mr M, I do not quite see that. How do you make it out?'

Lady Holland, he thought, was a woman of 'considerable talents and great literary acquirements' – high praise from so erudite a critic as Macaulay. But though she was gracious to him personally, he was dismayed by her manner to others, particularly to Allen:

> He really is treated like a negro slave. 'Mr Allen, go into the drawing room and bring me my reticule.' 'Mr Allen, go and see what can be the matter that they do not bring up dinner.' 'Mr Allen, there is not enough turtle soup for you. You must take gravy soup or none.'

'Yet I can scarcely pity the man,' he added. 'He has an independent income [as warden of Dulwich College] and if he can stoop to be ordered about like a footman, I cannot so much blame her for the contempt in which she treats him.'[7]

The relationship between Allen and the Hollands was a complex one. Holland habitually consulted him on political matters and he was much respected by Holland's colleagues in the Cabinet, particularly Grey. Despite her high-handed behaviour, Lady Holland relied on him totally in the practical affairs of life and the dependence between them seems to have been mutual. He had his own rooms at Holland House, and was so much part of life there that his study was known as Allen's Room by each succeeding generation. 'You are yourself like health,' Holland once told him. 'Once never feels your value more than when you are absent.'[8]

Soon after Macaulay's first visit to Holland House Sydney Smith arrived from his rectory in Yorkshire for an extended stay. Thanks to Whig patronage he was at last about to receive advancement in the Church. From September that year he would become resident Canon of St Paul's – a promotion all the sweeter since it brought him into easy range of Holland House. 'Some of the best and happiest days of my life I have spent under your roof,' he once told Lady Holland, 'and though there may be in some houses, particularly those of our eminent clerics, a stronger disposition to pious exercises... I do not believe all Europe can produce as much knowledge, wit and worth as passes in and out of your door under the nose of Thomas the porter.'[9]

Macaulay knew Smith already and had visited him in the country; it was he who first christened him 'the Smith of Smiths'. At Holland House he got the full flavour of Smith in company. His sense of fun, Macaulay wrote, was inexhaustible, and unlike Samuel Rogers, whose wit was carefully prepared, Smith always spoke from the impulse of the moment. Rogers would usually fall silent when Smith was talking; he preferred it when the company divided and he could have a smaller audience to himself. Neither, however, was a match for Macaulay. 'Now Macaulay,' said Smith after one of his long monologues, 'when I am gone you will be sorry you have never heard me speak.'[10]

There would always be laughter and good company at Holland House, but the atmosphere that summer was heightened by the dramas surrounding the Reform Bill. In the House of Commons, the battle to get it through the committee stage was being waged with increasing bitterness. The Tories, determined on a policy of obstruction, used every delaying tactic they could find, fighting it line by line against a background of growing anger in the country. 'The bill, the whole bill, and nothing but the bill' was the cry; the fear of revolution should it not go through was very real.

The government resisted all attempts to modify the bill, making it clear that the House would sit till Christmas, or the following Christmas if necessary, till it went through. The date of the usual summer recess slipped by; for three sweltering months in the hot and crowded conditions of the lower chamber, the debate raged back and forth. Finally on the morning of 22 September the bill was passed on its third reading and was presented to the House of Lords that same day. 'There seemed a preconcerted silence and moderation on the opposition benches,' wrote Holland in his journal, 'and they received the distant day of Monday 2nd Octr, named for the second reading, and even the hint that little time would be allowed between that stage and the committal, with great composure.'[11]

It was plain that this was just the calm before the storm. The government knew there was bound to be a majority against them in the Lords and had already discussed the idea of creating additional peers to carry the bill through. But Grey was reluctant to bring things to a crisis, and it was unlikely that the king would agree to do so. On 3 October, when Grey rose to move the second reading of the bill, he relied on his own eloquence, and the danger of the consequences should it be rejected, to make his case. His speech, delivered with a fire that recalled the great days of Burke and Fox, was the start of a five-day debate, which lasted till the small hours of each morning. The high spot was a speech by Brougham, who reached the climax of his peroration by falling on his knees as he pleaded with the house, 'I warn you, I implore you, yea on my knees I supplicate you – Reject not this Bill.'[12] He had drunk at least a bottle and a half of mulled port during his speech, noted Holland, and had some difficulty in getting up again.

Holland had attended the whole debate, though he did not speak, and he stood with Grey in a little group as they awaited the result of the division. Holland, wrote a spectator, 'was a little excited, but Grey was tranquil and smiling, as if they had been dividing on a road bill... No stranger would have imagined that a measure was decided that might occasion the land to be deluged in blood.'[13]

The bill was thrown out by 41 votes, their numbers including 21 peers who were proprietors of nomination boroughs. 'May not a man do what he likes with his own?' the Duke of Newcastle had demanded, when his right to nominate his own MP was questioned, and the feeling that nomination seats were private property, about to be seized without compensation, accounted for the resistance of some borough owners. The Church too feared a diminution of its privileges and the bishops voted 20 to two against the bill. Their votes, with those of the borough owners, noted Holland, 'made up the number... by which we were beat.'[14]

The defeat of the bill was greeted with a wave of fury. There were riots all over the country; mobs broke the Duke of Wellington's windows at Apsley House and razed the Duke of Newcastle's house in Nottingham to the ground; bishops were burnt in effigy; Tory peers and clergy went in fear of their lives. Till then there had been few mass protests; the one exception, a peaceful demonstration by starving agricultural labourers the previous autumn, had been ruthlessly dealt with by Melbourne as Home Secretary. Three men were executed, another 457 transported, in an assize that stained the government's reputation and cast a new light on the supposedly genial Melbourne's character. But there were no troops in the country sufficient to deal with a general uprising. In the Commons debate, which followed the bill's rejection in the Lords, Macaulay summed the contradictions of the situation:

> I know only two ways by which societies can permanently be governed
> – by public opinion or by the sword... I understand how the peace
> is kept in New York. It is governed by the assent and support of the
> people. I understand also how the peace is kept at Milan. It is by the
> bayonets of the Austrian soldiers. But how the peace is to be kept
> in England by a government acting on the principles of the present
> opposition, I do not understand.[15]

The Reform Bill had become far more than a party measure. Even those who aspired to a far wider suffrage rested their hopes on it as a first step, and radicals and working-class associations were as ardent in its support as the middle classes it would chiefly benefit. At the other side of the spectrum was the king, whose fears that the bill was too democratic could only be calmed by the tact and patience of his aristocratic ministers. Ironically, perhaps, it was only an aristocratic ministry that could have channelled such varying demands through Parliament and presided successfully over the loss of its monopoly of power. In 1831, however, this happy outcome was still far from certain and the first question to be decided was whether the government would leave office after being defeated in the Lords.

Lady Holland was appalled at the prospect. 'Mama's agony at the idea of going out was monstrously diverting, if it were not one's mother,' reported Charles Fox to his brother.

> 'Your Papa is what I feel about... now really I cannot say how much
> it vexes me to think of him.' I said, 'Why I do not think in two days, if

you would *let* him go to H.H., he would even think of it; *you* would, I know, be sorry.'

'Ha ah, you are quite wrong. If you knew of the little things, the sort of old recollections that all come back to him, the little feeling of doing good, of moderating some people, of softening prejudices, foreign politicks, the great hobby of his Uncle, of France and England, and still more his own.'

I interrupted and most impudently (I don't mean to her impudent and Allen was only present!) said, 'Oh you mean Mama, that he and old Talleyrand are to keep the peace of Europe, don't you?'

My Lady looked angry, and of course was quick enough to say immediately, 'Oh, you may hold your Father cheap, &c., &c.' However, my shot told, which was all I wanted.[16]

Fortunately for Lady Holland's peace of mind the question was quickly decided. At the insistence of the king Grey agreed to stay on in office, but only on condition that the king support a new version of the bill, unchanged in its main outlines, though possibly including some minor alterations. This would be presented at the beginning of the next session, normally due to open in February, but brought forward to early December in view of the urgency of the situation. Riots in Bristol, during which the mob took control for three days and burned down the prison and other public buildings, showed how fragile law and order had become. Meanwhile the growth of pro-reform unions, theoretically committed to peaceful protest but threatening from the sheer weight of their membership, made matters still more pressing. The brief period before Parliament reassembled on 6 December was a time of multiple negotiations – with the leaders of the unions, which were tolerated but forbidden to carry arms; with the 'waverers', or undecided peers; with the king; with differing shades of opinion in the Cabinet itself. Holland's journal for this period is full of fascinating sidelights: the queen cutting Grey at a court reception; Durham, the most left-wing of the bill's promoters – he was commonly known as Radical Jack – in a fury with his father-in-law Grey, because he had not been given an earldom; Wellington stirring up doubts among the waverers, and alarming the king with his forecasts of disaster: 'He's so d—d cunning,' said Melbourne's brother Frederick Lamb. 'People don't know him; he's the cunningest fellow in the world.'[17]

The Tories in the Commons were in a chastened mood when Parliament reopened and the second reading of the bill of 17 December was carried by a majority of two to one, many Tories deliberately abstaining. But would it be possible to get it through the House of Lords without the creation of new peers, and if not, would the king agree to make them? This was the controversy still to be resolved when the House adjourned for Christmas the next day.

22

The Triumph of Reform

THE winter of 1831–32 was one of great economic and social misery. Unemployment, strikes and industrial unrest were rife; rick-burning and the destruction of property in rural areas were so frequent that insurance premiums rose from two to ten per cent. The arrival of cholera in Scotland the previous summer had brought fresh distress; over the next 15 months, as the epidemic moved southward, it took a toll of 50,000 victims. It was the poor, living in the crowded and insanitary conditions of the big industrial towns, who suffered most, but fear of the disease spread through all classes. In London the outbreak was largely confined to the East End and the area round the docks, though there was talk of moving Parliament to Oxford should the disease reach Lambeth.

In the fevered atmosphere of the time even cholera took on a political dimension: it was an alarm put about by the anti-Reformers, declared one Union member. The Reform Bill dominated every other issue; a second rejection by the Lords, in most people's opinion, would lead to civil war. The new bill, though basically unchanged, had included some minor modifications which, it was hoped, would make it more acceptable to the moderate Tories. But the outcome was still far from certain, and despite the reluctance of the king (much influenced by his wife's hostility to reform) Grey had obtained a written promise that he would create additional peers if all else failed.

The majority of the Cabinet, including Holland, was in favour of an immediate creation, possibly of 50 or 60 peers, in order to ensure the bill would pass its second reading. Grey however was doubtful about the wisdom of doing so, at least until the results of the vote were known. He felt it would set a dangerous precedent, and alienate the undecided. His colleagues were torn between their loyalty to him and their feeling that delay would be disastrous. Holland made it clear he disagreed with Grey, but promised to support him if it came to a vote.

The strain of the bill was beginning to tell on those concerned. The bluff Lord Althorp was so overwrought about its passage through the Lords that he removed the pistols from his room for fear he should be tempted to shoot himself. Durham, who had recently lost his eldest son, was moody and irascible; Brougham, foul-mouthed against the royal ladies, the 'Begums' as he called them. Grey, above all, was getting cold feet about the whole affair. Essentially loyal to his caste, he feared the damage to the House of Lords if its powers were over-ridden by the creation of new peers. 'Indeed,' wrote Holland in his journal for 6 March,

> his rooted aversion to that necessary and useful expedient broke out more forcibly when he was goaded by Durham, than I had ever hitherto known. He bitterly lamented that he had undertaken a task in the government of this Country for which he was too old and quite unfit; acknowledged that had he foreseen that such a measure as making 60 Peers, which he termed *an act of violence unparalleled in our history and equivalent to a Destruction of the House of Lords* could have been contemplated, he would never have proposed the Reform Bill; and with great earnestness declared that he wished

any one of his colleagues would free him from a responsibility that overwhelmed him. [1]

It was only a momentary outburst. Grey's standing in the country and the respect he inspired in his colleagues made the idea of challenging his leadership unthinkable. In the end, after heated discussions, he prevailed on the Cabinet to postpone the creation of new peers till after the second reading of the bill. With the king's promise to create them as a backstop, he felt they could wait till they knew what numbers were required. His decision was probably the right one; a premature creation of new peers might well have antagonized some of those who voted for the bill. As it was when the House of Lords divided for its second reading on 14 April, there was a majority of nine in its favour.

The worst danger, that the bill would be defeated, had been averted. But the government's majority was very small and the Tories had not yet shot their bolt. Their aim was to whittle away at the bill in committee with a series of minor amendments, on each of which it would be difficult for the government to demand new peers, but which collectively would destroy its character. On 7 May, when the debate of the bill in committee began, the former Tory Chancellor Lord Lyndhurst introduced a motion to postpone consideration of the disenfranchising clauses (abolishing rotten and nomination boroughs) until after the enfranchising clauses had been debated.

The plot, wrote Holland in his journal,

> was obviously to get the Management of the bill entirely in their own hands, to shake the confidence of the people in the Government, and then to mutilate or impair our measure in such a way that would force us in honour to resign on some point which neither King nor Country would support in making peers. [2]

The motion was passed by a majority of 41 votes. But Lyndhurst had over-reached himself. By defying the government on a point of procedure, rather than attacking the bill clause by clause, he offered Grey an ideal chance to take a stand. 'The bill, the whole bill and nothing but the bill' had been the slogan on which the measure had been presented to the country; in suggesting that it should be debated in two parts, he had breached this basic principle. Grey was quick to seize his opportunity. Casting aside his earlier hesitations, he announced that the government would resign unless they were allowed to create sufficient new peers to pass the bill in its entirety.

Three months earlier the king had agreed to do this as a last resort. But his mind had been worked on by Wellington and the queen in the meantime, and his attitude had changed considerably. He knew that some measure of reform was inevitable, but now leant towards a more moderate version which would get through the Lords without the trouble of creating new peers. On 9 May, he accepted the government's resignation and turned to Wellington to form an administration.

The days that followed were known as the 'days of May'. Years later Lord John Russell would recall them as the only moment in his life when Britain was in real danger – and Russell, we must remember, had lived through all the dramas of the Napoleonic war. Civil war was suddenly in sight. Instead of the spontaneous outbreaks of the previous year there was a feeling of silent but determined resistance, of violence still in check but waiting to erupt. Mass meetings were held across the country, communications established between political unions of all complexions, and plans for resisting taxes, barricading town centres and arranging simultaneous demonstrations put in preparation. In London, the radical leader Francis Place campaigned for a run on the banks – 'To stop the duke, go for gold.' The king's carriage was mobbed whenever it ventured out in public. Europe as well as Britain held its breath. 'So intense was the interest taken in our domestick affairs during these six or seven days,' wrote Holland, 'that neither the Cholera nor the death of Casimir Périer [the French prime minister]... were deemed worthy of much notice, and even at Paris, I have been assured that the Publick were much more interested with the dismissal of our Premier than with the illness and death of theirs.'[3]

Wellington had agreed to form a government out of loyalty to the king. He now accepted that only an extensive measure of reform, along the lines proposed by Grey, would calm public feeling, though he hoped to make its terms 'as little noxious' as possible. But none of the Tories in the Commons, including their leader Robert Peel, were prepared to make the volte-face necessary, and for all his prestige he was unable to form a government. On 18 May, after nine days of fruitless negotiations, Wellington abandoned the attempt.

The ball was now in Grey's court, and since he refused to take office unless new peers were created, the king was finally forced to give in. The promise to make them was enough; faced with prospect of being swamped by new peers, the chief opponents of the bill decided to abstain from voting. A few remained defiant to the end: one Tory peer, reported Holland, arraigned Grey at the top of his voice for subverting the constitution and degrading the Lords, threatening him with 'revolution and bloodshed, remorse on his death and damnation afterwards.'[4] Grey remained unmoved by the opposition's fury, and on 4 June, after only six days in committee, the third reading of the bill was carried by 106 votes to 22.

The king accepted the verdict grudgingly. He had been greatly shaken by the hostile reaction of the public towards him and refused to go down to the Lords to give the royal assent in person; after the way he had been treated by the populace, he declared, he would feel disgusted by their applause. The government refrained from pressing him. 'There is evidently a fear of *exciting* him (that is the term),' wrote

Holland, 'and I hear it whispered that his dinners and his wine tend to aggravate the said excitement.'[5]

In the absence of the king Holland was one of the six commissioners appointed to pass the Reform Bill in the House of Lords on 7 June; the others were Grey, Brougham, Lansdowne, Durham and Wellington's brother Lord Wellesley. A contemporary print depicts the scene. The commissioners are seated in front of the throne, with Brougham as Lord Chancellor presiding. The government benches are full, those of the Tory opposition are empty, and members of the House of Commons stand at the bar. In contrast to the wild rejoicing that was taking place across the country Holland's comments in his journal are low-key. But they exude a quiet sense of pride.

> We were six in our robes and I reflected with some satisfaction that five of us were members of the old opposition who uniformly maintained the principles of peace and reform, and that the three bills I had hitherto sat to pass were the abolition of the Slave Trade, the alteration of the Game Laws, and the Reform Bill.[6]

Holland had spoken very little during the debates on the Reform Bill. He was humble about speaking in public, lamenting the 'strange and culpable nervousness' which made it an ordeal for him to do so. His admiration for the superior powers of Grey was without the slightest tinge of envy. In one of the last and most heated debates, when a bad cold gave him an excuse not to speak, he had the satisfaction, he wrote,

> of hearing many of my thoughts far better expressed and many of my expressions and points better delivered by Lord Grey, than I could have done, in his admirable reply which in spirit, judgement, recollection and reasoning would have been an extraordinary display at

any time and from any man, and was surely after a fatiguing debate of four nights and at six of clock in the Morning... from a man of near seventy years almost miraculous.[7]

Grey was the hero of the Reform Bill, and hailed as such across the country. Even diehard radicals, who saw it only as a stage on the road to full democracy, admitted that it was a great bill when it was passed. It would have been impossible to get anything more radical through Parliament at the time. Often timid and discouraged, and at heart more conservative than most of his Cabinet, Grey had risen to its challenge. He had been backed by the force of popular opinion. Just over 30 years ago George III had struck Fox's name off the Privy Council for drinking to the 'sovereignty of the people'. In the words of Grey's biographer, G.M. Trevelyan, the wheel had come full circle.

For Holland too the wheel had come full circle. His uncle's three great aims had been achieved: Catholic Emancipation had been won; the bill to abolish slavery was in preparation and would be passed the following year; the long campaign for electoral reform had reached its climax in the Reform Bill. Holland House had been intimately involved in each, helping to bridge the gap between radicals and Tories, between abolitionists and slave owners, and lending its grandeur, its intellectual sparkle and its aristocratic credentials to the cause of reform. Holland had fulfilled his role as Fox's heir.

Lady Holland, as a hostess, had also had played a vital part. Tory writers had long lamented that they had no one like her on their side. Even though she was no longer a beauty she had lost none of the magnetism that had characterized her in her younger days. It was her skill as a social impresario, directing and orchestrating the diverse and powerful personalities who frequented Holland House, that made its gatherings so attractive and successful. She was highly conscious of what she was trying to do. Her idea of a successful party, she once remarked to Henry, was one in which there was 'not one person [present] who was not remarkable for sense, wit, acquirement or some other distinguishing quality'.[8] She might well have complained – and she did – of 'the interminable business of the Reform Bill' – but she put the whole force of her salon behind it.

Lady Holland was frequently accused of trying to influence politics behind the scenes – as a woman at that time she had no chance of doing anything more. But neither she nor Holland was ever exclusively concerned with political matters. Books, ideas and conversation would always have their place and even at the height of the debates on the Reform Bill there were many evenings at Holland House when politics was hardly mentioned. In his journal for 16 January 1832, for instance, Holland abandons Cabinet matters to describe an especially congenial dinner party at which Melbourne, Jeffrey and Sydney Smith were among those present.

> Scarce any politicks were talked about... The origin of the Edinburgh Review, at the instigation of Sydney Smith, Horner... and Jeffray at the flat of the latter in Buccleuch Square in Edinburgh (now 30 years ago), was described with great humour by Sydney. He told us he had further proposed to adapt for a motto
>
> We cultivate literature on oats
> Musam meditamur avena
>
> but that the two Scotsmen [Horner and Jeffrey] vehemently protested. I scarcely ever heard more wit, learning and good sense in any Society and the remainder of the evening did not fall off when Talleyrand came in and closed it with anecdotes, both political and literary, in which his conversation abounds.[9]

On another evening shortly after, Talleyrand came round to read the first part of his memoirs, 'beautifully written, full of wit and *feeling*'. The aged cynic was unexpectedly shy and nervous when he read them:

> They spoke with great taste and delicacy but with deep and natural feeling of the conduct of his parents, and Mother in particular, who neglected and slighted him in his childhood and forced him into the Church when grown up, from an indulgence of their own passions of family pride and wounded vanity on his becoming lame from an accident in infancy. We sat up till three. I could have sat up till sunrise and from thence to sunset to hear these memoirs.[10]

It is a touchingly human glimpse, not only of Talleyrand himself, but of the respect and affection with which he regarded his friends at Holland House.

23

Elder Statesman

T H E general election which followed the Reform Bill in December 1832 was an overwhelming victory for the Whigs. 'I have never seen so many bad hats in my life,' remarked Wellington as he surveyed the reformed House of Commons. A new age was opening and though Holland would remain Chancellor of the Duchy of Lancaster, with one short intermission when the Whigs were out of office, until his death eight years later, he was becoming a faintly anachronistic figure. Like Grey he was a product of the enlightened eighteenth-century aristocracy; like Grey he revered the memory of Fox. His greatest contribution had been to keep the Foxite flame alive through the long years of opposition. With the Whigs now firmly in the saddle, the political role of Holland House had become less important.

Electoral reform had been part of Fox's agenda, but only in a limited sense and as a counter to the powers of the Crown and the executive. Holland did not take his ideas much further. He believed in an extension of the franchise as a response to the changing demands of society, but it was a franchise based on property with an interest in preserving good order and the country's institutions. It was right that popular opinion should be respected, but he never subscribed to the idea of universal suffrage and would have been amazed at the developments of the next 90 years. He was 58 in 1832 and for him at least the Reform Bill of that date was a convenient resting place.

If Fox's aims had been achieved at home there was still much to be done in foreign policy. In welcoming the French Revolution Fox had made himself the patron saint of liberal movements across Europe. From the very first Holland House had been home to political refugees from reactionary regimes, and even if the Russian ambassadress, Princess Lieven, representing the most absolutist power of all, was a frequent visitor, she came there for the company, not the politics. It would have been hard to find much sympathy at Holland House for Russia's brutal suppression of the Polish national rising in 1831, and when the exiled Polish leader, Prince Czartoryski, came to London in January 1832 he received an enthusiastic welcome from the Hollands despite the Lievens' protest that he was '*un criminel d'état*'. 'Lord Palmerston dined two days running with us *on purpose* to meet him...' Lady Holland told Henry triumphantly. 'Esterhazy [the Austrian ambassador] made a point of calling & sitting an hour with him. In short everything that can prove sympathy & deep interest to him personally he has found here.'[1]

Holland's sympathy for the cause of Polish independence had been tempered by the knowledge that Britain had no realistic chance of influencing events there. In Portugal and Spain, however, civil wars between reactionaries and constitutionalists in the early 1830s seemed to offer greater opportunities. Holland, as expected, took the liberal side, though his proposals that Britain should act with France to intervene in both countries were consistently turned down. Palmerston shared none of his Francophilia, or belief in France's good intentions, and had no desire to become embroiled in foreign adventures in partnership with the French. He deeply distrusted Talleyrand; Grey, by contrast, had now succumbed to the wily diplomat's charm. Writing to her brother Count Benckendorff in Russia in 1832, Princess Lieven described their varying reactions to the French ambassador. 'Grey is devoted to him, Palmerston detests him, Lord Holland tells him all the Cabinet secrets.'[2]

Even though Princess Lieven was exaggerating, Holland's indiscretions could drive his colleagues to distraction, though, as in the case of Belgium, they often served a useful purpose. His knowledge of foreign affairs and personalities, fed by the constant flow of foreign visitors to Holland House, was immense. (Macaulay, on one of his first visits there, was amazed by the 'jabber' of different languages at table.) Though often infuriated by Holland's meddling, Palmerston respected his judgement and experience, and as a special courtesy to Holland arranged that all Foreign Office despatches should be automatically circulated to him for his perusal. However much they differed over France, Palmerston was always glad to have his views, and Holland's support for constitutionalist causes in the rest of Europe was largely in tune with his own.

Parallel to Holland's interest in foreign policy was his concern for Irish affairs, and he was once more in close correspondence with Anglesey, who had returned to Ireland as Lord Lieutenant in December 1830. Catholic Emancipation had averted civil war, but there were still grievances enough to fuel violence and near anarchy.

Religion remained a burning issue, above all where tithes for the Church of Ireland were concerned. It was intolerable that the impoverished Catholic peasantry should be forced to subsidize an alien Church, and under the leadership of O'Connell vast anti-tithe meetings were being held across Ireland. Holland, like Anglesey and the more liberal members of the Cabinet, would have been glad to see concessions introduced at once. But their way was blocked by the House of Lords, and by those, like the Irish Secretary, Edward Stanley, who had religious scruples about the sanctity of the Established Church – and its revenues – in Ireland. Meanwhile behind resistance to paying the tithe lurked the more ominous possibility that the next step would be resistance to paying rent to alien landlords, and that law and order would break down altogether. Throughout the 1830s the Cabinet was torn between policies of coercion and conciliation, and it was on a disagreement over the Irish question that Grey finally resigned in July 1834. He was 70 and had long wanted to retire. Only two months after the Reform Bill was passed he had discussed the possibility of doing so with Holland. '[He] spoke feelingly and earnestly on his situation,' wrote Holland on that occasion,

> and, comparing the prospects of his declining years and energies with that of continual and increasing labour and excitement, avowed a disposition if not a determination to retire shortly... I avoided much conversation on it and only urged postponement of all such plans, especially as there was the prospect of a recess for three months to recruit his health and spirits and it was essential to his glory to launch and steer out of port the great vessel of Reform he had constructed.[3]

Grey had accepted Holland's urging at the time, but when the moment came he was delighted to retire to a tranquil old age in Northumberland where, according to Creevey, who visited him there, 'he could not have felt more pleasure from carrying the Reform Bill, than he does apparently when he picks up half a crown at cribbage.' Holland, who had known Grey in his ups and downs, his indecisions and his moments of greatness, took pride in their long association. A few days before his own death in 1840, Holland wrote some lines in verse; they were found on his dressing table after he died:

Nephew of Fox and friend of Grey,

Enough my meed of fame,

If those who deigned to observe me say,

I injured neither name.[4]

It was a characteristically modest summing up of his political career.

Meanwhile, a new prime minister had to be found. After a brief period of hesitation the king sent for Melbourne, then Home Secretary. 'Many thought his decision would not have been so absolutely or promptly taken if the queen had been in England [she was visiting her family in Germany],' wrote Holland, 'for she misunderstands Lord Melbourne's paradoxes and humour and, affecting or feeling many religious scruples, thinks his principles too loose.'[5]

Lady Holland was delighted to see another friend of Holland House in power. 'Her anxiety to see William [Melbourne] you may guess,' wrote Charles Fox to Henry the next day. 'I believe she wants to make Papa Foreign Secretary at least. However it will be as much as she can do to persuade him to remain Ch. Duchy Lancaster, as he considered himself yoked to Lord Grey.'[6]

Their sister Lady Lilford, now married and safely out of her mother's control, wrote to Charles in a similar vein: 'My Lady and Mary [Charles's wife],' she reported, 'took a drive late in the evening, the latter not at all knowing *where* she was to go. And who do you suppose they *did* visit? Lord Melbourne, the Prime Minister of three days! They found him extended on an ottoman, *sans* shirt, *sans* neckcloth, in a profound slumber.'[7]

Holland stayed on as Chancellor of the Duchy of Lancaster in Melbourne's Cabinet. Lady Holland put a good face on the appointment. 'Nothing could have induced yr Father to have remained in this mutilated Govt,' she told Henry, 'but that it is a legacy of Lord Grey's & urged by him.'[8]

Melbourne's first government was short-lived. The king had never really trusted him and when the party leader Althorp was forced to leave the Commons for the Lords following the death of his father Lord Spencer, the king used the excuse of his departure to disband the government. He first turned to Wellington, but the duke, who felt that the government should be led from the Commons, suggested Peel instead. Peel loyally took on the task, but with a minority in the Commons he was in an impossible position and in April 1835, after only five months in power, he resigned and the king was forced to take back Melbourne. Lord John Russell took on the leadership of the House of Commons, and Holland, though increasingly incapacitated by gout, returned to his old post as Chancellor of the Duchy of Lancaster. 'For myself,' he confided in his journal,

> I am only annoyed at having so good a place when I can do nothing for it, and I told Melbourne, Lansdowne and Johnny [Russell] that I was ashamed of accepting the office, though I must own it was so agreable and convenient to me that I could not refuse. It is in truth kind to have me at all and certainly, helpless as I am, it is the seat I can fill with least discredit to myself as well as most profit to myself.[9]

As well as the interest and occupation it provided, Holland's appointment had practical advantages. The position had a salary of £3,000 a year, an important resource, since the West Indian estates and Ampthill were running at a loss; for some time he had been making up his income by the sale of building land from the Holland House estate. As a member of the government he also had considerable powers of patronage (an accepted fact of political life at the time) and was able to use his influence to further his son Henry's diplomatic career. In June 1835 Henry was promoted to be minister in Vienna where, since the ambassador (Melbourne's brother) was ill, he found himself in charge, and where he and his wife – '*les petits Reynards*' as they were called – soon became a great success. 'Give [the Viennese] a fiddle to waltz to, a supper to eat and treat them with an indifference approaching insolence, and you will be adored,'[10] he told his mother cynically.

In 1833, after numerous love affairs, Henry had married Lady Mary Augusta Coventry, daughter of the Earl of Coventry. Her parents were separated, and she had been brought up in Rome by her mother, with whom, it appears, Henry had had a mild flirtation some years earlier. The marriage took place in Florence, with none of his family being present, but he brought her to meet them in London shortly afterwards. Vivacious and very small – 'decidedly under three feet in height', commented Creevey[11] – she quickly won her father-in-law's heart, and even Lady Holland confessed herself delighted with her 'little doll'.

A further family pleasure followed when Lady Holland was reunited with her Webster daughter Harriet, after more than 30 years of separation. It was Henry, who had met her some years previously, who brought about the reconciliation. 'Tell me *frankly* what you think of her,' Lady Holland asked him eagerly. 'Is she pretty, clever, pleasing? In short, what is she? I had a very obliging note expressing much kindness & good affection. I hope her daughter [also called Harriet] is a nice girl and will be satisfactory to her.'[12] The first meeting, which took place at Lady Affleck's house in the summer of 1834, went off well, and thereafter Harriet and her husband Admiral Fleetwood Pellew became regular visitors to Holland House. It was hard to recognize in the stately figure of their hostess the desperate young woman who had pretended her daughter was dead rather than let her be taken from her.

In February 1835 Lady Affleck died at the age of 88. She had always been on the best of terms with her daughter (apart from refusing to see her while she waited for her divorce) and she left Lady Holland her little 'nutshell' of a house in South Street. It was a great economy for the Hollands who no longer had to hire lodgings in London while Parliament was sitting, and as a further bonus it was only a few doors down from Melbourne, who had preferred to stay in his own house rather than move to 10 Downing Street. He would drop in there on his way home as easily as he did at Holland House.

Like Lord John Russell, now the Leader of the Commons, Melbourne had always been part of the Hollands' inner circle. Holland never had the reverence for him that he had for Grey, but his respect for him increased as he watched him grow into his role as prime minister, acting with a decisiveness and grasp of essentials that his indolent manner would not have led one to imagine him capable of. Even at his busiest, however, Melbourne always had time to relax at Holland House, where he could be found browsing in the library, discussing the early fathers of the Church with Allen or sitting with his feet on one of Lady Holland's drawing-room chairs, his laughter always the loudest in the room. The Hollands had stood by him faithfully through all the dramas of his marriage with Caroline Lamb. They would do so again the following year when he was involved in a new scandal, this time in an action brought against him for adultery by the husband of Sheridan's granddaughter, the beautiful Mrs Norton.

Caroline Norton's relationship with Sheridan had been the first link in her friendship with Melbourne, who had known the playwright well in his last years and even contemplated writing his life. In 1830, when the Whigs came to power, she had written to Melbourne, reminding him of his old acquaintance with her grandfather and asking him to find a job for her husband. Melbourne obliged with a place as a police magistrate for Norton, at the same time embarking on a romantic, but probably platonic, friendship with his wife. In 1836, a scandal blew up when Norton (urged on, it was thought, by the prime minister's political opponents) sued Mrs Norton for divorce, naming Melbourne as the co-respondent. Not everyone believed Melbourne's denial of misconduct with Mrs Norton – '*forse era ver ma non però credibile*,'[13] noted Holland – but the flimsiness of the evidence, and the meanness and spite which had motivated Norton's action, so disgusted the jury that Melbourne was acquitted.

It was generally agreed that Norton was a brute. But Mrs Norton was a highly colourful character, too witty and free-spoken to please conventional opinion, and though she had been found innocent her reputation was inevitably tarnished by her trial. It never affected her welcome at Holland House; the Hollands had their own morality and loyalty to old friends was one of them. As for Melbourne, who had been more harassed by the affair than he cared to admit, the trial proved a blessing in disguise. 'The whole Publick as well as the political adherents of Lord Melbourne sincerely rejoiced at the favorable verdict,' wrote Holland,

> and the more respectable of the Tories, especially the Duke of Wellington himself, discountenanced every attempt to affix any imputation on the private character either of Lord Melbourne or the Lady... The incident from which the vulgar of the tories hoped and the liberals at home had apprehended much, turned out so well that it rather endeared Lord Melbourne to the popular party than estranged him from them.[14]

Even William IV, who much preferred the Tories to the Whigs, refused to make capital out of Melbourne's difficulties. As the affectionate father of ten illegitimate children he was in no position to throw stones. Writing to Lady Holland a few days before the case was quashed, Melbourne's nephew William Cowper told her: 'There is a story going about that the King, when told that Lord Melbourne would not [after an unfavourable verdict] be fit to be his minister, replied, "Then I am not fit to be King."'[15]

24

'This Wretched Day'

O N 20 June 1837, William IV died, after reigning for just seven years. Holland, as we know, had pursued a lifelong policy of opposition to the Crown while Allen, his closest political confidant, was an outright republican. But he was sincerely moved at the news of the king's death. For all the ramblings and eccentricities which had earned him the nickname of Silly Billy, William IV had proved to be an exemplary king whose decency, common sense and determination to do his duty as he saw it had carried the monarchy safely into the mid nineteenth century. 'He was on the whole,' wrote Holland, 'the best king of his race and perhaps of any race we have ever had, and the one who has left the greatest name as a Constitutional Sovereign and the first Magistrate of a free and improving nation.'

Holland's son Charles and his wife Mary, together with the queen and all his other children, had been constantly at the king's bedside; the king died holding Mary's hand. From them and others Holland received first-hand descriptions of his final days. One incident, recorded in his diary, struck him particularly:

Early in the morning of Sunday, 18th. June he [the king] was thought by Lady Mary, Sir Herbert Taylor and the queen, who were present, to have said, 'I hope I may live to see the sunset of this *horrible* day'; the last word but one was very indistinct nor could they divine his reason for terming the day *horrible* as he expressed no other impatience and his sufferings did not appear aggravated... In relating the circumstance to Lord Munster [the king's eldest son] *he* quickly remarked that the word he intended to use was 'Memorable' for the day was the Anniversary of the Victory of Waterloo. Accordingly, before the sun set or the poor king expired, which was not till 2 AM of the 20th, the usual flag presented by the Duke of Wellington arrived and Lord Munster, with attentive and affectionate presence of mind, hastened into the room and laid it at the feet or across the knees of the expiring king who still had strength enough of mind to raise his hand and touch it and to murmur, tho' inarticulately, 'Glorious, Glorious.'[1]

It is one of those vignettes that light up Holland's journal of his years in office, giving it an immediacy often lacking in his formal memoirs. Never intended for publication, he wrote it, he explained, with the idea of providing material for himself or subsequent historians, and had kept it most faithfully during the momentous period when the Reform Bill was being debated. Since then he had written it intermittently and had laid it aside altogether during the few months when the Whigs were out of office. 'I am no longer behind the scenes,' he had written, 'and neither listen nor prompt. I may therefore close my book.'[2] He had taken up his pen again when Melbourne returned to power.

Shortly before he died, William IV sent a secret message to Victoria (bypassing her interfering mother the Duchess of Kent) advising her, if possible, to continue with the existing ministry. In the election that followed his death, the Whigs had held the majority, and the queen had accordingly taken his advice. She was a warm supporter of the government's liberal politics at home and abroad, noted Holland, and had a strong predilection for her uncle Leopold, whose recent elevation to the Belgian throne, she seemed to think, identified her family's interests with a constitutional monarchy. 'This is lucky for the interests of freedom,' wrote Holland,

> though perhaps it is rather mortifying to philosophy to perceive how much the destinies of Europe and the institutions and happiness of Mankind, still depend, in spite of the pretended march of intellect, schoolmasters, the representative system, the press or what not, on the accidental character and will of a girl of 18![3]

Holland might distrust the monarchy as an institution but he was charmed by the young Queen Victoria herself. 'Our little Queen has made courtiers of us all and of me among them,'[4] he wrote to Henry. When he first dined at court, she paid so much attention to him and Melbourne after dinner that the lord-in-waiting came over and whispered to Melbourne that Lord Hertford, who was sitting nearby, was showing signs of discontent at being neglected. The situation was saved when Holland tactfully asked the queen to wheel his chair from her side to the whist table and the mollified Hertford was then called to take his place.

Lady Holland, of course, was not invited to court; in fact she was more excluded from royal circles than before. William IV had frequently dined at Holland House, leaving Queen Adelaide behind. But the easy-going Regency morality which had continued into his reign came to an end with the accession of a woman to the throne. No one was more concerned that the young queen's reputation should be above reproach than Melbourne. Even though Lady Holland was one of his dearest friends he asked her not to visit her daughter-in-law, who had a grace-and-favour house at Windsor Castle, while the queen was in residence. 'I know if you do that, it will lead to discussions which you will not like,' he told her frankly. 'I believe I do wrong in telling you this, as I know it will give you a great desire to come; and if I said it did not signify, you would probably think nothing of it.'[5] Lady Holland, however, took the hint and did not visit Mary till the queen was gone. There was no escaping the double standards of the day. Queen Victoria, who took a lively interest in Lady Holland – not unmixed with jealousy, for Melbourne went to Holland House far too often for her liking – once asked him if she minded. 'He shook his head,' the queen recorded in her journal,

> and said, 'Perpetually; oh! She feels it very much'... [I] said, I thought perhaps she mightn't mind the exclusion; Lord M. said, 'Oh, she feels it deeply; there's nobody who doesn't feel it; I have never known anyone who didn't feel it; many don't wish to go, but they don't like the exclusion.'[6]

It might have consoled Lady Holland to have seen Victoria's entry for 15 February 1838. 'Lord Melbourne dines with Lady Holland tonight,' she wrote; 'I *wish* he dined with me!'[7]

Melbourne's relationship with the queen in the early days of her reign was perhaps the most important attachment of his life. Half avuncular, half in love, he was enchanted by her ingenuousness, her vitality, her directness, and by her obvious hero-worship of him. Even so, there were moments when he needed to escape from the stiffness of court life to the fun and sophistication of Holland House. Holland might be confined to a wheelchair, Lady Holland's sharp tongue might show no signs of mellowing, but they still presided over the best company in London. 'Such is the social despotism of this strange house...' wrote the diarist Charles Greville.

> Though everybody who goes there finds something to dislike or ridicule in the mistress of the house, or its ways, all continue to go;

all like it more or less; and whenever by the death of either, it shall come to an end, a vacuum will be made in society which nothing will supply. It is the house of all Europe; the world will suffer by its loss; and it may with truth be said that it will eclipse the gaiety of nations.[8]

Among the newcomers to Holland House in the late 1830s was the young Charles Dickens, recently sprung to fame as the author of *The Pickwick Papers* and *Oliver Twist*. It was Lady Holland, ever alert to new talent, who sought him out, though her query to Sir Edward Bulwer-Lytton as to whether Boz was presentable annoyed him by its condescending tone. Dickens however was delighted to be invited to Holland House but nervous enough to hope his friend, Serjeant Talfourd, through whom Lady Holland had sent the invitation, would be able to accompany him on his first visit. He first went there – with Talfourd – in August 1838. 'We have had the author of *Oliver Twist* here,' reported Holland to his sister. 'He is a young man of 26, very unobtrusive, yet not shy, intelligent in countenance and altogether prepossessing. It was too large a company of strangers to bring out the fun which must be in him.'[9]

Thereafter Dickens dined at Holland House from time to time, and embarked on an intermittent correspondence with Lady Holland, who was a warm admirer of his work. He once apologized for a muddle over dates – he had forgotten a previous engagement when accepting an invitation to Holland House – on the grounds that he had been distracted 'by some imaginary persons [the Nickleby family] whose affairs have reached such a very complicated pitch just now that they sometimes confuse me in my recollection of my own.'[10] When *Nicholas Nickleby* was published as a single volume (having appeared in instalments previously) he presented Lady Holland with a copy. The accompanying note is worth quoting in full.

In begging you, my lady Holland to accept from me a copy of Nickleby in a dress which will *wear* better than his every-day clothes, I am not influenced by any feeling of vanity or any supposition that you will find in the book, a solitary charm to which you have not done more than justice. I must not scruple to say that I am actuated by a most selfish feeling, though, for I wish to have the gratification of acknowledging your great kindness, and I do not know how I can better do so than by this poor token; which I venture to send you – not for its own sake (for that would be presumptuous indeed) but simply and solely for the reason I have just mentioned.[11]

It was common to cast Lady Holland as the bad fairy of Holland House, ascribing all its good points to her husband. But for all her eccentricities and autocratic ways, her personality was as much a draw as his. (The proof of this could be seen after Holland's death, when she continued to attract distinguished guests to the little 'nutshell' of her house in South Street.) As her relationship with Byron had shown, she had a real feeling for literature – though not for the Lake Poets – and neither he nor Dickens would have wasted time on someone whose opinion they did not respect. Henry Fox, incidentally, did not share his mother's admiration for the latter's novels. 'I am very glad you did not send me *Nicholas Nickleby*,' he wrote,

as I dare say I should not be more successful in reading that, than in getting thro' the more celebrated and admired of that author's works. I completely agree with what Lady Carlisle said about them. 'I know there are such unfortunate beings as pickpockets and street walkers. I am very sorry for it and very much shocked at their mode of life, but I own I do not much wish to hear what they say to one another'... I suspect, when the novelty and the fashion of admiring them dies down they will sink to their proper level.[12]

So much for Henry's literary opinions.

In September 1838 the Hollands embarked on what would be their last visit to Paris. They stayed in some splendour at the Bristol Hotel, with Allen, Rogers and Macaulay (just returned from four years in India) in close attendance. Their old friend Princess Lieven, now living in Paris, and estranged from her husband, who had been replaced as Russian ambassador in London three years earlier, was full of gossip about their doings. 'I see the Hollands a great deal,' she reported to Melbourne's sister Lady Cowper. 'They appear to be delighted with Paris. She is in very good spirits, flattered by everyone's attentiveness to her.'[13] And to Grey a fortnight later, 'Lord Holland dined at Court. Lady Holland did not go; but the Queen sent her all her boxes for the theatres, by which piece of attention Lady Holland appeared to be much gratified.'[14]

Louis Philippe went out of his way to entertain the Hollands. He offered to show Lady Holland round Versailles (she refused on account of her health) and granted Holland a private audience lasting two hours. 'What a very clever fellow he is!' wrote Holland. 'It would be wrong in a Whig to laud a King for too much proficiency in government, but certainly one talks to no man in this country and few in any, whose conversation convinces one more that he is qualified to be the Minister of a great nation.'[15]

The Hollands returned to London on 5 November, well pleased with their visit. Three days later Melbourne, who had been staying with Queen Victoria at Windsor, told her he was leaving for London the next morning. The queen could not conceal her mortification. 'He said "I should like to stay [away] Saturday",' she confided to her journal.

'Must you *really*?' said I, much vexed; 'I want to dine at Holland House; it's as well to hear what he has got to say; I'll come back Sunday', he replied. 'You *must*', I said. I was selfish enough to be quite cross inwardly at this announcement... I said I dreaded Lord and Lady Holland's return, as I knew she would get hold of him; and that Holland House was a great attraction, and that I was jealous of it.[16]

For Melbourne it was probably Holland's discussions with Louis Philippe and his prime minister Count Molé which were of greater interest than the charms of Lady Holland. Like Palmerston he was well aware of Holland's pro-French bias, but his first-hand impressions were obviously of value, and it would be pleasant to talk them over in the congenial atmosphere of Holland House.

Meanwhile things were not going well for the government. The first years after the Reform Bill had witnessed great reforms; the Poor Law and the Factory Acts, however inadequate by later standards, were at least an attempt to deal with some of the social evils brought about by agrarian unemployment and the industrial revolution. Since then the pace of progress had slowed down. New troubles had arisen on the horizon: the rise of Chartism, agitation against the Corn Laws, a narrowly averted rebellion in Canada. The radicals had abandoned the Whigs in disgust at their lack of decision, O'Connell and the Irish MPs were unreliable allies, Melbourne himself was weary and discouraged. The administration limped on till the spring of 1839, when in a vote to suspend the constitution of the legislative assembly in Jamaica (where the planters were in open defiance of the government) the radicals combined with the Tories and the government's majority was reduced to only five. Melbourne resigned, and the queen, on the advice of Wellington, sent for Peel.

The queen had burst into tears on hearing the news of Melbourne's resignation, but she behaved with scrupulous correctness towards Wellington and Peel, and according to Holland abstained from any consultation with Melbourne or her former ministers. But she did not conceal her sadness at parting with them, and it was perhaps for this reason that Peel insisted that she also change her ladies-in-waiting, many of whom were the wives or relatives of leading Whigs, as a sign of her confidence in the new government. The queen indignantly refused. When Peel politely remonstrated with her, arguing that Ladies of the Bedchamber under a reigning queen were in the same position as Lords under a king, she smartly replied 'that it did not place them in the House of Lords or give them votes and political influence, and that she did not see why, if *her Ladies* were *her Lords*, the Parliament should have given her eight Lords besides.'[17] A king who had practised his craft for 40 years could not have played his part better, thought Holland, who recorded the exchange.

The upshot of the Bedchamber dispute, as it was called, was that Peel refused to form a government without having the entire disposal of the royal household, including the ladies-in-waiting, in his hands. The queen took his decision as final, and Melbourne was accordingly recalled. The whole episode had been badly mishandled by Peel, whose awkward manner had helped to stiffen the young queen's resistance. 'Had the D[uke] of W[ellington] conducted the negotiation it would probably have gone well,' Lady Holland told Henry, 'but Peel's vulgarity, stiffness and grasping, wounded the feelings of the high spirited Princess.'[18]

The new government was in as weak a position as before and it was obvious that Peel was only biding his time. His moment would come in May 1841, when the government's majority was reduced to only one vote, and the Tories were swept back to power in the election that followed. Holland did not live to see the defeat of his party. His health was in decline and his gout was increasingly painful and debilitating. But he continued to attend Cabinet meetings when he could, his greatest interest as ever being in foreign affairs. For the last 18 months of his life he was deeply involved in discussions over the Near Eastern crisis which had arisen when the Viceroy of Egypt,

Mehmet Ali, declared independence from the Ottoman Empire, occupied Syria and, in June 1840, defeated the Turkish army sent to crush him. The French, who had close links with Egypt, were sympathetic to Mehmet Ali; the other great powers, concerned at the threat to the Ottoman Empire, were prepared to take strong measures against him. For Holland, to whom the Anglo-French entente was crucial, the prospect of a breach with France was deeply disturbing. When Palmerston announced his intention of drawing up a joint treaty with Russia, Austria and Prussia, pledging the four powers to maintain the integrity of the Ottoman Empire, without reference to France, Holland's first thought was to resign. But he was afraid of damaging the administration if he did so: 'The near balance of parties in Parliament,' he wrote in his journal for 8 July;

> the old adherents of Mr Fox who were partial to my name; the resemblance of the questions relating to peace to those upon which they had formerly adhered to Mr Fox and had been accustomed to support under him and with me... made me apprehend that my resignation, old and worn out as I was, might in fact [lead to] a dissolution of the Government.[19]

Even in the last days of Holland's life, the memory of his uncle was still potent. Melbourne indeed was fearful of upsetting the government's fragile hold on power, and it was finally agreed that Holland and another colleague, Lord Clarendon, should attach a dissenting minute to the record of the Cabinet's decision.

The French were furious when the proposal for the Treaty became known, even threatening to go to war on behalf of Mehmet Ali. Palmerston was convinced they were bluffing, but Holland, with several of his Cabinet colleagues, was desperately anxious that a face-saving compromise should be found. He continued to propound his views at Holland House, much to Palmerston's exasperation. 'Holland really quite foolish and superannuated,' complained Lady Palmerston to her brother Frederick Lamb, 'but with name and following and dinners, and activity of proselitism that was quite extraordinary, very good friends in the main with P[almerston] but thinking it fair to have all this cabal against him... in short friendly, but just as he would in opposition.'[20]

Drawing-room dissension was one thing; more serious were stories that reports of disagreements in Cabinet had reached Paris and Vienna, and that Holland House was said to be the source. Tactfully Melbourne suggested that the Hollands should exercise discretion. 'I know not what can be done except to take care that as little of political affairs transpires in conversation as possible,' he wrote to Holland on 18 October; 'but this is inconsistent with a *salon* which has many advantages and some disadvantages, and more particularly when matters of great importance are pending.'[21]

The Hollands entertained as usual on 19 and 20 October. On the morning of 21 October Holland woke up feeling very ill, with vomiting and a seizure of the bowels, and the family doctors were sent for. His symptoms, the effect thought the doctors of 'internal gout', became more alarming as the day went on and he gradually lapsed into semi-consciousness. It was obvious that the Eastern crisis was still preying on his mind, for 'Egypt', 'Syria' and 'Palmerston' were among the last intelligible words he uttered. 'Illness – Illness', wrote Lady Holland in the dinner book that evening. He died the following morning.

'This wretched day,' read the entry for 22 October, 'closes all the happiness, refinement and hospitality within the walls of Holland House. E.V.Hd.'

Allen's diary, written as Holland lay dying, contained a single word: 'Alas.'

25

Leaving the Stage

H OLLAND'S funeral took place at Milbrook, in the church near Ampthill, where his daughter Georgiana was buried. At his request, the funeral was private, with only members of the family and household present. Letters of condolence poured into Holland House from both sides of the Channel. The queen sent messages of deep concern; Melbourne, who confessed himself stunned, confided to a friend that it was the heaviest blow, both personal and political, he had ever received. A subscription for a monument in Westminster Abbey was set up by Lansdowne and his friends, and Holland's bust by Edward Baily now stands at the west end of the north aisle. But his most important memorial perhaps was the famous essay by Macaulay which appeared in the *Edinburgh Review* for May 1841.

Its opening pages were devoted to Holland's family history and his political career – the essay was ostensibly a review of his contributions to the Journal of the House of Lords. But it was as a host and friend that Macaulay recalled him best, and he ended his essay with a paean of praise for Holland House and all it had meant to those who had known it in its heyday. Like Scott, he feared that it would be soon be engulfed by the ever-increasing spread of London.

The time is coming when perhaps a few old men, the last survivors of our generation, will in vain seek, amid new streets, and squares, and railway stations, for the site of that dwelling, which in their youth was the favourite resort of wits and beauties, of painters and poets, of scholars, philosophers, and statesmen... They will recollect how many men, who have guided the politics of Europe, who have moved great assemblies by reason and eloquence, who have put life into bronze or canvas, or who left to posterity things so written that it will not willingly let them die, were there mixed with all that is loveliest and gayest in the society of the most splendid of capitals... They will remember above all, the grace, and the kindness far more admirable than grace, with which the princely hospitality of that ancient mansion was dispensed... They will remember, too, that he whose name they hold in reverence was not less distinguished by the inflexible uprightness of his political conduct than by his loving disposition and winning manners. They will remember that in the last lines which he traced he expressed his joy that he had done nothing unworthy of the friend of Fox and Grey; and they will have reason to feel similar joy, if, in looking back upon many troubled years, they cannot accuse themselves of having done anything unworthy of men who were distinguished by the friendship of Lord Holland.[1]

Lady Holland lived on for five years after her husband. They were years marked with disagreements with her children. Holland had left her Holland House and Ampthill for her lifetime; Holland House would then go to Henry, and Ampthill to Charles, with Ampthill reverting to Henry when Charles (who was childless) died. But there were large debts to be paid. Ampthill eventually had to be sold and some of the paintings and articles of furniture from both houses, which had been left to Lady Holland absolutely, were sold or given away. The bitterness both brothers felt over these depredations – especially the sale of Ampthill – led to angry scenes. 'You know well how you have been towards your children for years and years,' wrote Charles after one such occasion, 'you know the things you have said of them, you know the things you have said of those they love, you know the jealousy you have shown of their being with him whom they loved above all the world.' And when Allen, called in as a mediator, remarked that Lady Holland had always loved her children 'perhaps too fondly and indulgently for their own good', Charles riposted furiously. Had he not witnessed ('alas silently') the way that Mary had been treated 'from her very birth to womanhood?' Either Allen had 'no observation at all' or he was ready to 'assert anything as a partisan.'[2]

Caroline Fox, as usual, did her best to smooth things over between the children and their mother. Although their characters were so different she understood her sister-in-law well, and knew how deeply she felt Holland's death. 'Poor Lady Holland,' she wrote to her friend Lady Calcott,

> has lived a life of excitement and so *out of acquaintance* with herself or the resourses of her own mind, that she needs perpetually the excitement of society and the aid of others. I deeply and sincerely feel for her; tho' her way of feeling is so different from my own, it is not less profound and perhaps more incurable.[3]

Lady Holland, it was true, found her best solace in social activity, and she was borne up by the kindness of her friends, Melbourne, the Lansdownes, the Palmerstons, the Dukes of Devonshire and Bedford, Lord John Russell and many others. For some time she could not bear to live at Holland House, preferring to stay with Caroline at Little Holland House, where she brought her own cook and servants, and invited her own guests. Caroline, who dined early for reasons of health, would join the other ladies when they left the dining room.

In September 1841, Lady Holland returned to Holland House itself, Caroline kindly offering to keep her company. The house was filled with family friends, the gardens were bright with her favourite dahlias, but she complained of 'a *stillness*' that struck her to the heart and left for a rented house in Brighton after only a week. She returned to Holland House from time to time till the death of Dr Allen, in March 1843, made living there seem impossible. 'H.H. is out of the question,' she wrote to Henry; 'I would & might have tried it, but for this second loss, which has deprived me of my prop & companion, friend & protector.'[4]

Allen had lost all relish for life after Holland's death, wrote Caroline to Henry, and had neglected to take the various remedies which, as a doctor, he knew would have helped to prolong it. In his will he asked to be buried at Milbrook as near as possible to Georgiana and her father and that on the stone above his body the words 'Buried at his own desire close to the objects of his dearest affection' be added to his name. He left his treasured bust of Georgiana by Westmacott to Henry.

One loss followed another. Mrs Charles James Fox, whom the family had always visited regularly at St Anne's Hill, had died aged 92, the previous year. In February 1845, Sydney Smith died, after several months of illness. Dickens, calling at South Street shortly afterwards, found Lady Holland crying for her old friend. 'It is a sad scene, the last – the last act of life,' Smith had written to her in September;

> to see beauty and eloquence, sense, mouldering away... to witness the barren silence of him who charmed us with his exuberance... to gaze upon wrinkles and yellowness and incurvations where we remember beautiful forms and smiles and smoothness and the blush of health... but here I recollect I am not in the pulpit, so I stop.[5]

Lady Holland had been stricken by Smith's death. But worse was to follow when Caroline Fox died after a stroke in July the same year. The two women had grown closer after Holland's death and had found comfort in each other's company, Caroline once admitting that without Lady Holland she would have lost all contact with the outside world. (Her lifelong companion, Miss Vernon, had died some years before.) Despite these losses, Lady Holland continued to entertain and dine out in London, where she had taken a larger house in South Street, and to go on stately visits to old friends in the country.

In October 1845, while she was staying with the Lansdownes at Bowood, she caught a severe chill, which was followed by a bilious attack, but recovered enough to go on giving dinners on her return to London. The dinner book, now kept by Harold Doggett, her page, listed 62 guests for dinner over the first eight days of November. On 9 November, when a party of 12 had already assembled, she collapsed and was forced to take to her bed. 'Great stupor and general prostration of strength,' wrote Doggett in the dinner book, which from then on was a record of her worsening condition. 'She evinced during her illness a very philosophical calmness and resolution, and perfect good humour,' reported Greville, 'aware that she was dying and not afraid of death. The religious people don't know what to make of it. She never seems to have given the least sign of religious belief.'[6]

Henry Webster, Mary Lilford and Charles Fox hastened to be with her. Henry, in Florence, was in less of a hurry to return, though it would have been difficult for him to have done so in time. On the evening of 16 November Doggett wrote in the dinner book, 'My Lady is evidently sinking.' She died in the early hours of 17 November. She was buried at Milbrook next to her husband.

Difficult to the last, she had made a controversial will. Some clauses were straightforward: legacies and annuities to her servants;

£1,000 to Charles who would also receive half the income from the sale of Ampthill; silver and jewellery to Mary Lilford; a number of drawings and paintings to friends, including a sketch of Talleyrand for Macaulay. Henry, of course, would inherit Holland House and its contents, together with his mother's Jamaican estates (worth exactly nothing, according to Brougham), and an income of £7,000 a year. But she left the bulk of her disposable property, a valuable estate in Kennington, subject to mortgages and an annuity to Henry, to Lord John Russell for his lifetime, with a reversion to the Lilford family on his death. When Russell, who heard the terms of the will in advance, tried to remonstrate with her, Lady Holland told him firmly: 'I hate my son[s]; I don't like my daughter.'[7] Russell, in fact, put things right by using his life interest in the property to insure his life for £15,000, so that the Lilfords would receive the estate unencumbered on his death.

More galling for Henry than the Kennington legacy was the fact that his mother left his father's collection of papers relating to Charles James Fox, which Holland had been preparing for publication, to Russell rather than him, with the wish that he should bring them out as soon as possible. (*The Memorials and Correspondence of Charles James Fox*, edited by Russell, were published in 1853.) For Henry there was only the contemptuous proviso that Russell should give him those 'papers relating to the Fox family that he should deem fit.'[8] In the event, Russell handed all the rest of Holland's papers over and Henry put them to good use when he edited and published his father's memoirs of the Whig party ten years later.

Lady Holland had made it difficult for her family to mourn her deeply. 'I wish she loved us as much as she loves all of you,'[9] her son Charles once said sadly to one of the intimates of Holland House. But for the wider world she left a gap which it was impossible to fill. 'Though she was a woman for whom nobody felt any affection,' wrote Charles Greville (unfairly, since her close friends had remained devoted to her),

> and whose death will therefore have excited no grief, she will be regretted by a great many people, some kindly, more from selfish motives, and all who had been accustomed to live at Holland House and continued to be her *habitués* will lament over the fall of the curtain on that long drama, and the final extinction of a social light which illuminated and adorned England and even Europe for half a century. The world has never seen and never will see again anything like Holland House.[10]

Epilogue

HENRY, the fourth Lord Holland, had no heir, and after his widow's death in 1889 Holland House passed to the fifth Earl of Ilchester, the great-great-grandson of the first Lord Holland's brother. Over the years substantial areas of the outlying land were developed for building, but some 60 acres of parkland were still intact when in September 1940 the house was largely destroyed by incendiary bombs. As staff and firemen battled to save the burning building, the steward saw a fox race over the lawn and disappear into the surrounding woods. It was hard not to see it as a symbolic ending.

Holland House was too badly damaged for its owner, the sixth Lord Ilchester, to rebuild after the war, and in 1951 the house and 52 acres round it were sold to the London County Council. As Holland Park it has given joy to nearly three generations of Londoners. Every summer Opera Holland Park stages its performances against the background of the ruined building, the music wafting across the gardens and echoed by the cry of peacocks from the woods. Even though it is a public space the park still has the feeling of a private estate, and the benevolent spirit of the third Lord Holland, personified in his statue, seems to preside there. The Guyanese writer and poet, Sir Theodore Wilson Harris, recounts a strange experience. In 1959, having just arrived in London, and knowing nothing of the history of Holland House, he was entering the park with his wife. As he went in he heard a man's voice say clearly, 'Come in. Come in. You are welcome.' There was no one around and his wife heard nothing.

Harris became fascinated by the story of Holland House, reading up about its history and evoking its landscape in his mysterious, poetic novel *Da Silva da Silva's Cultivated Wilderness*. Let us follow its hero, a painter, as he too visits Holland Park:

> I entered the park from Abbotsbury Road, ascended the avenue of limes to the statue of Lord Holland with the pond at its back. Paused for a while to make a sketch of green-headed ducks. The place is unique. Oaks, birches, chestnuts, cedars. Priceless woodland…
>
> Took the paved path through rose bushes lit like lamps, curled flame, then across the stretch of green with its gnarled sentinel tree, down into the old Dutch garden and up to the fountain under the clock.
>
> Fish in the pool were darting, red, gold and silver. A sudden bird flew through the fountain with a human voice, wing touching water… Genie of paradise.'

At moments like these the noise of London is forgotten. Past and present seem to come together, and the Hollands and their friends do not seem very far away.

Notes

Chapter 1 · Nephew of Fox

1   Ayling, p. 40.
2   Ibid., p. 40.
3   Kelly, *Sheridan*, p. 107.
4   Ibid., p. 108.
5   Fox, *Memorials*, vol. 2, p. 370.
6   Ayling, p. 167.
7   FR, p. 13.
8   Fox, *Memorials*, vol. 1, p. 346.
9   Ibid., vol. 2, p. 370.
10 Ibid., vol. 2, p. 102.
11 Ibid., vol. 3, p. 79.
12 Ibid., vol. 3, p. 80.
13 Ibid., vol. 3, p. 89.

Chapter 2 · Lovers' Meeting

1   JELH, vol. 1, p. 125.
2   Keppel, p. 54.
3   Ibid., p. 48.
4   JELH, vol. 1, p. 125.
5   Ibid., vol. 1, p. 125.
6   Ibid., vol. 1, p. 131.
7   Ibid., vol. 1, p. 132.
8   Ibid., vol. 1, p. 138.
9   Ibid., vol. 1, p. 145.
10 BLHHM, Lord Holland to Caroline Fox, 25 January 1795. Holland is quoting from Dryden's *All for Love*, Act I, Scene I.
11 Ibid., July 1796.
12 Ibid., July 1796.
13 Ibid., July 1796.
14 JELH, vol. 1, p. 147.
15 PCLG, vol. 1, p. 162. ['ne vous déplaise': 'if you please'; 'Un tel hymen...': 'Such a union is heaven on earth'; the latter is a quotation from Voltaire's play *L'Enfant prodigue*.]

Chapter 3 · In Opposition

1   JELH, vol. 1, p. 147.
2   Ibid., vol. 1, p. 159.
3   Ibid., vol. 1, p. 159.
4   Ibid., vol. 1, p. 159.
5   PCLG, vol. 1, p. 164.
6   The first Marquess of Lansdown spelt his name without an 'e'.
7   BLHHM, Lord Holland to Caroline Fox, 20 July 1797.
8   Ibid., 31 July 1797.
9   Keppel, p. 76.
10 Ayling, p. 106.
11 JELH, vol. 1, p. 149.
12 Ibid., vol. 1, p. 141.
13 Ibid., vol. 1, p. 244.
14 Ibid., vol. 1, p. 255.
15 Ibid., vol. 1, p. 274.
16 BLHHM, Lord Holland to Caroline Fox, January 1798.
17 Fox, *Memorials*, vol. 3, p. 143.
18 JELH, vol. 1, p. 187.
19 Ibid., vol. 1, p. 257.

Chapter 4 · Foreign Adventures

1   JELH, vol. 2, p. 62.
2   Macaulay, 'Lord Holland', p. 216.
3   BLHHM, Lord Holland to Caroline Fox, March 1800.
4   JELH, vol. 2, p. 256.
5   JELH, vol. 1, p. 210.
6   Ibid., vol. 1, p. 211.
7   Keppel, p. 108.
8   JELH, vol. 2, p. 90.
9   Ibid., vol. 2, p. 125.
10 Ibid., vol. 2, p. 131.
11 Kelly, *Sheridan*, p. 239.
12 HOH, p. 179.
13 BLHHM, Lord Holland to Caroline Fox, August 1802.
14 JELH, vol. 2, p. 149.
15 ['*C'est tout...*': 'It's completely different here'.]
16 Keppel, p. 120.

Chapter 5 · 'The Best and Greatest Man...'

1   SJLH, p. 186.
2   Fox, *Memorials*, vol. 4, p. 79.
3   MWP, vol. 1, p. 164.
4   SJELH, p. 157.
5   PCLG, vol. 2, p. 96.
6   Stanhope, p. 133.

7   PCLG, vol. 2, p. 162.
8   MWP, vol. 1, p. 244.
9   Ibid., vol. 1, p. 253.
10 Creevey, p. 82.
11 JELH, vol. 2, p. 174.
12 PCLG, vol. 2, p. 209.
13 Ibid., vol. 2, p. 211.
14 MWP, vol. 1, p. 272.

Chapter 6 · Edinburgh Reviewers

1   Liechtenstein, vol. 1, p. 182.
2   Pearson, p. 97.
3   Smith, *Letters*, vol. 1, p. 107.
4   PCLG, vol. 2, p. 118.
5   MWP, vol. 1, p. 245.
6   PCLG, vol. 1, p. 217.
7   Pearson, p. 140.
8   PCLG, vol. 2, p. 313.
9   Macaulay, *History of England*, p. 215.
10 Smith, *Peter Plymley's Letters*, Letter III.
11 Ibid., Letter I.
12 Pearson, p. 119.
13 Smith, *Letters*, vol. 1, p. 123.
14 HOH, p. 225.
15 JELH, vol. 2, p. 228.
16 PCLG, vol. 2, p. 335.
17 BLHHM, Lord Holland to Caroline Fox, 9 October 1808. The quotation is from Dryden's 'To My Dear Friend Mr Congreve'.

Chapter 7 · Spanish Journeys

1   BLHHM, Lord Holland to Caroline Fox, 7 November 1808.
2   Quoted in the appendix to SJELH, p. 250.
3   BLHHM, Lord Holland to Caroline Fox, 2 February 1809.
4   L. Mitchell, *Holland House*, p. 227.
5   SJELH, p. 376.
6   BLHHM, Lord Holland to Caroline Fox, May 1809.
7   SJELH, p. 371.
8   PCLG, vol. 2, p. 349.
9   Keppel, p. 179.
10 FMWP, p. 121.
11 Ibid., p. 128.

Chapter 8 · Enter Byron

1   FMWP, p. 123.
2   BLJ, vol. 2, p. 168.
3   Blessington, p. 185.

4   JELH, vol. 2, p. 231.
5   BLJ, vol. 4, p. 327.
6   Moore, *Journals*, vol. 1, p. 62.
7   BLJ, vol. 9, p. 14.
8   Liechtenstein, vol. 1, p. 158.
9   Pearson, p. 108.
10 Kelly, *Sheridan*, p. 88.
11 BLJ, vol. 3, p. 231.
12 PCLG, vol. 2, p. 123.
13 Ibid., vol. 2, p. 235.
14 Keppel, p. 180.
15 Liechtenstein, vol. 1, p. 157.
16 Smith, *Letters*, vol. 1, p. 250.

Chapter 9 · Towards Waterloo

1   FMWP, p. 128.
2   Ibid., p. 157.
3   BLJ, vol. 2, p. 191.
4   Sheridan, *Letters*, vol. 3, p. 227.
5   PCLG, vol. 2, p. 495.
6   FMWP, p. 180.
7   Keppel, p. 193.
8   BLJ, vol. 3, p. 76.
9   Creevey, p. 189.
10 Ibid., p. 189.
11 Ibid., p. 189. ['ce n'est point un homme...': 'he's not a man, he's a system'; 'pour produire...': 'for producing conscripts'; 'c'est une classe...': 'it's a class he would like to suppress'.]
12 Blessington, p. 21.
13 Gooden, p. 229.
14 Ibid., p. 230.
15 FMWP, p. 196.
16 Smith, *Letters*, vol. 1, p. 250.
17 Keppel, p. 205.
18 Ibid., p. 205.
19 L. Mitchell, *Holland House*, p. 258.
20 Keppel, p. 213.
21 Ibid., p. 213.
22 L. Mitchell, *Holland House*, p. 259.
23 Keppel, p. 214.
24 HCG, vol. 1, p. 56.

Chapter 10 · Defenders of Napoleon

1   Tangye Lean, p. 186.
2   Giles, p. 51.
3   FMWP, p. 229.

4 Sanders, p. 114.
5 Grosskurth, p. 234.
6 Elwin, p. 140.
7 Langley Moore, p. 48.
8 BLJ, vol. 5, p. 30.
9 Ibid., vol. 5, p. 53.
10 Keppel, p. 257.
11 Ibid., p. 199.
12 Lamb, vol. 1, pp. 244–47.
13 Creevey, p. 264.
14 Cecil, p. 160.

Chapter 11 · At Home at Holland House

1 Keppel, p. 240.
2 Ibid., p. 240.
3 HCG, vol. 1, p. 121.
4 Keppel, p. 243.
5 Ibid., p. 243.
6 FMWP, p. 249.
7 Keppel, p. 144.
8 Liechtenstein, vol. 1, p. 176.
9 Smith, *Letters*, vol. 1, p. 227.
10 FMWP, p. 259.
11 Keppel, p. 237.
12 Creevey, p. 260.
13 Keppel, p. 238.
14 Ibid., p. 238.

Chapter 12 · The Trial of Queen Caroline

1 Keppel, p. 238.
2 FMWP, p. 261.
3 Brougham, vol. 3, p. 325.
4 Tangye Lean, p. 77.
5 FMWP, p. 270.
6 Ibid., p. 272.
7 Ibid., p. 285.
8 Ibid., p. 289.
9 Fraser, p. 223.
10 Creevey, p. 346.
11 FMWP, p. 295.
12 PCLG, vol. 2, p. 548.
13 ['*L'empereur Napoléon…*': 'The Emperor Napoleon to Lady Holland, as a token of satisfaction and respect'.]
14 Keppel, p. 227. The abduction and subsequent execution of the Bourbon Duke of Enghien in 1804 was generally regarded as one of Napoleon's blackest crimes.

15 Ibid., p. 227.
16 Tangye Lean, p. 200.

Chapter 13 · 'A House of All Europe'

1   A. Mitchell, p. 154.
2   Ibid., p. 43.
3   FR, p. 139.
4   L. Mitchell, *Holland House*, p. 205.
5   FMWP, p. 303.
6   Creevey, p. 357.
7   L. Mitchell, *Holland House*, p. 208. ['*ne font que jouer...*': 'are only play-acting'.]
8   Creevey, p. 249.
9   L. Mitchell, *Holland House*, p. 129.
10 Creevey, p. 347.
11 Ibid., p. 347.
12 Keppel, p. 254.

Chapter 14 · Reforming Campaigns

1   FMWP, p. 308.
2   Holland, introduction to Horace Walpole, *Memoirs of the Last Ten Years of the Reign of George II.*
3   FMWP, p. 309.
4   Creevey, p. 609.
5   Greville, p. 90.
6   Liechtenstein, vol. 1, p. 275.
7   FMWP, p. 394.
8   Ibid., p. 398.
9   L. Mitchell, *Holland House*, p. 97.
10 BLHHM, William Wilberforce to Lord Holland, 3 April 1820.
11 Ibid., 4 January 1822.
12 Brougham, vol. 3, p. 330.

Chapter 15 · Family Matters

1   CHH, p. 25.
2   LELHS, p. 11.
3   CHH, p. 19.
4   Ibid., p. 62.
5   Keppel, p. 273. ['*épouseurs*': 'suitors'.]
6   HCG, vol. 1, p. 384. ['*gênéd*' (the 'd' is Lady Granville's anglicization): 'embarrassed'; '*gêne*': 'embarrassment'.]
7   Keppel, p. 262.
8   Marchand, vol. 3, p. 1,055. ['*Le Diable Boiteux*': 'The Lame Devil'.]
9   LELHS, p. 20.
10 BLJ, vol. 11, p. 59.
11 Keppel, p. 201.

12 Ibid., p. 200.
13 Moore, *Memoirs*, 6 July 1821.
14 Ibid., 4 November 1821.
15 Marchand, vol. 3, p. 1,253.
16 H. Fox, *Journal*, pp. 213–16.

Chapter 16 · A Surrogate Son

1   L. Mitchell, p. 26.
2   C H H, p. 49.
3   D N B.
4   C H H, p. 36.
5   A. Mitchell, p. 173.
6   D N B.
7   A. Mitchell, p. 175.
8   Creevey, p. 248.
9   H C G, vol. 1, p. 360. ['to her alentours': 'to those around her'.]
10 Ibid., p. 360. ['la plus belle...': 'the most beautiful, the most magnificent, the most piquant (of creatures), her wit sparkles in her eyes, her soul reveals itself in her charming face'.]
11 Keppel, p. 274.
12 L. Mitchell, *Holland House*, p. 26. ['dans l'intérieur...': 'in the bosom of the family'.]
13 Smith, *Letters*, vol. 1, p. 434.
14 A. Mitchell, p. 190.

Chapter 17 · Party Confusions

1   C H H, p. 81.
2   B L H H M, Lord Holland to Henry Fox, May 1827.
3   Ibid., 5 June 1827.
4   A. Mitchell, p. 194.
5   B L H H M, Lord Holland to Henry Fox, 5 June 1827.
6   Ibid., 9 January 1827.
7   L E L H S, p. 58.
8   B L H H M, Lord Holland to Henry Fox, 3 July 1827.
9   C H H, p. 79.
10 L E L H S, p. 58.
11 C H H, p. 81.
12 B L H H M, Lord Holland to Henry Fox, January 1828. ['*Alors comme alors*': 'We'll see' (approximately); '*pour trancher le mot*': 'to put it bluntly' (approximately).]
13 C H H, p. 82.

Chapter 18 · Irish Affairs

1   L E L H S, p. 29.
2   Ibid., p. 32.
3   Keppel, p. 258.

4 LELHS, p. 80.
5 Ibid., p. 80.
6 Sanders, p. 219.
7 Ibid., p. 218.
8 Scott, *Journal*, 17 May 1828.
9 PRONI, Lord Holland to Lord Anglesey, 18 March 1828.
10 Ibid., 13 June 1828.
11 Anglesey, p. 200.
12 Ibid., p. 201.
13 PRONI, Lord Holland to Lord Anglesey, 11–28 August 1828.
14 Ibid., 6 October 1828.
15 Anglesey, p. 210.
16 Ibid., p. 211.
17 PRONI, Lord Holland to Lord Anglesey, 8 January 1829.
18 Anglesey, p. 213.

Chapter 19 · The July Revolution

1 LELHS, p. 95.
2 Anglesey, p. 215.
3 Kelly, *Ireland's Minstrel*, p. 97.
4 Russell, vol. 6, p. 54.
5 Ibid., p. 80.
6 LELHS, p. 109.
7 Hobhouse's entry in Moore's *Life of Byron*.
8 LELHS, p. 77.
9 CHH, p. 117.
10 BLHHM, Holland House dinner book.
11 Kelly, *The Young Romantics*, p. 44.
12 BLHHM, Lord Holland to Henry Fox, 24 August 1830.
13 L. Mitchell, *Holland House*, p. 272.

Chapter 20 · The Whigs in Power

1 Duff Cooper, p. 331.
2 FR, p. 40. ['*C'était donc...*': 'So it was your father who wasn't so good-looking.']
3 L. Mitchell, *Holland House*, p. 23. ['*Elle fait semblant...*': 'She pretends she knows everything, because it makes her seem important, and what she doesn't know she invents.']
4 Liechtenstein, vol. 1, p. 158. ['*C'est pour gêner...*': 'It's to make things awkward for everybody.']
5 L. Mitchell, *Holland House*, p. 278.
6 Ibid., p. 278.
7 Zamoyska, p. 149.
8 CHH, p. 130.
9 Somerset, p. 136.
10 CHH, p. 136.
11 PRONI, Lord Holland to Lord Anglesey, 2 February 1831.

12 Smith, *Letters*, vol. 2, p. 534.
13 Keppel, p. 291.

Chapter 21 · 'The Bill, the Whole Bill and Nothing but the Bill'

1 L. Mitchell, *Holland House*, p. 19.
2 CHH, p. 145. ['*Malade...*': 'Ill and dying seem to be synonymous to her'.]
3 HCG, vol. 1, p. 169.
4 G.O. Trevelyan, *Life and Letters*, vol. 1, p. 205.
5 Ibid., vol. 1, p. 207.
6 Pearson, p. 108.
7 G.O. Trevelyan, *Life and Letters*, vol. 1, pp. 212–13.
8 Keppel, p. 365.
9 Pearson, p. 106.
10 Ibid., p. 181.
11 HHD, p. 58.
12 G.M. Trevelyan, *Lord Grey of the Reform Bill*, p. 308.
13 Ibid., p. 310.
14 HHD, p. 64.
15 Journal of the House of Commons, 10 October 1831.
16 CHH, p. 146.
17 HHD, p. 85.

Chapter 22 · The Triumph of Reform

1 HHD, p. 147.
2 Ibid., p. 176.
3 Ibid., p. 178.
4 Ibid., p. 188.
5 Ibid., p. 189.
6 Ibid., p. 190.
7 Ibid., p. 169.
8 LELHS, p. 129.
9 DHH, p. 115.
10 Ibid., p. 117.

Chapter 23 · Elder Statesman

1 LELHS, p. 127.
2 Keppel, p. 301.
3 HHD, p. 202.
4 Liechtenstein, vol. 1, p. 134.
5 HHD, p. 159.
6 Keppel, p. 306.
7 Ibid., p. 306.
8 LELHS, p. 151.
9 HHD, p. 290.
10 Keppel, p. 319.

11 Creevey, p. 315.
12 LELHS, p. 143.
13 HHD, p. 345. [*'forse era ver...'*: 'It may be true, but it doesn't seem credible to me'; Lord Holland is quoting from Ariosto's *Orlando Furioso* (I.lvi).]
14 Ibid., p. 345.
15 Keppel, p. 310.

Chapter 24 · 'This Wretched Day'

1   DHH, p. 366.
2   Ibid., p. 278.
3   Ibid., p. 372.
4   Keppel, p. 311.
5   CHH, p. 225.
6   Keppel, p. 313.
7   Ibid., p. 313.
8   Ibid., p. 298.
9   CHH, p. 241.
10 Dickens, *Letters*, vol. 1, p. 98.
11 Ibid., vol. 1, p. 99.
12 CHH, p. 245.
13 Keppel, p. 326.
14 Ibid., p. 326.
15 CHH, p. 247.
16 Keppel, p. 328.
17 HHD, p. 398.
18 LELHS, p. 177.
19 HHD, p. 398.
20 Palmerston, p. 235. Melbourne's sister, Emily Cowper, had married her long-term lover, Palmerston, after her husband's death two years before.
21 Cecil, p. 499.

Chapter 25 · Leaving the Stage

1   Macaulay, *Edinburgh Review*, May 1841.
2   CHH, p. 296.
3   Ibid., p. 285.
4   Keppel, p. 368.
5   Pearson, p. 321.
6   Greville, p. 161.
7   Peel, p. 71.
8   CHH, p. 346.
9   Ibid., p. 354.
10 Greville, p. 161.

Bibliography

Abbreviations

BLHHM   Holland House Papers, British Library [Add. MSS 51318–52254]

BLJ   Byron, Lord, *Letters and Journals*, ed. Leslie Marchand, 12 vols., 1972–82

CHH   Ilchester, Earl of, *Chronicles of Holland House, 1820–1900*, 1937

DNB   *Dictionary of National Biography*, First Series, 1885–1900

FMWP   Holland, third Lord, *Further Memoirs of the Whig Party During My Time*, ed. Lord Stavordale, 1905

FR   Holland, third Lord, *Foreign Reminiscences*, ed. fourth Lord Holland, 1850

HCG   Granville, Harriet, Countess, *Letters*, ed. Hon. F. Leveson-Gower, 1894

HHD   Holland, third Lord, *The Holland House Diaries, 1831–1840*, ed. Abraham D. Kriegel, 1977

HOH   Ilchester, Earl of, *The Home of the Hollands, 1605–1820*, 1917

JELH   Holland, Lady, *The Journal of Elizabeth, Lady Holland*, 2 vols., ed. Lord Ilchester, 1908

LELHS   Holland, Lady, *Letters of Elizabeth, Lady Holland to Her Son*, ed. Lord Ilchester, 1946

MWP   Holland, third Lord, *Memoirs of the Whig Party During My Time*, ed. fourth Lord Holland, 2 vols., 1852–54

PCLG   Granville, Earl, *The Private Correspondence of Lord Granville Leveson-Gower, First Earl Granville*, ed. Castalia, Countess Granville, 1916

PRONI   Correspondence between Henry William Paget, First Marquess of Anglesey and Lord Holland, 1827–39, Public Record Office of Northern Ireland [D619/27]

SJELH   Holland, Lady, *The Spanish Journal of Elizabeth, Lady Holland*, ed. Lord Ilchester, 1910

Books

All titles are published in London unless otherwise stated.

Airlie, Mabell, Countess of, *In Whig Society*, 1921

Anglesey, Marquess of, *One Leg: The Life and Letters of Henry William Paget, First Marquess of Anglesey*, 1961

Ayling, Stanley, *Fox: The Life of Charles James Fox*, 1991

Bell, Alan, *Sydney Smith*, Oxford, 1980

Bernard, J.F., *Talleyrand*, 1973

Bessborough, Earl of, *Lady Bessborough and Her Family Circle*, 1940

Blessington, Countess of, *Conversations with Lord Byron*, 1834

Briggs, Asa, *The Age of Improvement*, 1979

Brougham, Lord, *Historical Sketches of Statesmen Who Flourished in the Time of George III*, 1839

Broughton, Lord, *Recollections of a Long Life*, 1909

Byron, Lord, *Letters and Journals*, ed. Leslie Marchand, 12 vols., 1972–82

Byron, Lord, *Poetical Works*, 1863

Cecil, Lord David, *Melbourne*, 1965 [one-volume edition of *The Young Melbourne* and *Lord M.*]

Clayden, P.W., *Rogers and His Contemporaries*, 1889

Creevey, Thomas, *The Creevey Papers*, ed. Sir Herbert Maxwell, 1912

Denny, Barbara and Starren, Carolyn, *Kensington Past*, 1956

Dickens, Charles, *Letters*, vol. 1, ed. Madeleine House and Graham Storey, Oxford, 1965

Dictionary of National Biography, First Series, 1885–1900

Duff Cooper, Alfred, *Talleyrand*, 1932

Elwin, Malcolm, *Lord Byron's Wife*, 1962

Esher, Viscount, *The Girlhood of Queen Victoria*, 1912

Fairweather, Maria, *Madame de Staël*, 2005

Foreman, Amanda, *Georgiana, Duchess of Devonshire*, 1998

Fox, Charles James, *The Memorials and Correspondence of Charles James Fox*, ed. Lord John Russell, 4 vols., 1853–57

Fox, Hon. Henry Edward, *Journal, 1818–1830*, ed. Earl of Ilchester, 1923

Fraser, Flora, *The Unruly Queen: The Life of Queen Caroline*, 1996

Giles, Frank, *Napoleon Bonaparte: England's Prisoner*, 2001

Gloag, M.K., *Holland House, Kensington*, 1906

Gooden, Angelica, *Madame de Staël: The Dangerous Exile*, Oxford, 2008

Granville, Earl, *The Private Correspondence of Lord Granville Leveson-Gower, First Earl Granville*, ed. Castalia, Countess Granville, 1916

Granville, Harriet, Countess, *Letters*, ed. Hon. F. Leveson-Gower, 1894

Greville, Charles, *The Greville Memoirs*, ed. Christopher Lloyd, 1947

Gross, John, *The Rise and Fall of the Man of Letters*, 1969

Grosskurth, Phyllis, *Byron*, Toronto, 1997

Herold, J. Christopher, *Mistress to an Age: A Life of Madame de Staël*, New York, 1958

Hilton, Boyd, *A Mad, Bad, Dangerous People? England, 1783–1846*, Oxford, 2008

Hobhouse, Christopher, *Fox*, 1934

Holland, Lady [wife of Sir Henry Holland], *A Memoir of the Reverend Sydney Smith by His Daughter, Lady Holland, with a Selection from His Letters*, ed. Mrs Austin, 2 vols., 1855

Holland, Lady, *Letters of Elizabeth, Lady Holland to Her Son*, ed. Lord Ilchester, 1946

Holland, Lady, *The Journal of Elizabeth, Lady Holland*, 2 vols., ed. Lord Ilchester, 1908

Holland, Lady, *The Spanish Journal of Elizabeth, Lady Holland*, ed. Lord Ilchester, 1910

Holland, third Lord, *Foreign Reminiscences*, ed. fourth Lord Holland, 1850

Holland, third Lord, *Further Memoirs of the Whig Party During My Time*, ed. Lord Stavordale, 1905

Holland, third Lord, *Memoirs of the Whig Party During My Time*, ed. fourth Lord Holland, 2 vols., 1852–54

Holland, third Lord, *Some Account of the Life and Writings of Lope Felix de Vega Carpio*, 1806

Holland, third Lord, *The Holland House Diaries, 1831–1840*, ed. Abraham D. Kriegel, 1977

Holland, third Lord, *The Opinions of Lord Holland as Recorded in the Journal of the House of Lords*, ed. Dr Moylan, 1841

Holland, fourth Lord, *The Journal of Henry Edward Fox, 4th Lord Holland*, ed. Earl of Ilchester, 1923

Howell-Thomas, Dorothy, *Duncannon: Reformer and Reconciler, 1781–1847*, 1992

Hurd, Douglas, *Robert Peel*, 2007

Ilchester, Earl of, *Chronicles of Holland House, 1820–1900*, 1937

Ilchester, Earl of, *The Home of the Hollands, 1605–1820*, 1917

Ilverstein, Gry, *Impressions of Holland House*, 2002

Johnson, Paul, *The Oxford Book of Political Anecdotes*, Oxford, 1975

Kee, Robert, *The Most Distressful Country*, 1972

Kelly, Linda, *Ireland's Minstrel: A life of Tom Moore*, 2006

Kelly, Linda, *Richard Brinsley Sheridan*, 1997

Kelly, Linda, *The Young Romantics, Paris 1827–1837*, 1976

Keppel, Sonia, *The Sovereign Lady: A life of Elizabeth Vassall, Third Lady Holland, with Her Family*, 1974

Lamb, Lady Caroline, *Glenarvon*, 1816

Langley Moore, Doris, *The Late Lord Byron*, 1961

Lawday, David, *Napoleon's Master: A Life of Prince Talleyrand*, 2009

Liechtenstein, Princess [adopted daughter of the fourth Lord Holland], *Holland House*, 2 vols., 1874

Lieven, Princess, *The Lieven–Palmerston Correspondence*, trans. and ed. Lord Sudeley, 1943

Longford, Countess of, *Wellington: Pillar of State*, 1974

Longford, Countess of, *Wellington: The Years of the Sword*, 1969

Macaulay, Thomas Babington, 'Lord Holland', *Critical and Historical Essays*, vol. 3, 1854

Macaulay, Thomas Babington, *The History of England in the Eighteenth Century*, ed. Peter Rowland, 1980

Marchand, Leslie, *Byron*, 1957

McCarthy, Justin, *Sir Robert Peel*, 1891

Mitchell, Austin, *The Whigs in Opposition, 1815–1830*, Oxford, 1967

Mitchell, Leslie, *Holland House*, 1980

Mitchell, Leslie, *The Whig World*, 2005

Moore, Thomas, *Memoirs of the Life of the Right Honourable Richard Brinsley Sheridan*, 1823

Moore, Thomas, *Memoirs, Journal and Correspondence of Thomas Moore*, ed. Lord John Russell, 8 vols., 1856

Moore, Thomas, *The Journal of Thomas Moore*, ed. Wilfred S. Dowden, 6 vols., 1983–91

Paget, Julian, *Wellington's Peninsular War*, 1990

Pakenham, Thomas, *The Year of Liberty*, 1969

Palmerston, Lady, *The Letters of Lady Palmerston*, ed. T. Lever, 1957

Pearson, Hesketh, *The Smith of Smiths*, 1934

Peel, Lady Georgiana, *Recollections*, ed. Edith Peel, 1920

Quennell, Peter, *Byron: The Years of Fame*, 1976

Roberts, R. Ellis, *Samuel Rogers and His Circle*, 1910

Rogers, Samuel, *Recollections of the Table Talk of Samuel Rogers*, ed. A. Dyce, 1856

Russell, Lord John, *Early Correspondence, 1805–1840*, ed. Rollo Russell, 1913

Sanders, Lloyd, *The Holland House Circle*, 1908

Scott, Sir Walter, *The Journal of Sir Walter Scott*, ed. W.E.K. Anderson, Oxford, 1972

Sheppard, F.H.W., ed., *Survey of London*, vol. 37 [Northern Kensington], 1973

Sheridan, Richard Brinsley, *The Letters of Richard Brinsley Sheridan*, ed. Cecil Price, 3 vols., Oxford, 1966

Smith, Rev. Sydney [published anonymously], *Letters on the Subject of the Catholics to My Brother Abraham Who Lives in the Country by Peter Plymley*, 1807 [Gutenberg facsimile]

Smith, Rev. Sydney, *The Letters of Sydney Smith*, 2 vols., ed. Nowell C. Smith, Oxford, 1953

Somerset, Anne, *The Life and Times of William IV*, 1980

Stanhope, Earl, *Life of the Right Honourable William Pitt*, 1867

Starren, Carolyn, *The Families of Holland House*, 2012

Tangye Lean, Edward, *The Napoleonists: A Study in Political Disaffection*, Oxford, 1970

Trevelyan, G.M., *British History in the Nineteenth Century and After*, 1937

Trevelyan, G.M., *Lord Grey of the Reform Bill*, 1920

Trevelyan, G.O., *The Life and Letters of Lord Macaulay*, Oxford, 1935

Walpole, Horace, *Memoirs of the Last Ten Years of the Reign of George II*, ed. Lord Holland, 1822

Wilson Harris, Theodore, *Da Silva da Silva's Cultivated Wilderness*, 1977

Zamoyska, Priscilla, *Arch Intriguer* [life of Princess Lieven], 1957

Journals and Periodicals

'Speech of Lord Holland in the House of Lords on the second reading of the bill for the repeal of the Constitution and Test Acts', House of Lords, 1828

Chancellor, V.E., 'Slave-owner and anti-slavery: Henry Richard Vassall Fox, 3rd Lord Holland, 1799–1840', *Slavery and Abolition*, December 1980, pp. 263–75

Manuscript Sources

Holland House Papers, British Library [Add. MSS 51318–52254], in particular:

Correspondence between Lord Holland and Caroline Fox [51731–51743]
Correspondence between Lord and Lady Holland [51730]
Correspondence between Lord Holland and his son Henry [51748–51757]
Letters to and from William Wilberforce [51820]
Holland House dinner books, 1799–1845 [51950–51957]

Correspondence between Henry William Paget, first Marquess of Anglesey and Lord Holland, 1827–39, Public Record Office of Northern Ireland [D619/27]

Transcription of Hobhouse's entries in Doris Langley Moore's copy of Moore's *Life of Byron*, now in the collection of Jack Wasserman (courtesy of Peter Cochran)

Index

In this index, Henry signifies Henry Richard Vassall Fox, 3rd Baron Holland; Elizabeth signifies his wife, Lady Holland.

Bessborough, Henrietta Frances (cont.)
in Italy, 11–12; visits newly-married
Henry and Elizabeth, 20; visits Holland
House, 23; welcomes Elizabeth from
travels, 43; and Fox's health decline, 47;
on Elizabeth's political involvement,
52, 65; on Hollands' wartime visit to
Spain, 57; and Granville's marriage to
Harriet Cavendish, 63; relations with
Elizabeth, 64; and daughter Caroline
(Lamb), 74, 160; friendship with Henry,
74–5; on Hollands' view of Napoleon,
81; on death of Napoleon, 115; death,
125
Boddington, Charles, 138
Bonaiuti, Serafino, 104
Bonaparte, Joseph, King of Spain, 56
Bonaparte, Lucien, 87
Bouverie, Mrs Edward, 46
Bowood (house), Wiltshire, 119
Bristol: riots (1831), 192
Britain: war with France (1803), 41; in
coalition against France (1805), 43;
invasion threat from France, 43
Brooks's Club, London, 100, 119
Brougham, Henry, Baron: co-founds
Edinburgh Review, 50; frequents
Holland House, 51, 125; reviews Byron,
68; defends Caroline of Brunswick,
81–2, 113; temporary absence from
Holland House, 123; on Hollands' view
of slavery abolition, 134; and Spanish
affairs, 146; and Henry's welcome of
Louis Philippe's accession, 175; barony,
181; as Lord Chancellor under Grey,
181; abuses royal ladies, 195; and
passing of 2nd Reform Bill in Lords
(1832), 199; *Statesmen in the Time of
George III*, 110, 134
Brown, Mrs (housekeeper), 136
Bulwer-Lytton, Sir Edward (*later* 1st
Baron Lytton), 216
Bunbury, Sir Henry, 91
Burke, Edmund, 49
Buxton, Thomas Fowell, 131
Byron, Annabella, Lady (*née* Milbanke),
94–6, 172–3
Byron, George Gordon, 6th Baron: and
Lady Caroline Lamb, 65, 73–4, 83;
welcomed to Holland House salon,

67, 69–70, 74, 90; speech in Lords, 69;
disparages Lake Poets, 71; prologue
on reopening of Drury Lane, 79–80;
on Madame de Staël, 84; sympathy
for Napoleon, 90, 94; marriage
breakdown, 94–5; leaves England
for good, 95; Caroline Lamb attacks,
96; defends Elizabeth's acceptance of
legacy from Napoleon, 116; Elizabeth's
reservations on, 138–9; friendship with
Henry Fox, 138; death in Greek War
of Independence, 139–40; memoirs,
140–1; Moore writes biography, 171–2;
relations with Elizabeth, 217; *The
Bride of Abydos*, 74; *Childe Harold's
Pilgrimage*, 69–70; *English Bards and
Scots Reviewers*, 68–9, 74; *Hours of
Idleness*, 68; 'Sympathetic Address to a
Young Lady' (poem), 67, 69

Calcott, Maria, Lady (*née* Dundas), 225
Campbell, Colonel Neil, 87, 91
Campbell, Thomas, 76
Canada: near-rebellion, 219
Canning, George: at Eton with Holland,
6; Toryism, 50; and Hollands' leaving
for Spain (1808), 57; as Foreign
Secretary, 118; friendship with
Henry, 124; hostility to Grey, 145,
152; opposes parliamentary reform,
146; and Spanish affairs, 146–7; and
party divisions, 151; as prime minister
(1827), 152, 155–6; accepts Catholic
Emancipation, 153; dines at Holland
House, 154; illness and death, 156
Canova, Antonio, 87, 93
Carlisle, Frederick Howard, 5th Earl of,
116
Caroline of Brunswick, Queen of George
IV: quarrels with husband, 81–2;
proposed divorce and trial, 113–14,
118, 124; denied access to coronation,
and death, 115
Castlereagh, Robert Stewart, Viscount:
suicide, 118
Catholic Association (Ireland), 131, 164
Catholic Emancipation: in Ireland,
27, 130–1; George III opposes, 36;
discussed in Commons, 42, 44; Henry
supports, 42, 79, 163; *Edinburgh*

July Revolution (1830), 175, 179;
supports Mehmet Ali in Egypt, 221
French Revolution: outbreak, 6; Fox
welcomes, 7, 9, 36, 38, 204; Henry's
attitude to, 7; and Terror, 9
Friends of the People, 181

George III, King: hostility with Charles
James Fox, 3–5, 49; madness
(porphyria), 6, 65; in love with Lady
Sarah Lennox, 30; opposes Catholic
Emancipation, 36, 53; press attacks on,
50; death, 113; removes Fox from Privy
Council, 200
George IV, King (*earlier* Prince of
Wales, *then* Prince Regent): C.J. Fox
influences, 4; vacillates on Catholic
Emancipation, 42; dines at Holland
House, 55; condemns Granville's
marriage to Harriet Cavendish, 63;
attitude to Whigs, 65–7, 78, 82, 100,
145; regency, 66; quarrels with wife
Caroline, 81; honours Lous XVIII,
85; succession to, 104; unpopularity,
104; proposed divorce, 113; succeeds
to throne, 113; opposes Catholic
Emancipation, 118, 130, 145, 158,
166, 169; state visit to Ireland (1821),
130; relations with Parliament, 146;
supports Canning, 155–6; accepts
Catholic Emancipation, 169; satirized
by Tom Moore, 171; death, 173
Glorious Revolution (1688), 36, 49
Goderich, Frederick John Robinson,
Viscount (*later* 1st Earl of Ripon),
156–7
Godoy, Manuel de, Duke of Alcudia, 41,
56, 120–1
Godwin, William, 110
Gower, Lord Francis, 165
Graham, Sir James, 182
Granville, Granville Leveson-Gower,
1st Earl: travels with Henry, 10–11;
affair with Lady Bessborough, 11, 14,
43; on Websters, 12; and Fox's health
decline, 47; and Hollands leaving for
Spain (1808), 57; marriage to Harriet
Cavendish, 63; and Hollands' view of
Napoleon, 81; viscountcy, 102; dines at
Holland House, 174

Granville, Harriet, Countess (*née*
Cavendish): marriage to Granville, 63;
visits Elizabeth after fall of Napoleon,
89; on Elizabeth's soirées, 102; on
Hollands in Paris, 148, 150; visits
Holland House, 160, 164; on Elizabeth's
political influence, 186
Greek War of Independence (1821–32),
139
Grenville, Thomas, 121
Grenville, William Wyndham Grenville,
Baron: and Catholic Emancipation
controversy, 42, 53; heads government
(1806), 44; Prince of Wales dislikes,
65; Prince of Wales offers place in
coalition, 66; votes for suspension
of habeas corpus, 101; alliance with
Henry ends, 112
Greville, Charles, 120, 128, 160, 215, 229
Grey, Charles (*later* 2nd Earl; *earlier*
Viscount Howick): parliamentary
reform proposals, 22, 119, 181; visits
Holland House, 24, 69; title, 45; as
Foreign Secretary, 51–2; seeks peace,
59; and war in Spain, 61; in Lords, 63;
Prince of Wales dislikes, 65; Prince
Regent offers place in coalition,
66; as leader of Whigs, 94, 101; ill
health, 101; and abolition of slavery,
133; hostility to Canning, 145, 152;
disfavours alliance with Tories, 151;
declines to join Canning's government,
152–3, 155; on Catholic Emancipation,
154; mocks Goderich, 157; George
IV opposes appointment to office,
158; view of Talleyrand, 178; forms
government (1830), 180–1; introduces
Reform Bills (1831–2), 182–4, 189–90,
195–7, 199–200; respects Allen,
188; retains office after rejection of
Reform Bill, 192; opposes appointing
new peers, 195–6; resignation and
reappointment as prime minister
(1832), 197–8; and passing of Second
Reform Bill in Lords (1832), 199;
resigns (1834), 206
Guiccioli, Contessa Teresa, 142

habeas corpus: suspended (1817), 101,
144; suspension repealed (1818), 109